I0836835

HUME'S HISTORY OF ENGLAND. From the latest London trade-edition, reprinted on large type to correspond with the London edition of Macaulay's History. 6 vols. 8vo, cloth. $9.

"These volumes are honorable to the taste, enterprise, and liberality of the publishers, and creditable to the country." — *Boston Atlas.*

"A finer library edition of the great historian of England we have never seen." — *New York Commercial Advertiser.*

ENCYCLOPÆDIA BRITANNICA. Eighth edition, revised, enlarged, and brought up to the present time. Edited by Thomas Stewart Traill, M. D., F. R. S. E., Professor of Medical Jurisprudence in the University of Edinburgh. With upwards of five hundred engravings on steel, and many thousands on wood. To be comprised in 21 vols. 4to. Vols. I. II. and III. now ready. Cloth. $5.50 per volume.

*** This edition has undergone careful revision and extensive alterations, so as to accommodate it to the improved taste and advanced intelligence of the times. The editor has secured the co-operation of the most eminent living authors, who have contributed treatises in the various departments of Science, Literature, the Arts, Manufactures, Commerce, Statistics, and General Knowledge, to supersede those now rendered obsolete by the progress of discovery, improvements in the arts, or the general advancement of society.

MEMOIRS AND CORRESPONDENCE OF FRANCIS HORNER, M.P. Edited by his Brother, Leonard Horner, Esq., F.R.S. 2 vols. 8vo, cloth. $4.50.

MACKINTOSH'S LIFE. — Memoirs of the Life of the Right Honorable Sir James Mackintosh. Edited by his Son, Robert James Mackintosh. From the second London edition. Portrait. 2 vols. 8vo, cloth. $4.50.

"More choice, indeed, than the English edition, and quite worthy of a book so agreeable and popular." — *Daily Advertiser.*

WILKINSON'S ANCIENT EGYPTIANS. — A Popular Account of the Ancient Egyptians. Revised and abridged from his larger work. By Sir J. Gardner Wilkinson. Illustrated with five hundred wood-cuts. 2 vols. post 8vo, cloth. $3.

CARTAPHILUS. — Chronicles selected from the Originals of Cartaphilus, the Wandering Jew, embracing a period of nearly six centuries. Now first revealed to and edited by David Hoffman. Vols. I. and II. 8vo, cloth. $5 per vol. (Vol. III. in press.)

"Mr. Hoffman has succeeded in producing a volume of intense interest." — *English Review.*

HEBER'S (BISHOP) POETICAL WORKS. Uniform with the Aldine Poets. Portrait. Fifth edition. Foolscap 8vo, cloth. $1.25.

RAMSHORN'S LATIN SYNONYMES. — Dictionary of Latin Synonymes. For the use of Schools and Private Students. With a complete Index. By Lewis Ramshorn. Translated from the German by Francis Lieber. New edition. 1 vol. 12mo, half morocco. $1.

WINTHROP'S HISTORY OF NEW ENGLAND. — History of New England, from 1630 to 1649. By John Winthrop, first Governor of the Colony of the Massachusetts Bay. From his original manuscript. With Notes by James Savage. New edition. 2 vols. 8vo, cloth. $4.50.

NORTON'S GENUINENESS OF THE GOSPELS. — Evidences of the Genuineness of the Gospels. By Andrews Norton. Second edition. 3 vols. 8vo, cloth. $5.

NORTON'S TRACTS ON CHRISTIANITY. — Tracts concerning Christianity. By Andrews Norton. 1 vol. 8vo, cloth. $1.50.

ELIOT'S HISTORY OF LIBERTY. — History of Liberty. Part I.: The Ancient Romans. Part II.: The Early Christians. By Samuel Eliot. 4 vols. 12mo, cloth. $5.

BANCROFT'S HISTORY. — History of the United States. Vols. IV. and V., being vols. I. and II. of the History of the Revolution. By Hon. George Bancroft. 8vo, cloth.

"His work is and must be the standard history of the country, and as such should reach every family, and be studied by every person who would be acquainted with the events of our past existence." — *New Haven Journal.*

"The further this work proceeds, the more do we feel that it must take its place as an essentially satisfactory History of the United States." — *London Athenæum.*

SPARKS'S CORRESPONDENCE OF THE REVOLUTION. Being Letters from Eminent Men to George Washington, from the Time of his taking Command of the American Army to the End of his Life. Edited by Jared Sparks. 4 vols. 8vo, cloth, $9; royal 8vo, $12.

SOCIAL THEORIES. — Considerations on some Recent Social Theories. 16mo, cloth. 75 cts.

PARKER'S THEISM. — Sermons of Theism, Atheism, and the Popular Theology. By Theodore Parker. 1 vol. 12mo, cloth. $1.25.

THE BREUGHEL BROTHERS. Translated from the German of the Baron Von Sternberg. By Dr. G. Henry Lodge. Illustrated by Billings. Small 4to, cloth. $2.

MISCELLANEOUS WORKS IN PRESS.

BACON'S WORKS. — The Works of Francis, Lord Bacon. From the complete English edition, by Basil Montague. 12 vols. 8vo.

PLUTARCH'S LIVES. Partly from Dryden's Translation, and partly from other hands. The whole carefully revised and corrected. With some Original Translations by the editor, A. H. Clough, Esq., late Fellow of Oriel College, Oxford. 5 vols. 8vo.

HUME'S PHILOSOPHICAL WORKS. — The Philosophical Writings of David Hume. 4 vols. 8vo.

NORTON'S TRANSLATION OF THE GOSPELS. — A Translation of the Four Gospels. With Notes. By Andrews Norton. 2 vols. 8vo.

PIERCE'S MECHANICS. — A Treatise on Analytic Mechanics. By Benjamin Pierce, LL.D., Perkins Professor of Astronomy and Mathematics in Harvard University. 1 vol. 4to.

DON QUIXOTE. Translated from the Spanish by Motteux. With a Life of the Author, and copious Notes. By J. G. Lockhart. 4 vols. 12mo.

ADAMS'S WORKS. — Life and Works of John Adams, second President of the United States. Edited by his Grandson, Charles Francis Adams. Vols. I. and X.

AMES'S LIFE AND WORKS. — The Life and Works of Fisher Ames. Edited by his Son, Seth Ames, Esq. 2 vols. 8vo.

LYELL'S MANUAL OF GEOLOGY. New edition. — Manual of Elementary Geology; or, the Ancient Changes of the Earth and its Inhabitants, as illustrated by Geological Monuments. By Sir Charles Lyell. Fifth and entirely revised edition. Illustrated with maps, plates, and wood-cuts. 8vo, cloth. (Nearly ready.)

THE

POETICAL WORKS

OF

JAMES THOMSON.

VOLUME I.

BOSTON:
LITTLE, BROWN, AND COMPANY.
M.DCCC.LIV.

CAMBRIDGE:
STEREOTYPED AND PRINTED BY METCALF AND COMPANY,
PRINTERS TO THE UNIVERSITY.

TO

JAMES FORBES YOUNG, ESQ., M. D.

DEPUTY LIEUTENANT OF THE COUNTY OF SURREY,

THIS MEMOIR

IS INSCRIBED, AS A SLIGHT TESTIMONY OF THE

ESTEEM AND REGARD OF HIS FRIEND

N. HARRIS NICOLAS.

CONTENTS.

VOL. I.

"The articles marked with an asterisk have never before appeared in any edition of Thomson's Poems, and some of them are printed for the first timefrom the Author's own Manuscript." *Edit.* 1830.

MEMOIR OF THOMSON.

BY SIR HARRIS NICOLAS.

"Tutored by thee, sweet Poetry exalts
Her voice to ages ; and informs the page
With music, image, sentiment, and thoughts,
Never to die!"

JAMES THOMSON was the eldest son of the Reverend Thomas Thomson, of Ednam, in the shire of Roxburgh, at which place the Poet was born on the 11th of September, 1700. Less has been said of his parents than they merit, and from the slight manner in which they have been noticed the idea may have arisen that he was of obscure origin. His father was well descended; and his mother was Beatrix, the daughter and co-heiress of Mr. Trotter, of Fogo,* a genteel family in the neighbourhood of Greenlaw in Berwickshire. Mr. Thomson was licensed to preach on the 17th of June, 1691, was ordained minister

* "1693, Oct. 6. The said day Mr. Thomas Thomson, minister of Ednam, and Beatrix Trotter, in the parish of Kelso, gave up their names for proclamation in order to marriage." Some notices of Mr. Thomson occur in "Kirkwood's Plea before the Kirk." 4to. London, 1698. Mrs. Thomson's sister married first Mr. Hume, and secondly the Rev. Mr. Nicolson, minister of Preston and Buncle.

of Ednam on the 12th of July, 1692, married in 1699, and was removed to Sudden, or Southdean, near Jedburgh, about 1701, the year after the Poet's birth, and died under remarkable circumstances, at Southdean, in 1718. Though his worth was of that unostentatious kind which only entitles him to the praise of being a good father, a good husband, and a good man, performing his clerical duties with pious diligence, and who

> "This noble ensample to his shepe he yaf,
> That first he wrought and afterwards he taught,"

nearly all human goodness comprised in that character.

At an early period of the Poet's life, his dawning talents attracted the attention of Mr. Riccalton, minister of the neighboring parish of Hobkirk, a man of some literary genius, and a judicious friend of his father, who consented that he should superintend his son's education. He was placed at school in Jedburgh,* and the care

* The school was then kept in the aisle of Jedburgh Church. Dr. Somerville, formerly Minister of Jedburgh, says in a letter dated the 24th of April, 1795, "Of Thomson's having attended the school here, there is no doubt, for when I came here twenty years ago several survived who had been his companions, and some of them his class-fellows. When I made application for a new school-house to the heritors, in 1778, on account of the ruinous state of the old one, I was told by the person who was then the Provost, that he thought that the aisle of the Church might again be employed for that purpose ; that greater men than any of the present generation had been educated there, for it was the place of the school

this gentleman bestowed upon him was well rewarded by the success that attended his exertions.

Nor was Mr. Riccalton his only friend. Sir William Bennet, of Chesters, near Jedburgh, who was distinguished for his wit, honoured him with his kindness, and invited him to spend his summer vacations at his seat. Under the auspices of these generous friends, and of Sir Gilbert Elliot of Minto,* Thomson wrote various pieces; but on the first of every January he destroyed most of his labours in the preceding year, and celebrated the annual conflagration by some humorous verses, stating his reasons for their condemnation. A poetical epistle, addressed to Sir William Bennet, and written in his fourteenth year, and a characteristic little poem addressed to his favourite sister on her parting with her cat, have, however, been lately discovered, and will be found in this edition of his works.

From Jedburgh young Thomson was, in March, 1715, sent to the University of Edinburgh, being intended for the Church; but, before he had been three years there, he lost his father, who died so suddenly that he did not see him before his decease, a circumstance which greatly increased his

when Mr. Thomson and himself attended it. The time of Thomson's attending school here was, I conjecture, from the year 1712 downwards." —*MS. in possession of the Publisher.*

* The Poet's uncle, and his cousin Robert Thomson were gardeners at Minto.

grief. His widowed mother, who was left with nine children slenderly provided for, was advised to remove to Edinburgh, where she remained, living in an economical manner, until her son James had completed his studies.

It appears that Thomson had a great horror of supernatural powers, and that his fear of ghosts and goblins afforded much amusement to his fellow collegians. His bedfellow knowing that he was afraid to remain alone in the dark, quietly left him one night while he was asleep. On waking he rushed out of the room roaring like a frightened child, and calling loudly upon his landlady for assistance. Dr. Somerville, who relates this anecdote upon the authority of Mr. Cranston, late minister of Ancrum, who lodged in the same room with the Poet at Edinburgh, attributes his weakness on this subject to the following circumstance. "The belief in ghosts, witches, fairies, &c. was so exceedingly prevalent at the beginning of this century, that it would have been deemed heretical in any clergyman to have called in question their existence, or even their palpable interposition. One of the last appearances of these tremendous agents happened, (I am speaking in the language of the vulgar,) at Woolie, in the parish of Southdean, where Mr. Thomson was minister. Even since I entered into life, it was necessary to speak guardedly upon the subject of the Woolie Ghost, and I myself have more than once given offence by my silence upon the subject. The sequel of the story I have heard, not at second hand, but from the lips of a person, and that of rank and education above the vulgar. Mr. Thomson, the father of the Poet, in a fatal hour was prevailed upon to attempt laying the evil spirit. He appointed his diet of catechising at Woolie, the scene of the ghost's exploits, and beheld, when he had just begun to pray, a ball of fire strike him upon the head. Overwhelmed with consternation, he could not utter another word, or make a second attempt to pray. He was carried home to his house, where he languished under the oppression of diabolical malignity, and at length expired. Only think what an impression this story, I do not say fact, I say this story, for of it there can be no doubt, must necessarily have made upon the vigorous imagination of our young Poet."

In 1719 Thomson became a student of divinity, and performed exercises in February, 1720, February, 1722, and May, 1724, which is the last time his name is mentioned in the books; and those records also prove that he did not take a Master of Arts' degree, nor obtain any bursary. Among his contemporaries at the University, where their friendship commenced, were David Malloch, or Mallet, who contributed several pieces to the "Edinburgh Miscellany," and Patrick Murdoch, his subsequent biographer; but his earliest, and one of the warmest of his friends, was Dr. Cranston, to whom the following, which is the first of Thomson's letters that has been found, was addressed:—

"Edinburgh, Dec. 11, 1720.

"Sir,

"I received yours, wherein you acquaint me that mine was very acceptable to you. I am heartily glad of it; and to wave all ceremony, if any thing I can scribble be entertaining to you, may I be damned to transcribe dull books for the press all my life if I do not write abundantly. I fondly embrace the proposal you make of a frequent correspondence this winter, and that from the very same principle you mention; and when the native bright ideas which flow from your good humour have the ascendant over those gloomy ones that attend your profession, I expect you will not be a wanting.

"You will allege that I have the advantage over you, being in town, where daily happen a variety of incidents. In the first place you must know, though I live in Edinburgh, yet I am but little conversant in the beau monde, viz. concerts, balls, assemblies, &c. where beauty shines and coxcombs admire themselves. If nature had thrown me in a more soft and indolent mould, had made me a Shapely or a Sir Fopling Flutter, if fortune had filled my pockets, (I suppose my head is empty enough as it is,) had I been taught to cut a caper, to hum a tune, to take a pinch, and lisp nonsense with all the grace of fashionable insipidity, then I could—what could I have done? hardly write; but, however, I might have made a shift to fill up a half sheet with 'rat me,' 'damn me,' &c. interspersed with broken characters of ladies gliding over my fancy like a passing image over a mirror. But if both nature and fortune had been indulgent to me, and made me a rich, finished gentleman, yet would I have reckoned it a piece of my greatest happiness to be acquainted with you, and you should have had entertainment if it was within the circle of wit and beauty to afford it; but alas! as it is, what can you expect from the Divinity hall or a Tippeny cell? It must be owned, indeed, that here in Edinburgh, to us humble sons of Tippeny, if beauty were as propitious as wit sometimes, we would have no reason to complain of the superior fortune of the fluttering generation; and O! ye foolish women, who have thus bewitched you? is it not wit that immortalizes beauty, that heightens it, and preserves it in a fresh eternal bloom? And did ever a fop either justly praise or admire you? but perhaps what I am railing at is well ordered, and if there was such a familiar intercourse betwixt wit and beauty as I would have, wit would degenerate into softness and luxury, and lose all its edge and keenness! it would dissolve in sighs or burst in nonsense. Wit and beauty thus joined would be, as Shakespeare has it, making honey a sauce to sugar; and yet another would say that beauty, divine beauty! enlivens, heightens, and refines wit; that even wit is the necessary result of beauty, which puts the spirits in that harmonious motion that produces it, that tunes them to that ecstasy, and makes them dart through the nerves, and sparkle in the eyes! — but whither am I rambling? What I am going to propose is, and you see there is great need for it, that you would in your next settle our correspondence into some order, and acquaint me on what subject you would have me write to you, for on news of any kind I shall soon run aground.

"You write to me that Mass John* and his quadruped are making a large eccentrical orbit, together with two or three wallets full of books, which I suppose will be multiplied into several more of papers before they return; belike they may have taken a trip into China, and then we shall have his travels. There is one thing I hear storied, God forbid it be true! that his horse is metamorphosing into an ass; and by the last accounts I had of it, its lugs are shot up into a strange length, and the cross was just beginning to dawn upon its shoulders; and, besides, as it one day was saluting a capful of oats, wonderful to tell! it fell a-braying. I wish Nanny Noble were so comfortably settled as you hint. Tell Mass John, when you see him, that I have a bundle of worthies for him, if once I had received his packet.

"There are some come from London here lately, that teach natural philosophy by way of shows by the beat of drum, but more of that afterwards. I designed to have sent you a manuscript poem, but I have no time till next week. Yours heartily,

"James Thomson."

While at the University, Thomson contributed three articles to a volume entitled "The Edinburgh Miscellany," printed in that city in 1720,

* Thomson alludes in many of his letters to some friend by this appellation, and the Earl of Buchan observes, that it was "undoubtedly the Rev. Mr. J. Wilson, Minister of the Parish of Maxton in Roxburghshire, a particular friend of Dr. Cranston of Ancrum, and of Thomson."

by a club called the Athenian Society. One of them, "On a Country Life, by a Student of the University," and signed with the initial of his name, shows how early the love of rural scenery and pursuits took possession of his mind, and may be deemed the first conceptions of "The Seasons." His productions were rather severely treated by some learned persons into whose hands they fell; and one of his biographers has laboured to prove the want of taste of his judges. This charge is probably unjust, for early pieces afford slight indication of his future powers; and the criticism was far from destroying his attachment to the Muses.

It is said that Mr. Hamilton, the Divinity Professor of Edinburgh, having given Thomson a Psalm as an exercise, he made so poetical a paraphrase of it, that the professor and the audience were equally surprised; that after complimenting the writer, Mr. Hamilton told him that if he expected to be useful in the Ministry he must restrain his imagination, and adopt language more suited to a country congregation; and, according to Dr. Johnson, one of the expressions was indecent if not profane. This story, though not without some foundation, inasmuch as Thomson did write a paraphrase of the 104th Psalm, is disproved by incontrovertible facts. No paraphrase in verse of a Psalm could possibly have been admitted as an exercise at the University; and the subject referred to was a prose lecture, or dissertation, on part of the 119th Psalm; but as it may have been written in too flowery a style, and been too redundant in poetical imagery, the censure said to have been pronounced by the Divinity Professor possibly occurred.* That this circumstance did not, as has also been asserted, alter his views with respect to the Church is evident from his stating, in some letters from London, that he still intended to be ordained.

This piece having fallen under the notice of Mr. Auditor Benson, he expressed his admiration of it; and added, that if the author came to London, he had no doubt his merit would be properly encouraged. When this remark was communicated to Thomson, he determined to try his fortunes in the English metropolis.

Dr. Cranston furnished him with an introduction to two friends, one of whom was Mr. Elliot, probably a brother of Sir Gilbert Elliot. Towards the end of February or at the beginning of March, 1725, about a fortnight before his departure for London, he wrote the following letters to Dr. Cranston. The observations on a future state, which occur in the second of these letters, is the earliest expression of the Poet's religious opinions that has been discovered; and his correspondence, as well as his works, prove that they never varied:—

* From the information of David Laing, Esq.

"Edinburgh, February or March, 1725.

"Dear Sir,

"I received yours, and can never sufficiently resent the regard for my welfare that you show in them. You are so modest as to desire me to correct any thing I see amiss in your letter to Mr. Elliot, and you will transcribe it again; but I assure you I am not so vain as to attempt it: if there was no other thing to bind me to a good behaviour but your recommendation and character of me, I could go great lengths of mortification to answer them. Your letter to my cousin, I do not doubt, will be considerably useful to me, if I can find him out. I remember I heard that Mr. Colden's letter was very serviceable to George Brown. I do not doubt but if Mr. Colden was advertised, I might have one too, and there will be time enough, for our ship sails not this fortnight, yet during that time, if it can contribute any thing to your diversion, you shall hear from me every opportunity, and when I go to London, you may lay your account of paying out some sixpences. If you have leisure, I could wish to hear from you before I go away, notwithstanding your apostolical conclusion, which I believe is as sincere, and will be as effectual, as the best of them. I am yours,

"J. T."

TO DOCTOR CRANSTON, AT ANCRUM.

"Dear Sir,

"I received yours, by which I find you have been as much concerned as Mr. Colden indifferent about me; he, good man, recommends me to God Almighty: very well; but I wish he had exerted something more of the layman on that . . . for, to be deeply serious, the . . . . Father of mankind beholds all . . . offspring with a melting eye . . . needs none to prompt him to acts of goodness, so that I cannot conceive for what purpose people's prayers for one another are, unless it be to stir up humane and social dispositions in themselves. I have gotten several recommendations, and am promised more afterwards, when I am fixed on any particular view, which would make them more pointed and effectual; I shall do all that is in my power, act, hope, and so either make something out, or be buried in obscurity. There is, and I am persuaded of it, I triumph in it, another life after this, which depends as to its happiness on our virtue, as this for the most part on our fortune. My spirits have gotten such a serious turn by these reflections, that although I be thinking on Misjohn, I declare I shall hardly force a laugh before we part, for this I think will be my last letter from Edinburgh, for I expect to sail every day; well, since I was speaking of that merry soul, I hope he is as bright, as easy, as dégagé, as susceptible of an intense laugh as he used to be; tell him when you see him that I laugh in imagination with him, ha! ha! ha! Mass John, how in the name of wonder dragged you so much good humour along with you through the thorny paths of systems and school divinity, considering the many hardy attempts you have had to epitomize . . . . and so forth — whenever I began to rust in these —— exercises, the doctor cleared me — well, may wit, humour, and everlasting joy surround you both, and if I but at any time . . . kindle up the laugh from London, I shall be sure to ha . . . . returned upon . . . . with greater force.

"Yours, while I am

"James Thomson."

"If you have the opportunity to be at Maxton, in Mr. Wilson's, there you will find a treasure of a good comrade, called Peter Murdoch, who will stay there these eight days."

Thomson embarked at Leith in March, 1725; and soon after his arrival in London he found himself destitute of money. His first want, says Dr. Johnson, was a pair of shoes; who adds that he had many letters of introduction; but, having tied them up in a handkerchief, they were stolen from him; an accident sufficiently disastrous to a young stranger, in the metropolis, to explain his condition.

His first letter to Dr. Cranston, after he came to London, was dated on the 3rd of April, 1725. It expresses many fears for his success, and is interesting from the account which he gives of the impression made upon him by his first visit to the theatres. Amidst many playful remarks, and some levity in his criticism on the actors, and especially on the actresses, there is an anxiety manifested about his future career, which shows that the state of his resources and the uncertainty of his plans rendered his mind ill at ease:—

"London, April 3, 1725.

"Dear Sir, I wish you joy of the spring.

"I had yours some days since, the only letter I received since I came from Scotland. I was almost out of humour at the letter I wrote for to Mr. Elliot, since it so curtailed yours to me; I went and delivered it, he received me affably enough, and promised me his assistance, though at the same time he told me, which every one tells me, that it will be prodigiously difficult to succeed in the business you know I design. However, come what will come, I shall make an effort, and leave the rest to Providence. There is, I am persuaded, a necessary fixed chain of things, and I hope my fortune, whatever it be, shall be linked to diligence and honesty. If I should not succeed, in your next advise me what I should do. Succeed or not, I firmly resolve to pursue divinity as the only thing now I am fit for. Now if I cannot accomplish the design on which I came up, I think I had best make interest and pass my trials here, so that if I be obliged soon to return to Scotland again, I may not return no better than I came away: and to be deeply serious with you, the more I see of the vanity and wickedness of the world I am more inclined to that sacred office. I was going to bid you suppress that rising laugh, but I check myself severely again for suffering such an unbecoming thought of you to enter into my mind — so much for business.

"The playhouse is indeed a very fine entertainment, though not to the height I expected. A tragedy, I think, or a fine character in a comedy gives greater pleasure read than acted; but your fools and persons of a very whimsical and humorous character are a delicious morsel on the stage; they indeed exercise my risible faculty, and particularly your old friend Daniel, in Oroonoko, diverted me infinitely: the gravedigger in Hamlet, Beau Clincher and his brother, in the Trip to the Jubilee, pleased me extremely too. Mr. Booth has a very majestic appearance, a full, harmonious voice, and vastly exceeds them all in acting tragedy. The last act in Cato he does to perfection, and you would think he expired with the 'Oh! that ends it.' Mr. Wilks, I believe, has been a very fine actor for the fine gentleman and the young hero, but his face now is wrinkled, his voice broken; and age forbids the youthful, clear Cibber [?]; I have not seen much of his action yet. Mills and Johnstoun are pretty good actors. Dicky Norris, that little comical, toothless devil, will turn his back and crack a very good jest yet: there are some others of them execrable. Mrs. Oldfield has a smiling jolly face, acts very well in comedy. . . . . . . Mrs. Porter excels in tragedy, has a short piercing voice, and enters most into her character, and if she did not act well she could not be endured, being more disagreeable in her appearance than any of them. Mrs. Booth acts some things very well, and particularly Ophelia's madness in Hamlet inimitably; but then she dances so deliciously, has such melting lascivious motions, airs, and postures, ... indeed the women are generally the handsomest in the house, and better actors than the men, but perhaps their sex prejudices me in their favour. These are a few of the observations I have made hitherto at Drury Lane Theatre, to which I have paid five visits, but have not been at the New House yet. My purse will not keep pace with my inclinations in that matter. O! if I had Mass John here, to see some of their top fools, he would shake the scenes with laughter. Give my service to him. Tell him I laugh at the thoughts of him, and should be very glad to hear from him. You may send your letters to my mother in Edinburgh in a line inclosed, desiring her to send them to me, which I have directed her to do, frank. However, you may send the next directly to me, to your cousin's care, and perhaps I shall fall upon a more expedite way. I must for the present stop here, and subscribe myself Yours sincerely,

"JAMES THOMSON."

On the 10th of May, 1725, a few weeks after Thomson left Edinburgh, he lost his mother, whom he loved with all a son's tenderness, and to whose talents and virtues he was eminently indebted for the cultivation of his own. In the poem which he wrote to her memory, he thus feelingly adverts to the moment when he took his last leave of her: —

"When on the margin of the briny flood
Chill'd with a sad presaging damp I stood,
Took the last look, ne'er to behold her more,
And mix'd our murmurs with the wavy roar,
Heard the last words fall from her pious tongue,
Then, wild into the bulging vessel flung,
Which soon, too soon, convey'd me from her sight,
Dearer than life, and liberty, and light!"

Among the few persons of rank to whom Thomson became known in London, was Lord Binning, eldest son of Thomas, sixth Earl of Haddington, who had married Rachel, daughter and heiress of George Baillie of Jerviswood, Esq. by Lady Grizel Hume, eldest daughter of Patrick, first Earl of Marchmont. It appears from the following letter to Dr. Cranston, which is particularly valuable for the information it affords of Thomson's situation and prospects, that he had undertaken to teach Lord Binning's eldest son Thomas, afterwards seventh Earl of Haddington, then a child five years old, to read. Thomson was, it seems, then a resident with the Hamilton family, near East Barnet: —

"East Barnet, July 20, 1725.

"Dear Doctor,

"I cannot imagine the meaning of this long silence, unless my last letter has not come to your hand, which was written two or three months since. I would have seconded it, though unanswered, before now, but one thing and another, particularly the severe affliction of my mother's death, incapacitated me for entertaining my friend. Now I am pretty much at ease in the country, ten miles from London, teaching Lord Binning's son to read, a low task, you know, not so suitable to my temper, but I must learn that necessary lesson of suiting my mind and temper to my state. I hope I shall not pass my time here without improvement, the great design of my coming hither, and then, in due time, I resolve, through God's assistance, to consummate my original study of divinity; for you know the business of a tutor is only precarious and for the present. I approve, every day more and more, of your advice to your brother John, as to the direction of his study; if well pursued, it is as honourable, useful, and certain a method of living as one, in his or my circumstances, could readily fall into . . . . contemptible notions of things at home, and romantic ones of things abroad; perhaps I was too much affected that way, but I hope in the issue it shall not be worse for me . . . . what he seemed to be fond of, viz. surgery. It is, as you cannot but know, the merest drug here in the world. Scotland is really fruitful of surgeons, they come here like flocks of vultures every day, and, by a merciful providential kind of instinct, transport themselves to foreign countries. The Change is quite full of them, where they peruse the ship-bills and meet the sea captains. Pray let John know my sentiments in this matter, because through a giddy discontent I spoke too slightly to him of the study which he has now so happily espoused. I am not now in London, so cannot acquaint you with any thing that passes there within my narrow observation. Being there on Sunday last, I heard that all was very dead both with respect to the scribblers of politics and poetry. As for news you never want too many of them, they increase proportionally to their distance from their source, like rivers, or, since I am in the way of similes, like Discord, as the poets personate her . . . . small at first, but in a short time her body reaches from the zenith to the nadir, and her arms from one pole to the other, which is the case of fame. To sound as fame is, when great actions make a great noise [?]. So news are a noise commonly about nothing. As for poetry, she is now a very strumpet, and so has lost all her flame, life, and spirit, or rather a common strumpet, passes herself upon the world for the chaste heaven-born virgin. All my other letters from this, if you will favour me with an answer, shall smell of the country. I need not tell you, I have a most affectionate regard for you, and it will give me as real a satisfaction to hear from you as any man : it will be a great pleasure to me likewise to hear of Mr. Riccalton's welfare, who deserves encouragement as much as any preacher in Scotland. Mass John and his horse also would make a very good paragraph: give my service to them both; to Mrs. and Miss Cranston, John, &c. Yours sincerely,

"J. THOMSON.

"I cannot have a certain account whether Sir William Bennet has lost post or not. Your country news, though they may seem trifling, yet will be acceptable to me. My brother will readily wait upon you, who is just now setting up at Kelso."

Thomson's next letter to Dr. Cranston proves that he was much in want of money. He was then writing his "Winter," the idea of which he had, he says, taken from a poem by Mr. Riccalton, which sets at rest the dispute whether "Winter" was composed before or after his arrival in London. This letter is without the date of the year, but it must have been written in September, 1725; and, as the post mark was Barnet, he was no doubt still with Lord Binning's family: —

"DEAR SIR,

"I WOULD chide you for the slackness of your correspondence; but, having blamed you wrongfully last time, I shall say nothing until I hear from you, which I hope will be soon.

"There is a little business I would communicate to you before I come to the more entertaining part of our correspondence. I am going, hard task! to complain, and beg your assistance. When I came up here I brought very little money along with me, expecting some more upon the selling of Widehope, which was to have been sold that day my mother was buried. Now it is unsold yet; but will be disposed of as soon as it can be conveniently done, though indeed it is perplexed with some difficulties. I was a long time here living at my own charges, and you know how expensive that is; this, together with the furnishing of myself with clothes, linen, one thing and another, to fit me for my business of this nature here, necessarily obliged me to contract some debts. Being a stranger here, it is a wonder how I got any credit; but I cannot expect it will be long sustained unless I immediately clear it. Even now, I believe, it is at a crisis. My friends have no money to send me till the land is sold, and my creditors will not wait till then; you know what the consequences would be. Now the assistance I would beg of you, and which I know, if in your power, you will not refuse me, is a letter of credit on some merchant, banker, or such like person in London, for the matter of twelve pounds, till I get money upon the selling of the land, which I am at last certain of. If you could either give it me yourself, or procure it, though you do not owe it to my merit, yet you owe it to your own nature, which I know so well as to say no more on the subject; only allow me to add, that when I first fell upon such a project, the only thing I have for it in my present circumstances, knowing the selfish, inhumane temper of the generality of the world, you were the first person that offered to my thoughts as one to whom I had the confidence to make such an address.

"Now I imagine you seized with a fine, romantic

kind of a melancholy on the fading of the year; now I figure you wandering, philosophical and pensive, amidst the brown, withered groves, while the leaves rustle under your feet, the sun gives a farewell parting gleam, and the birds

'Stir the faint note, and but attempt to sing.'

"Then again, when the heavens wear a more gloomy aspect, the winds whistle, and the waters spout, I see you in the well-known Cleugh, beneath the solemn arch of tall, thick, embowering trees, listening to the amusing lull of the many steep, moss-grown cascades, while deep, divine contemplation, the genius of the place, prompts each swelling awful thought. I am sure you would not resign your part in that scene at an easy rate. None ever enjoyed it to the height you do, and you are worthy of it. There I walk in spirit, and disport in its beloved gloom. This country I am in, is not very entertaining; no variety but that of woods, and them we have in abundance; but where is the living stream? the airy mountain? and the hanging rock? with twenty other things that elegantly please the lover of nature? Nature delights me in every form; I am just now painting her in her most lugubrious dress for my own amusement, describing Winter as it presents itself. After my first proposal of the subject,

'I sing of Winter, and his gelid reign,
Nor let a rhyming insect of the Spring
Deem it a barren theme. To me 'tis full
Of manly charms; to me, who court the shade,
Whom the gay seasons suit not, and who shun
The glare of Summer, welcome, kindred glooms!
Drear, awful, wintry horrors, welcome all!' &c.

"After this introduction, I say,

'Nor can I, O, departing Summer! choose
But consecrate one pitying line to you;
Sing your last temper'd days, and sunny calms,
That cheer the spirits and serene the soul.'

"These terrible floods, and high winds, that usually happen about this time of the year, and have already happened here, (I wish you have not felt them too dreadfully;) the first produced the inclosed lines; the last are not completed. Mr. Riccalton's Poem on Winter, which I still have, first put the design into my head. In it are some masterly strokes that awakened me: being only a present amusement, it is ten to one but I drop it whenever another fancy comes across.

"I believe it had been much more for your entertainment if in this letter I had cited other people instead of myself, but I must refer that until another time. If you have not seen it already, I have just now in my hands an original of Sir Alexander Brand's, the crazed Scots Knight with the woeful countenance, you would relish. I believe it might make Mass John catch hold of his knees, which I take in him to be a degree of mirth only inferior to falling back again with an elastic spring. It is very elegantly printed in the Evening Post, so perhaps you have seen these panegyrics of our declining bard; one on the Princess's birthday, the other on his Majesty's, in three cantos: they are written in the spirit of a complicated craziness.

"I was in London lately a night, and in the old playhouse saw a comedy acted, called 'Love makes a Man, or the Fop's Fortune,' where I beheld Miller and Cibber shine to my infinite entertainment. In and about London this month of September near a hundred people have died by accident and suicide. There was one blacksmith, tired of the hammer, who hanged himself, and left written behind him this concise epitaph,

'I, Joe Pope,
Lived without hope,
And died by a rope,'

or else some epigrammatic muse has belied him.

"Mr. Muir has ample fund for politics in the present posture of affairs, as you will find by the public news. I should be glad to know that great minister's frame just now. Keep it to yourself. You may whisper it, too, in Mass John's ear: far otherwise is his late mysterious brother Mr. Tait employed, — started a superannuated fortune, and just now upon the full scent. It is comical enough to see him from amongst the rubbish of his controversial divinity and politics, furbishing up his ancient rustic gallantry.

"Yours sincerely, J. T.

"Remember me to all friends, Mr. Rickle, Mass John, Brother John, &c."

Thomson's earliest patron in London was Mr. Duncan Forbes of Culloden, afterwards Lord President of the Session; who is thus commemorated in "The Seasons":

"Thee, Forbes, too, whom every worth attends,
As truth sincere, as weeping friendship kind,
Thee, truly generous, and in silence great,
Thy country feels through her reviving arts,
Plann'd by thy wisdom, by thy soul inform'd;
And seldom has she known a friend like thee."

Having seen his poetry in Scotland, Mr. Forbes received him with kindness: recommended him to the Duke of Argyle, the Earl of Burlington, Sir Robert Walpole, Dr. Arbuthnot, Pope and Gay. Among Mr. Forbes's other friends, to whom he introduced Thomson, was Mr. Aikman, a gentleman moving in high society. The friendship of Aikman was so much appreciated by Thomson, that he wrote some verses on his death, in June, 1731. He was, however, perhaps more indebted for attention and kindness to Mr. Mallet, his school fellow, than to any other person. Mallet was then private tutor to the Duke of Montrose and his brother Lord George Graham. Thomson is supposed to have been introduced by Mallet to many brother poets and wits of the day; and he was assisted by him in negotiating the publication of his first work.

The poem of "Winter," which, reversing the natural order, proved the harbinger of "The Seasons," appeared in folio in March, 1726. As soon as the poem was published Mallet brought it to the notice of Mr. Aaron Hill, who then enjoyed a literary reputation scarcely inferior to that of Pope, and who possessed considerable influence. After Hill had read the piece, he stated his opinion of it in a letter to Mallet, which threw its author into such a tumult of joy, as to bring forth the following extraordinary letter:

TO AARON HILL, ESQ.

"April 5, 1726.

"SIR,

"HAVING seen a letter you wrote to my friend Mr. Mallet, on Saturday last, though I cannot boast the honour and happiness of your acquaintance, and ought with the utmost deference and veneration to approach so supreme a genius, yet my full heart is not to be repressed by formalities; and you must allow me the pleasure of pouring forth my best acknowledgments.

"I will not affect a moderate joy at your approbation, your praise: it pleases, it delights, it ravishes me! Forgive me for the lowness of the truth, when I vow, I'd rather have it than the acclamations of thousands: 'tis so sincere, so delicate, so distinguishing, so glowing, and what peculiarly marks and endears it, so beautifully generous. That great mind, and transcendent humanity, that appear in the testimony you have been pleased to give my first attempt, would have utterly confounded me, if I had not been prepared for such an entertainment, by your well-known character; which the voice of fame, and your own masterly writings, loudly proclaim.

"It would both be disingenuous, and rudely unjust, in me, after what you have observed, to dissemble my satisfaction at several passages in the poem: this let me say, that your reflections have entered into the very soul of my purpose, and, even to myself, cast a light over the whole.

"How rare, how happy, is it to find a judge whose discerning goodness overlooks the faults of what is well meant, at the same time that his fine enthusiastic taste improves the beauties. To you alone it belongs to write so inimitably, and to read so indulgently. If I wrote all that my admiration of your perfections, and my gratitude dictate, I should never have done; but, lest I tire you, I'll for the present rather put a violence on myself: only let me cherish one hope further — of being, some time or other, admitted into the most instructive and entertaining company in the world. I am, with the greatest devotion, Sir, your most obliged and most faithful, humble servant,

"James Thomson."

Mr. Hill's reply increased the poet's transports, and he thus acknowleged its receipt: —

TO AARON HILL, ESQ.

"April 18, 1726.

"Sir,

"I received yours with a soul awakened all to joy, gratitude, and ambition. There is such a noble excellence of mind, so much uncommon goodness, and generosity of heart, in every thing you say, as at once charms and astonishes me. As you think, imagine, and write, with a diviner warmth, superior to the rest of mankind; so the very praises you bestow, bear the stamp of eminence, and reflect stronger on yourself. While I meditate your encouraging lines, for a while I forget the selfishness, degeneracy, and cruelty of men, and seem to be associated with better and more exalted beings.

"The social love, of which you are so bright an example, though it be the distinguishing ornament of humanity, yet there are some ill-natured enough to degrade it into a modification of self-love, according to them, its original. Those gentlemen, I am afraid, mingle their tempers too much with their speculations. Self-love is, indeed, indispensably necessary for the well-being of every individual, but carries not along with it an idea of moral beauty and perfection; whereas social love is of quite another nature; the just and free exercise of which, in a particular manner, renders one amiable, and divine. The accomplished man I admire, the honest man I trust; but it is only the truly generous man I entirely love. Humanity is the very smile and consummation of virtue; it is the image of that fair perfection in the Supreme Being, which, while he was infinitely happy in himself, moved him to create a world of beings to make them so. The excellent ones of the earth, in the exercise of social love, feel it as much to be an original impulse, as the low world that blind affection, they bear themselves: nor are they, in the least, conscious of that forced, cold reasoning, by which it is deduced from so mean an original. How many deathless heroes, patriots, and martyrs have been so gloriously concerned for the good of mankind and so strongly actuated by social love, as frequently to act in direct contradiction to that of self? A great many more arguments might be adduced to prove, that social love is a nobler, independent principle, by itself, were not the secret sense, that every good man has of the matter, instead of a thousand.

"Your writings, while they glow with innumerable instances of strong thinking, and sublime imagination, are peculiarly marked with this beautiful benevolence of mind; and it is that which, at this time, has awakened, in me, these reflections.

"I am ravished with the hope you give me, of your

nearer acquaintance; and that it should ever prove unprofitable, is as impossible, as that it should not be, in the highest degree, delightful to, Sir, your most obliged and most faithful, humble servant,

"JAMES THOMSON."

Thomson paid his first visit to Mr. Hill on the 26th of April; and his delight and gratitude on the occasion were expressed in terms of the grossest adulation. It seems scarcely possible, even with the largest allowance for the difference in their positions, to understand how any man could write to another in such a strain. Poor Savage was of the party, and he is said to have "remained bleak and withered under the influence of Hill's conversation!" Not satisfied with lavishing his fulsome flattery on the father, he bestows a large share upon the daughter; and it is curious to find Hill in his verses to Thomson saying,

"... Would your wit be noised, reflect no more,
Let the smooth veil of flattery silk you o'er—"

TO AARON HILL, ESQ.

"April 27, 1726.

"SIR,

"WHEN I reflect how truly happy I was, yesterday, in your company, it is impossible for me to restrain my sense of it from breaking out into this acknowledgment. There is, in your conversation, such a beauty, truth, force, and elegance of thought, and expression; such animated, fine sense, and chastised fancy; so much dignity and condescension, sublimity and sweetness; in a word, such a variety of entertainment and instruction, as is beyond all admiration. Your smiles have all the encouraging power of humanity in them. What one says, is received with great taste and indulgence; and to listen to you, gives one a secret, and more ravishing pleasure, than to be the author of the best things in other company.

"There is downright inspiration in your society. It enlarges and exalts all the powers of the soul, chases every low thought, throws the passions into the most agreeable agitations, and gives the heart the most affecting sentiments — 'Tis moral harmony! It gives me an additional pleasure to reflect how justly pleased, too, Mr. Savage was.

"Nothing is, to me, a stronger instance of the unimprovable nature of that unhappy creature of whom you speak so compassionately, notwithstanding of the barbarous provocation he has given you, than his remaining bleak, and withered, under the influences of your conversation — a certain sign of a field that the Lord has cursed.

"There is none that renders human nature more amiable than you; and at the same time, none that renders the greatest part of it more contemptible: and to descend from your company, and mingle with the herd of mankind, is like Nebuchadnezzar's descending from a throne, to graze with the beasts of the field.

"Now I feast on reflection — and am like a poor man, that has brought as much from a rich entertainment with him, as must sustain him for many days afterwards. What charms and amuses me, in a particular manner, is, the account you gave us of that little seraph, the young Urania! Her elegant turn of mind; her innocence, and goodness, in the choice of her subjects; her fancy, judgment, and ambition, above her years; and the beautiful struggle of the last (it is unfair to call it vanity), occasioned by the rude stupidity of the school boy, are most agreeably surprising. What you, obligingly, observed of good company's being Ariosto's fountain of thirst, is remarkably true of yours — I shall long impatiently for the farther refreshment of it; and am, with the most entire regard, Dear Sir, your most obliged, and most faithful, humble servant, JAMES THOMSON."

"Winter" was inscribed* to Sir Spencer Compton, Speaker of the House of Commons, afterwards Earl of Wilmington, but Thomson's motive for selecting him as his patron is unknown. Dr. Johnson says the poem was unnoticed by Sir Spencer Compton until Aaron Hill roused his attention to it by some verses addressed to Thomson in the newspapers, which censured the great for their neglect of ingenious men. Of those verses some particulars occur in a letter from Thomson to Mr. Hill; but that letter is of most interest from its showing that he had left his situation in Lord Binning's family, and accepted the office of tutor to a young gentleman in an academy kept by Mr. Watts in Little Tower Street: —

* Mr. Bolton Corney says the dedication was written by Mallet.

TO AARON HILL, ESQ.

"Oldman's Coffee House,
May 24, 1726.

"Dear Sir,

"I hope that your uncommon goodness will forgive me, what I scarcely can forgive myself, my not having, hitherto, answered the last encouraging letter, and copy of verses, you honored me with. The approbation which, out of the fulness of a beneficent heart, you are pleased to give me, I am fond and ambitious of, next to that of Heaven: it is my best reward for what I have done, and a noble incitement to go on. When you approve, my whole soul is awaked and charmed. Pleasing is your praise, but severe is your satire. It is particularly marked with exalted sentiment, and generous contempt. There is a force in it, that strikes through the heart; and a majesty not to be expressed. In a word, it is the unaffected resentment of a great mind.

"It is impossible for me, in the compass of this letter, to say how much I admire every particular line; yet it is as impossible for me to restrain myself from dwelling on some.

'Smile at your vanish'd hope — convinced, too late,
That greatness dwells not, always, with the great.' *

I feel the first line too sensibly; and the last finely insinuates the absurdity of vulgar and hereditary greatness. Your sinking of the Lord's unlasting name in the depth of time, is pleasingly and nobly just: Sir John Falstaff sunk not with greater alacrity, in a lite-

* These lines were altered to,

"Fruitless dependance oft has found too late
That greatness rarely dwells among the great."

ral sense, than they and all their fopperies do in a metaphorical.

"I never read any thing more glorious, than the four following lines,

'Patrons are nature's nobles, not the state's;
And wit 's a title, no broad seal creates.
Kings, from whose bounty wealth's chief currents flow,*
Are poor in power, when they would souls bestow.'

They are the most divine triumph of merit and virtue, that was ever writ. The best way of displaying all their beauties is to read them a thousand and a thousand times over. Your description of the court-haunting, wink-observing bard, is so natural, that, if I am not mistaken, it may be found a picture of some living originals. The last paragraph is very strongly and delicately wrought off; but so favourable to me, as obliges me to suppress all sentiments, save such as flow from gratitude; with which my heart is as full, as yours is with goodness and perfection. You have given me fame; and what have I to return you, but the acknowledgment of a grateful soul?

"How powerfully was I charmed with the four acts of Elfrid, you were so condescendingly good as to read us! There is in them such a rich assemblage of all the excellencies of the best poetry, as is not anywhere to be found. I never met, before, with such a force, and dignity of passion. My heart trembles, yet, when I reflect. But I will not cramp my admiration into the small space this letter allows.

"Mr. Mallet is now gone into the country, where

* This line was changed to

"E'en Kings from whose high source all honours flow."

he justly expects to be vastly entertained, and instructed, by your correspondence. I have been somewhat melancholy since his departure, touched with these pensive emotions, parting with such a friend gives;

'Bounteous Creator of the tender heart!
Is there no world, where friends shall never part?
Be that our future lot, and of such bliss
Grant us an earnest, ere we die, in this.'

"I go, on Saturday next, to reside at Mr. Watts's Academy in Little Tower-street, in quality of tutor to a young gentleman there. Since you have been pleased to raise me, in some measure, to the new life of your favour, let me never fall from it, but frequently be allowed the honour of subscribing myself, dear Sir, your most obliged, and most devoted, humble servant,

"JAMES THOMSON."

The efforts of Mr. Hill, aided, it is said, by those of Mr. Thomas Whatley, a gentleman of acknowledged taste, who commended the work wherever he visited, soon exhausted the edition.*

* To this edition Thomson added the letters "M. A." to his name, but his right to do so is very doubtful, and it was omitted on every other occasion. Warton says, "when Thomson published his Winter in 1726, it lay a long time neglected, till Mr. Spence made honourable mention of it in his Essay on the Odyssey; which, becoming a popular book, made the Poem universally known. Thomson always acknowledged the use of this recommendation; and from this circumstance an intimacy commenced between the critic and the poet, which lasted till the lamented death of the latter, who was of a most amiable and benevolent temper. I have before me a letter of Mr. Spence to Pitt, earnestly

Accompanied, apparently by Mallet, Thomson waited upon Sir Spencer Compton on the 4th of June, 1726, and in the afternoon sent the annexed note to Mr. Hill:—

TO AARON HILL, ESQ.

"June 4, 1726.

"SIR,

"MR. BOWMAN and I are at Long's Coffee House, in Queen Square, Westminster; and, if it be consistent with your conveniency, would be glad to attend the honour and happiness of your company, as you shall be pleased to direct. Mr. Mallet left with me, what they call a Spanish cheese, which he begs you to accept of. At last, I have been with the Speaker, this morning; but would rather give you an account of my reception by word of mouth. We beg pardon for this freedom, which the delightful prospect of your company irresistibly tempts us to. I am, Sir, with the deepest respect, your most obliged, and most devoted, humble servant, JAMES THOMSON."

Not having seen Hill, he wrote to him again three days afterwards, giving him an account of his interview with the Speaker. The inconvenience of having excited a patron's liberality by reproaches is amusingly shown by the dilemma in which Thomson now found himself. Before receiving Sir Spencer Compton's donation, Mallet,

begging him to subscribe to the quarto edition of Thomson's Seasons, and mentioning a design which Thomson had formed of writing a descriptive poem on Blenheim; a subject that would have shone in his hands."

as well as Hill, had written verses upon his neglect of the Poet, which were intended to be prefixed to the second edition of "Winter," then in the press. But the Speaker's present rendered most of those verses inapplicable, if not unjust; and as they were too flattering to the Bard's vanity to be suppressed, he thus states his embarrassment, and prays Mr. Hill to alter his verses so that they might agree with the present state of the case:—

TO AARON HILL, ESQ.

"June 7, 1726.

"Dear Sir,

"Encouraged by that most divine of all virtues, your charming goodness, I frequently, you see, take the liberty to address you. On Saturday last I wrote to you, from a coffee-house in Westminster, but had the misfortune to hear you were gone out, only half an hour, before the letter was sent. Flattering myself, then, with some hopes of your company, I did not mention a copy of verses I had received, on Friday last, from Mr. Mallet, to be prefixed to the second edition of 'Winter;' and which I send you inclosed. That you should read them, was his particular desire, in the following terms:—'Offer my verses to Mr. Hill's perusal, and tell him, that I will not determine their fate, till I first learn his opinion of them: for I know him too nobly sincere, to indulge my vanity, at the expense of your credit. Say, likewise, that I will shortly venture to make use of that permission he so generously granted me, of writing to him, as often as my fear of becoming troublesome will let me.' All that I shall observe concerning them, to such a finished judge as you are, is, that their only glorious fault, if they have any, is an excess of that beautiful benevolence of mind, which, among a thousand other things, make you and him so greatly amiable.

"I hinted to you in my last, that, on Saturday morning, I was with Sir Spencer Compton. A certain gentleman, without my desire, spoke to him concerning me; his answer was, that I had never come near him: then the gentleman put the question, if he desired that I should wait on him; he returned, he did: on this, the gentleman gave me an introductory letter to him. He received me in what they commonly call a civil manner, asked me some common-place questions, and made me a present of twenty guineas. I am very ready to own, that the present was larger than my performance deserved; and shall ascribe it to his generosity, or any other cause, rather than the merit of the address.

"As the case now is, one of your infinite delicacy will be the best judge, whether it will be proper to print these two inimitable copies of verses I have from you, and Mr. Mallet, without such little alterations as shall clear Sir Spencer of that best satire I ever read. I shall say no more on that head; for if there be any reasons for such alterations, you will, of necessity, at one glance, see them in the strongest and finest light. Only this let me add, should you find that the case required some small alterations, and yet not indulge me with them, I shall reckon what my patron gave me, a fatal present. 'Tis a thought too shocking to be borne — to lose the applause of the great genius of the age, my charter of fame! for — I will not name it! But you are too good to plague me so severely. I expect this favour from Mr. Mallet, next post.

"When you honour me with an answer, for which I shall be anxious, please to direct for me at Mr. Watt's Academy, in Little Tower-street. I am, dear Sir, with the most hearty respect, your most devoted, and most humble servant, JAMES THOMSON."

On the 11th of June he sent Mr. Hill the proof sheets of the new edition of "Winter;" and it appears from the letter which accompanied them, that he took it for granted that Hill would comply with his wishes about the verses, but that Mallet found an excuse for not changing his lines, perhaps justly, considering that the generosity which was called into action only by shame well deserved the original reproach.

TO AARON HILL, ESQ.

"London, June 11, 1726.

"DEAR SIR,

"I HAVE been, for some days last past, in the country, else the enclosed sheets, to which you yourself have given the greatest sanction and value, should have waited on you ere now.

"It was your approbation that gave me, formerly, an equally just and noble satisfaction; and the continuance of it is my inviolable ambition. Since I put you to the trouble of altering your verses, I ought to give you an account why Mr. Mallet's were not altered likewise. The truth is, he promised me to alter them, as I wrote to you; but in a following letter told me, that, after several attempts, he found it absolutely out of his power; and, rather than lose them, I resolved to print them, as they at first were. To this resolution your last favourable letter, in a great measure, raised me: and who, that has a soul in him, could forbear to follow the advice you give me, in those generous lines?

'Heedless of fortune, then look down on state,
Balanced, within, by reason's conscious weight:
Divinely proud of independent will,
Prince of your passions, live their sovereign still.'

"I wish, that the declaration, from my heart, with regard to you, in the preface, may not be disagreeable. These sentiments I could not suppress; and they are but a faint expression of the full esteem and admiration I shall ever bear you. May I hope that one of the inclosed copies of my poem can be acceptable to a lady of Mrs. Hill's fine taste, and the young darling of the Muses, Urania, who, in such a tender age, has encountered with all the horrors of so rough a description? Shall I languish out a whole summer in the same city with you, and not once be re-inspired with your company? Such a happiness would much brighten my description of that season; from which, to fill out this letter, I venture to transcribe the following lines:

'Oft in this season, too, the horse, provoked,
While his big sinews, full of spirits, swell,
Trembling with vigour, in the heat of blood,
Springs the high fence; and o'er the field effused,
Darts on the gloomy flood, with steady eye,
And heart estranged to fear; his nervous chest,
The seat of strength! bears down th' opposing stream,
Luxuriant, and arrect: quenchless his thirst,
He takes the river, at redoubled draughts,
And, with wide nostrils, snorting, skims the wave.'

"In your last you were pleased to threaten me, as you term it, with a long letter. I beg you would be as exact, in the execution of your threatenings, as you always are, in the performance of your promises; which shall be submitted to, with the most cheerful resignation, by him who is, dear Sir, with the utmost devotion, your most obliged, and most obedient, humble servant, JAMES THOMSON."

To Thomson's great satisfaction, however, Mallet at last promised to alter his verses; but he was then in doubt how far Mr. Hill might be disposed to follow the example:

TO AARON HILL, ESQ.

"London, June 17, 1726.

"SIR,

"I HAD the inclosed for you, from Mr. Mallet this day, which emboldens me to give you the present trouble. He is so good as to promise me another copy of verses, next post, which gives me a very great pleasure: but my satisfaction is far from being complete, so long as I am uncertain of the like favour from you. Perhaps my forwardness, if not vanity, presumes too much on your goodness; but your already wondrous generosity, in this regard, has raised in me an expectation and ambition you ought, in all poetical justice, to satisfy. If you knew the gladness it would inspire into my heart, you would, certainly, steal a kind hour from your more important affairs, to smile upon my, I will not scruple to say, reasonable fondness. But by being importunate, I shall offer an injury to your ever-ready humanity.

"All that I shall further add is, that on Monday

next the Poem will be printed off. I am, Sir, with the utmost gratitude and regard, your most devoted, humble servant, JAMES THOMSON.

"P. S. The press, if you please, shall wait your leisure."

It would not be easy to ascertain if Mallet did alter his verses, but in those of Hill some changes seem to have been made.

In a long preface Thomson entered into a defence of Poetry, complained of the debasing subjects to which it was chiefly applied, and contended that the works of Nature are most calculated to produce poetical enthusiasm. He then expressed his gratitude to Mr. Hill and to Mr. Mallet for their verses, as well as to a lady, (according to Dr. Johnson, but too well known,) who had graced his poem with some lines under the signature of "Mira;" and he announced his intention of treating of the other Seasons.

"Winter" was universally read and almost as universally admired, and produced to the author the acquaintance of several ladies of rank, among whom were the Countess of Hertford, afterwards Duchess of Suffolk, Miss Drelincourt, daughter of the Dean of Armagh, who became Viscountess Primrose, and Mrs. Stanley; but the most valuable result of the Poem was the friendship of Dr. Thomas Rundle, afterwards Bishop of Derry. That learned person, finding the man to be as estimable as the Poet, honoured him with his friendship, spread his fame, and by introducing him to Sir Charles Talbot, afterwards Lord Chancellor, rendered him an important service.

In Thomson's next letter to Mr. Hill, who was then in Scotland, he thanks him for a flattering notice which he had published of "Winter," and sends him the news of the town:

TO AARON HILL, ESQ.

"London, Oct. 20, 1726.

"Dear Sir,

"Mr. Savage was so kind as to show me a letter you lately favoured him with, by which I had the true pleasure of learning your safe arrival at Berwick, intended tour, and halt at Inverness.

"It is with a mixture of joy, pride, and confusion, I read the favourable mention you were pleased to make of me: what unusual good fortune has thus intitled me to your kind regard? 'Tis nothing, sure, but your own generous goodness, which with your other many matchless perfections, shall ever be my love, and wonder, while truth and harmony are the objects of these passions.

"Every Muse, every Virtue, here, languishes for your return: to me your absence would be much severer, if my partial sympathy in the happiness of my native country did not alleviate the misfortune. I congratulate her on the presence of such a kind inspirer and candid observer: there, you may chance to find, in that neglected corner of the world, depressed merit, uninformed beauty, and good sense clothed in the rags of language. Nothing has appeared in print here, since your departure, unless it be some mushroomish pamphlets, beings of a summer's night, whose only merit is the violent propension with which they tend into oblivion. Memory abhors them, and their essence is, to die. I beg Mr. Pope's pardon, some of whose letters to Mr. Cromwell, were surreptitiously printed by Curll; and yet, though writ careless, and uncorrected, full of wit and gaiety. We have got, O rare! a rostrum, and an orator! since you left us; whose pretended great design is to restore primitive Christianity; and his hopeful candidates are all the beaus, and pretty powdered fellows about town. You were, a week or two ago, traduced by the praises of one of our journalists, who can no more understand the beauties of your writings, than you write to his understanding. A new torrent of Italian farces is lately poured in upon us. The advertisement, which just now lies before me, and begins thus — 'By his Majesty's command, at the King's Theatre in the Haymarket, to-morrow, being Friday the 21st of October, will be acted, by the company of Italian comedians newly arrived, a comedy called The Enchanted Island of Arcadia, or Arlequin King of the Forests,' &c. is such a maze of incredible impertinence, and promises so much folly, that it is to be presumed the house will be very full, and that, too, with persons of the first quality.

"May you soon return to town, resume the Plaindealer, and, if we are not devoted to destruction, restore the great dramatic taste by that tragedy, part of which I had the honour and sublime pleasure of hearing read, by the finest reader, as well as the finest author, in England.

"If your business will allow me one line, please to direct for me at the Academy in Little Tower-street. I am, dear Sir, your most obliged, faithful, humble servant, JAMES THOMSON."

Only one other letter to Mr. Hill has been found after March, 1727, for six years:—

TO AARON HILL, ESQ.

"Oldman's Coffee-house, Monday
morn. March 4. 1726-7.

"DEAR SIR,

"THE news of your safe arrival in town gave me a joy I have not felt since the receipt of your most agreeable letter from the north of Scotland. But while I have not the honour of seeing you, Westminster is at a more gloomy distance, than Skor-urran's snowy top.

"Mr. Mallet, and I, wish, with the fondest impatience, the happiness of your company: which, if we may hope this afternoon, we'll wait upon you, as you shall please to appoint, by a short line with the bearer. I will not make any apology for this freedom to one of your unbounded goodness. I am, with the most inviolable regard, dear Sir, your devoted humble servant, JAMES THOMSON."

Thomson's life for several years can only be traced in his works. It is probable, however, that he quitted the Academy in Tower-Street towards the end of 1726 or early in 1727, and trusted to his pen for subsistence. Some time in 1727 he published his "Summer," and "Britannia." He also issued "Proposals for printing by subscription 'The Four Seasons, with a Hymn on their Succession,'" "A Poem to the Memory of Sir Isaac Newton," and an "Essay on Descriptive Poetry," but the Essay never appeared. In this Advertisement he pledged himself that the separate publication of his "Spring" should not prevent "The Seasons" from being published in the ensuing winter. The Poem on the death of Sir Isaac Newton, which he dedicated, but with what advantage to himself is unknown, to Sir Robert Walpole, was published in that year. This dedication, which was omitted in all subsequent editions,* is worth preserving:

"To the Right Honourable Sir Robert Walpole, Knight of the most noble Order of the Garter.

"Sir,

"Since I have ventured to write a poem on a gentleman who is universally acknowledged to be the honour of our country as a philosopher, prompted by the same ambition I address it to her most illustrious patriot.

"Though by the wise choice of the best of Kings, you are engaged in the highest and most active scenes of life, balancing the power of Europe, watching over our common welfare, inform-

* In the original folio edition of the poem, the title page contains this motto:

"His tibi me rebus quædam divina Voluptas
Percepit, atque Horror; quod sic Natura tuâ vi
Tam manifesta patet ex omni parte retecta.
Lucretius."

ing the whole body of society and commerce, and even, like Heaven, dispensing happiness to the discontented and ungrateful; though thus gloriously employed, yet are you not less attentive, in the hour of leisure, to the variety, beauty, and magnificence of nature, nor less delighted and astonished at the discoveries of the incomparable Newton. The same comprehensive genius which way soever it looks must have a steady, clear, and unbounded prospect.

"But not to encroach any further on your important moments, all devoted to the good of mankind, I once more plead the dignity of my subject for my excuse in this approach, and beg leave to subscribe myself, with the sincerest veneration, Sir, your most faithful, humble servant,

"JAMES THOMSON."

It is said that he asked Lord Binning's permission to inscribe his "Summer" to him, but that nobleman generously sacrificed the compliment to his desire of advancing the Poet's interest; and at his lordship's suggestion, it was dedicated to the well known Mr. Bubb Dodington, then a Lord of the Treasury, in that humble strain of panegyric by which, happily, authors no longer disgrace themselves.

In his eulogy on Newton, Thomson was assisted by his friend Gray,* who, being well ac-

* John Gray, author of a Treatise on Gunnery, who in

quainted with the Newtonian Philosophy, furnished him with a sufficient idea of its principles to enable him to allude to the subject with correctness. "Britannia" owed its existence to the displeasure of the English merchants at the interruption of our trade by the Spaniards in America. Thomson was particularly alive to impressions of public liberty, and eagerly availed himself of a moment of political excitement to indulge his feelings.

In 1728, he published his "Spring," and dedicated it to Frances Countess of Hertford, wife of Algernon then Earl of Hertford, afterwards Duke of Somerset. This lady, whose generous intercession in favour of Savage preserved his life, not only patronized poetry, but was herself a votary of the Muses;* and her letters create a very favourable impression both of her heart and her understanding. If the dedication may be relied

1765 was elected Rector of Marischal College, Aberdeen, and died in 1769.

* On the 15th of May, 1748, the Countess of Hertford, in a letter to Lady Luxborough, noticed Thomson's Castle of Indolence in the following terms:—"I conclude you will read Mr. Thomson's Castle of Indolence: it is after the manner of Spenser; but I think he does not always keep so close to his style as the author of the School Mistress, whose name I never knew till you were so good as to inform me of it.——I believe the Castle of Indolence will afford you much entertainment; there are many pretty paintings in it; but I think the wizard's song deserves a preference:

'He needs no muse who dictates from the heart.'"

on, Spring "grew up under her encouragement," and Thomson was for one summer the guest of her ladyship at her country seat; but Johnson says he took more pleasure in carousing with her lord than in assisting her studies, and therefore was never again invited.

The tragedy of "Sophonisba," which was written and acted in 1729, was his next production; and such were the expectations excited by the author's fame, that the rehearsals were attended by splendid audiences: though, if Johnson be correct, nobody was much affected, and the company rose as if from a moral lecture. Among those who honoured the tragedy with particular regard was the Queen, to whom, on that account, it was dedicated. In the preface the author pleads in extenuation of the errors of the piece, that it was a first attempt: he explains his reasons for choosing its subject, and thanks Mr. Wilks, and more especially Mrs. Oldfield, for their powerful representations of Masinissa and Sophonisba, the latter having, he says, "excelled what even in the fondness of an author he could either wish or imagine."

The success of this tragedy on the stage was not great, though it went through four editions in the year 1730; and Dr. Johnson ascribes one cause of its failure to a foolish parody of the silly line, omitted in subsequent impressions,

> "Oh, Sophonisba, Sophonisba, O!"
> "O Jemmy Thomson, Jemmy Thomson, O!"

which was very generally repeated through the town. Johnson says, on the assertion of Savage, that Pope wrote the first part of the prologue; and as he could not be persuaded to finish it, that the remaining lines were added by Mallet; but the following passage in a letter from Pope to Aaron Hill, dated on the 29th of September, 1731, makes it very doubtful if Pope wrote any part of that prologue. In reply to Hill's request that he would furnish him with an epilogue to his tragedy of "Athelwold," Pope says, "You will, I am sure, be so candid and so reasonable as to conclude I would not decline writing your epilogue on any but a just reason, and indeed (to me) an invariable maxim which I have held these twenty years. Every poetical friend I have has my word I never would, and my leave to take the same refusals I made him ill if ever I wrote one for another; and this very winter Mr. Thomson and Mr. Mallet excuse me, whose tragedies either are to appear this season or the next."

A complete edition of the "Seasons" appeared in 1730, when "Autumn," which Thomson addressed to the Right Honourable Arthur Onslow, Speaker of the House of Commons, and the beautiful "Hymn" were first printed. A very material difference exists between the "Seasons" as they were then published and as they now stand. From time to time Thomson polished his work with great assiduity and success, perhaps from the anticipation that by it he would be best known to posterity. To this labour he was probably excited by an epistle from Somerville, who asks,

"Why should thy Muse, born so divinely fair,
Want the reforming toilet's daily care?
Dress the gay maid, improve each native grace,
And call forth all the glories of her face:
The accomplish'd nymph in all her best attire,
Courts shall applaud, and prostrate crowds admire;
For kind and wise the parent, who reproves
The slightest blemish in the child he loves.
Read Phillips much, consider Milton more,
But from their dross extract the purer ore.
Let perspicuity o'er all preside, —
Soon shalt thou be the nation's joy and pride."

Dr. Johnson admits that these revisions improved the poems in general: but he expresses his suspicion that they lost their *race*. A few examples of the benefit which they derived from reflection and criticism prove that this remark displays more ingenuity than taste; and as instances of the difference between early and subsequent editions of a Poet's lucubrations, they are sufficiently curious to deserve the space they will occupy.* His nephew Dr. Bell intended to publish an edition of "The Seasons" with all the variations; and in a letter to the Earl of Buchan in September, 1791, he said, "I have begun to col-

* See the end of the volume. Mr. Bolton Corney has clearly shewn the additions made to each edition of "the Seasons" in a tabular form. Altogether Thomson added 5541 lines.

late 'The Seasons,' — the edition 1730 with that of 1744. As I proceed in the work, I have more and more reason to think that my labour will not be unworthy of the attention of the public. A great many beautiful passages in the edition of 1730 are entirely struck out of all subsequent editions, and the other alterations made are considerable, far more than I had any conception of previous to collating them with accuracy. The improvements made on the edition 1744 will be taken notice of; they are highly important." Dr. Bell did not execute his design, but a duodecimo edition of "The Seasons" was published by Sibbald, at Edinburgh, in 1789, containing, at the end, the variations between the last and previous impressions.

Through the influence of Dr. Rundle, who, on sending Mrs. Sandys a copy of "The Seasons," observed, that it was "a volume on which reason bestows as many beauties as imagination," Thomson was chosen in 1730 by Sir Charles Talbot, then Solicitor General, to accompany his eldest son, Mr. Charles Richard Talbot, on his travels. With this accomplished young man he passed through France to Italy in parts of the years 1730 and 1731. Admitted to the best society, unembarrassed by pecuniary considerations, and encouraged by the rising influence and generosity of his patron to hope for a permanent independence, if not for a situation calculated for the display of talents, this must have been the happiest period of the poet's life, since nothing more can be desired than youth, fame, health, and competence in possession, with a bright perspective of future renown.

During his absence from England he appears to have kept up a correspondence with Mr. Bubb Dodington, to whom he had dedicated his "Summer;" and his letters,* which show that he was on terms of intimacy with that gentleman, justify a more favourable opinion of his epistolary powers than any others that have appeared. They are also interesting from his account of the impression which foreign scenes made upon his mind, and of his future intentions with respect to literature: —

"Paris, December 27, N. S. 1730.

"M. DE VOLTAIRE's Brutus has been acted here seven or eight times with applause, and still continues to be acted. It is matter of amusement to me to imagine what ideas an old Roman republican, declaiming on liberty, must give the generality of a French audience. Voltaire, in his preface, designs to have a stroke at criticism; and Lord have mercy on the poor similes at the end of the acts in our English plays, for these seem to be very worthy objects of his French indignation. It is designed to be dedicated to Lord Bolingbroke . . . .

"I have seen little of Paris, yet some streets and

* First printed in "Seward's Anecdotes," vol. v. p. 137, and again in the "Universal Magazine," for September, 1798.

playhouses; though, had I seen all that is to be seen here, you know it too well to need a much better account than I can give. You must, however, give me leave to observe, that amidst all that external and showy magnificence which the French affect, one misses that solid magnificence of trade and sincere plenty which not only appears to be, but is, substantially, in a kingdom where industry and liberty mutually support and inspirit each other. That kingdom I suppose I need not mention, as it is, and ever will be, sufficiently plain from the character. I shall return no worse Englishman than I came away.

"Your observation I find every day juster and juster, that one may profit more abroad by seeing than by hearing; and yet there are scarce any travellers to be met with, who have given a landscape of the countries through which they have travelled that have seen (as you express it) with the Muses' eye; though that is the first thing which strikes me, and what all readers and travellers in the first place demand. It seems to me, that such a poetical landscape of countries, mixed with moral observations on their government and people, would not be an ill judged undertaking. But then, the description of the different face of nature, in different countries, must be particularly marked and characteristic, the portrait-painting of nature."

"October 24, 1730.

"WHAT you observe concerning the pursuit of poetry (so far engaged in it as I am) is certainly just. Besides, let him quit it who can, and 'erit mihi magnus Apollo,' or something as great. A true genius, like light, must be beaming forth, as a false one is an incurable disease. One would not, however, climb Parnassus, any more than your mortal hills, to fix for ever on the barren top. No: it is some little dear retirement in the vale below that gives the right relish to the prospect, which, without that, is nothing but enchantment; and though pleasing for some time, at last leaves us in the desert. The great fat doctor of Bath,* told me that poets should be kept poor, the more to animate their genius. This is like the cruel custom of putting a bird's eye out, that it may sing the sweeter; but, surely, they sing sweetest amidst the luxuriant woods, whilst the full spring blooms around them.

"Travelling has long been my fondest wish, for the very purpose you recommend. The storing one's imagination with ideas all-beautiful, all-great, and all-perfect nature: these are the true materia poetica, the light and colours, with which fancy kindles up her whole creation, paints a sentiment, and even embodies an abstracted thought. I long to see the fields where Virgil gathered his immortal honey, and tread the same ground where men have thought and acted so greatly.

"But not to travel entirely like a poet, I resolve not to neglect the more prosaic advantages of it, for it is no less my ambition to be capable of serving my country in an active than in a contemplative way. At my times of leisure abroad, I think of attempting another tragedy, and a story more addressed to common passions than 'Sophonisba.' The Sophonisba people now-a-days must have something like themselves, and a public spirited monster can never interest them. If any thing could make me capable of an epic performance, it would be your favourable opinion in thinking

* Query, Dr. Cheyne?

so. But (as you justly observe) that must be the work of years, and one must be in an epic situation to execute it. My heart both trembles with diffidence, and burns with ardour at the thought. The story of Timoleon is good as to the subject matter, but an author owes, I think, the scene of an epic action to his own country; besides, Timoleon admits of no machinery except that of the heathen gods, which will not do at this time of day. I hope, hereafter, to have the direction of your taste in these affairs; and in the mean time, will endeavour to expand those ideas and sentiments, and in some degree to gather up that knowledge which is necessary to such an undertaking.

"Should the scenes and climates through which I pass inspire me with any poetry, it will naturally have recourse to you. But to hint a return from Young or Stubbs were a kind of poetical simony, especially when you yourself possess such a portion of the spirit."

"Rome, November 28, 1731.

"I WILL make no apology for neglecting to do myself the honour of writing to you since we left Paris. I may rather plead a merit in not troubling you with long scrawls of that travelling stuff, of which the world is full even to loathing. . . . . . . That enthusiasm which I had upon me, with regard to travelling, goes off, I find, very fast. One may imagine fine things in reading ancient authors; but to travel is to dissipate that vision. A great many antique statues, where several of the fair ideas of Greece are fixed for ever in marble, and the paintings of the first masters, are, indeed, most enchanting objects. How little, however, of these suffices! How unessential are they to life! they are, surely, not of that importance as to set the whole world, man, woman, and child, a-gadding. I should be sorry to be Goth enough to think them highly ornamental in life, when one can have them at home without paying for them an extravagant price. But for every one who can support it to make a trade of running abroad only to stare at them, I cannot help thinking something worse than a public folly. Instead of travelling so furiously, it were wiser and more public-spirited should they, with part of those sums of money spent that way, send persons of genius in architecture, painting, and sculpture, to study those arts abroad, and import them into England. Did they but once take root here, how they might flourish in such a generous and wealthy country! The nature of the great painter, architect, and statuary, is the same she ever was; and is no doubt as profuse of beauty, proportion, lovely forms, and real genius, as formerly she was to the sunny realms of Greece, did we but study the one and exert the other. In England, if we cannot reach the gracefully superfluous, yet I hope we shall never lose the substantial, necessary, and vital arts of life; such as depend on labour, liberty, and all commanding trade. For my part, I, who have no taste for smelling to an old musty stone, look upon these countries with an eye of poetry, in regard that the sisters reflect light and images to one another. Now I mention poetry, should you inquire after my Muse, all that I can answer is, that I believe she did not cross the channel with me. I know not whether your gardener at Eastbury has heard any thing of her among the woods there; she has not thought fit to visit me while I have been in this once poetic land, nor do I feel the least presage that she will. But not to lengthen out a letter that has no pretence to entertain you, give me leave only to add, that I can never lose the pleasing sense I have of your goodness to me; and it is a hope that I must flatter myself with your continuance of it upon my return to England; for which my veneration and love, I will be vain enough to say, increase every day, even to fondness and devotion. . . . . Lord Binning says that you are building a house in a very fine taste in London: there I am persuaded that we shall see not an uninhabitable whim of architecture, but an inhabitable house for the climate of England; where usefulness and convenience support beauty; and where beauty dignifies usefulness and convenience."

Thomson returned to England before the end of 1731. New scenes had rather excited than lessened his poetic ardour; and no sooner was he settled than he resumed his pen, choosing for his subject "Liberty."

It has been erroneously supposed by every biographer of Thomson, that immediately on his return he obtained the sinecure situation of Secretary of Briefs in the Court of Chancery, and that soon after he had commenced his poem his young friend Mr. Talbot died. The slightest attention to dates will show the error of these statements. Sir Charles Talbot did not become Chancellor until the 29th of November, 1733, and Mr. Talbot died in September in that year; so that great part of "Liberty" must have been written before his decease, and he did not live to witness the service which his father rendered to Thomson by appointing him to the office alluded to. The truth then appears to be, that, actuated either by gratitude to his patron, or by regard for his accomplished son, or probably by both feelings, the poet resolved to show his respect alike for the living and the dead, by prefixing to the first part of "Liberty" an address which should commemorate their worth. Mr. Talbot died in his twenty-fourth year, and Thomson's eulogy of him is marked by simplicity and tenderness.

In December, 1733, Aaron Hill sent Thomson his translation of Voltaire's "Zaire;" and the letter which contained his flattering comments on that performance, proves the correctness of the rumour that Thomson had exerted himself for the relief of poor old Dennis; who shewed his gratitude by writing some verses on Thomson's kindness: * —

TO AARON HILL, ESQ.

"Tuesday, December 18, 1733.

"Dear Sir,

"I have been almost entirely in the country since I had the honour of yours, and of the inclosed papers you were so good as to send me. The two or three days since my return to town have been rather hurried than employed in soliciting for the benefit of old Dennis. Your well-known and formerly experienced goodness

* Printed in the Gentleman's Magazine for 1733, p. 656. Dennis died on the 6th of January, 1734.

will, I hope, forgive me for having been so selfish as to keep your papers so long. Though I would have had some objections to your undertaking the translation of Zaire; now that it is so affectingly done, I should be very ungrateful, for the great pleasure it has given me, to think of them any more. In reading of Zara, I forget what it was that I objected to in Zaire. You have heightened it with more imagination, but with such a chastised one, as accords perfectly well with the nobler fervency of the heart. The sentiments and reflections, too, rise in the translation, and glow stronger, as well as the touches of the poetical pencil. Allow me to say, that, in these respects, I deeply feel the difference betwixt Mr. Voltaire and Mr. Hill. The more generous warmth of your heart more animates the scene, raises the dear tumult in the breast, and moves me much more. I observed nothing that I wished altered but a word here and there, which are mere trifles, and not worth regard. One, however, I will take the liberty to mention: it is in a speech of the first scene, which marks the civility and gallantry of France — "Where men adore their wives." The two last words I would change into — the fair. — I imagine you smiling at my important criticism, and ready to reply — that though the present French are not famous for adoring their wives, yet those in the good old unrefined days of St. Lewis might. If they do not now adore their wives, they perhaps do better, they make them easy. I shall long to renew the pleasure your play has given me at its representation. What attention I can contribute to the promoting of that, will greatly be its own reward. Mr. Dodington is expected, in a few days, from Ireland: he, I dare say, will warmly favour it, from a double cause — both the love of the fine arts, and his own pleasure. Had you but players equal to those Voltaire had, I would not doubt, in this instance, the taste of our countrymen — almighty nature is everywhere the same.

"Soon I propose to fix in Town for the winter, during which time I hope to pass several happy evenings in your company: Mr. Pope earnestly wishes the same. Believe me to be, most affectionately and sincerely, dear Sir, yours, &c.

"J. THOMSON."

The First Part of "Liberty" was published on the 27th of December, 1734; and the Second and Third Parts appeared in the following year.*

About this time Thomson's only brother John came to London, and acted as his amanuensis; but being attacked with consumption he returned to Scotland early in August, 1735. A letter which the Poet wrote on that occasion to Dr. Cranston is of much interest, not only from the fraternal kindness which it displays, but from the account he gives of his pecuniary affairs and expectations, and of his poem of "Liberty," three parts of which had been then published: —

* "Ancient and Modern Italy compared, being the First Part of Liberty. A Poem by Mr. Thomson. London, 1735. 4to." — "Greece, being the Second Part of Liberty, &c. 4to. 1735." — "Rome, being the Third Part of Liberty, &c. 4to. 1735."

"London, August the 7th, 1735.

"Dear Sir,

"The bearer hereof, my brother, was seized last spring with a severe cold, which seems to have fallen upon his lungs, and has reduced him to such a low condition that his physician here advises him to try what his native air can do, as the only remaining means of recovery. In his present melancholy circumstances, it gives me no small satisfaction to think that he will have the benefit of your directions: and for me to spend more words in recommending him to your care were, I flatter myself, a superfluous formality. Your old acquaintance Anderson attends him; and besides what is necessary to defray the expenses of their journey, I have only given my brother five guineas; choosing rather to remit him the money he will afterwards want, which shall be done upon the first notice.

"My brother's illness puts me in mind of that which afflicted you some years ago; and it is with the sincerest pleasure that I reflect on your recovery: your health I hope is perfectly established; health being the life of life, I will not make you the compliments which I justly could upon the subject; the sentiments of the heart are generally plain, and mine rejoices in your welfare.

"Should you inquire into my circumstances: They blossomed pretty well of late, the Chancellor having given me the office of Secretary of Briefs under him: but the blight of an idle inquiry into the fees and offices of the courts of justice, which arose of late, seems to threaten its destruction. In that case I am made to hope amends: to be reduced, however, from enjoyment to hope, will be but an awkward affair — awkward or not, hope and I (I hope) shall never part. Hope is the breath in the nostrils of happiness, when that goes this dies. But then one ought at the same time to distinguish betwixt the fair star of hope, and that meteor, court-expectation. With regard to the last, I subscribe to a new beatitude of Pope's or Swift's I think it is — Blessed is he who expecteth nothing, for he shall never be disappointed.

"You will see by the three first parts of a poem called 'Liberty,' which I send you, that I still attempt the barren but delightful mountain of Parnassus. I have poured into it several of those ideas which I gathered in my travels and particularly from classic ground. It is to consist of two parts more, which I design to publish next winter. Not quite to tantalize you, I send you likewise some of the best things that have been printed here of late, among which Mr. Pope's second volume of miscellanies is eminent, and in it his Essay on Man. The first volume of his Miscellany Poems was printed long ago, and is every where. His Letters were piratically printed by the infamous Curll. Though Mr. Pope be much concerned at their being printed, yet are they full of wit, humour, good sense, and what is best of all, a good heart. One Mr. Lyttleton, a young gentleman, and member of parliament, wrote the Persian Letters. They are reckoned prettily done. The book on the Sacrament is writ by Hoadley, Bishop of Winchester. All bigots roar against it, consequently it will work your Mass-Johns. I wish I could send you more entertainment of this kind: but a new gothic night seems to be approaching, the great year, the millenium of dulness. Believe me most affectionately yours,

"J. THOMSON.

"Remember me kindly to friends, and direct to me, should you favour me with a letter, at the Lancaster Coffee House, Lancaster Court, in the Strand, London."

On the 23d of August, Thomson again wrote to Aaron Hill, and commented freely on the low state of the theatrical art, and on the degraded condition of literature:—

TO AARON HILL, ESQ.

"August 23, 1735.

"DEAR SIR,

"UPON my return to Town, from Mr. Dodington's seat in Dorsetshire, where I had for some time been, I found your letter, about a month after its date. Had it been sent me in the country, I could not have neglected, till now, acknowledging the pleasure it, and the packet of Prompters you sent along with it, gave me. Though very happy in the company where I then was, yet cannot I help sincerely regretting the loss of that entertainment to which you was so good as to give me an invitation. With the greatest pleasure would I have beheld, and with the greatest zeal would I have countenanced, to the utmost of my little power, the revival of action, which seems on all our theatres to be now both dead and rotten. A friend of mine, who was there, did not, by what he told me, soften my loss.

"I was very much enlightened and warmed by the Prompters upon action: they present no less a strong and beautiful idea of what actors ought to be, than a mortifying one of what they are. As the stage is a powerful school of human polite morality, so nothing can contribute more to barbarize the age than the present condition of ours. There, human nature is represented in as awkward, false, and monstrous a manner, as the human form was by an ancient Gothic sculpture and painting. If that were all, it might be laughed at, and contemned: but since it tends, at the same time, to confound the head, and corrupt the heart; since crowds grow stupid, or barbarous, as they gaze; who can consider it in that view, without feeling an honest indignation? And what crowns the misfortune is, that there is no hope of its ever being otherwise: the root of the evil lies too deep to be plucked up. Was there ever an equal absurdity heard of, among a civilized people? That such an important public diversion, the school which forms the manners of the age, should be made the property of private persons; who, did they happen in the first instance, by an infinite chance, to be judges of the matter, yet may transfer that property to the most profligate, tasteless, and ignorant of mankind. But this, alas! is only one of the pillars of that vast temple of corruption, under which this generation, more than any other that ever boasted freedom, worships the dirty, low-minded, insatiable idol of self-interest. Even to this idol is every public work, which we have the soul to attempt, made an immediate sacrifice. — You see how much your Prompters have inflamed me; and the melancholy conclusion I draw from all is, that I never hope to see gentlemen of equal genius, taste, judgment, and generosity of heart, to the author of these Prompters, at the head of our theatres. I may, however, very well live to see all poetry reduced to magazine-miscellanies, all plays to mummery entertainments, and, in short, all learning absorbed into the sink of hireling scurrilous newspapers. Pardon this supposition in a letter to one, who, while he lives, will never suffer it wholly to take place: in the mean time, go on to stem the torrent of barbarism. I wish you could find an assistant, though never so weak a one, in, dear Sir, your most affectionate humble servant, JAMES THOMSON."

Dr. Cranston informed Thomson of the death of his brother, in a letter dated on the 23d of September, and he replied to it in the following month. His reflections on death are well expressed, and he says that in his opinion a future state of happiness consists in a progressive increase of beatitude. This letter is valuable also, because it contains some lines on the death of his young friend, Mr. Talbot, which were intended for insertion in "Liberty," instead of those which do occur:—

"London, October 20th, 1735.

"DEAR SIR,

"BEING but lately returned from Mr. Dodington's seat, in Dorsetshire, I only received yours of September the 23d, a few days ago. The account it brought me of my brother's death, I was pretty much prepared against, considering the almost hopeless condition he had for some time been in. What you mention is the true point of view wherein to place the death of relations and friends. They then are past our regret: the living are to be lamented, and not the dead. And this is so true and natural, that people when they grieve for the death of those they love, from a principle of compassion for the departed, without a return upon themselves, they envisage them in the article of death, and under the pains both real and imagined thereof; that is to say, they grieve for them whilst they were alive. Death is a limit which human passions ought not, but with great caution and reverence, to pass. Nor, indeed, can they easily pass that limit; since beyond it things are not clearly and distinctly enough perceived formally to excite them. This, I think, we may be sure of, that a future state must be better than this; and so on through the never-ceasing succession of future states; every one rising upon the last, an everlasting new display of infinite goodness. But hereby hangs a system, not calculated perhaps for the meridian in which you live, though for that of your own mind, and too long to be explained in a letter. I will conclude these thoughts by giving you some lines of a copy of verses I wrote on my friend, Mr. Talbot's death, and designed at first to be prefixed to 'Liberty,' but afterwards reduced to those you see stand there. Perhaps some time or other I may publish the whole.

'Be then the startling tear,
Or selfish, or mistaken, wiped away.
By death the good, from reptile matter raised,
And upward soaring to superior day,
With pity hear our plaints, with pity see
Our ignorance of tears; if e'er indeed,
Amid the woes of life, they quench their joys.
Why should we cloud a friend's exalted state
With idle grief, tenaciously prolonged
Beyond the lonely drops that frailty sheds,
Surprised? No, rather thence less fond of life,
Yet still the lot enjoying heaven allows,
Attend we, cheerful, the rejoining hour.
Children of nature! let us not reject,

Froward, the good we have for what we want.
Since all by turns must spread the sable sail,
Driven to the coast that never makes return,
But where we happy hope to meet again;
Sooner or later, a few anxious years,
Still fluttering on the wing, not much imports.
Eternal Goodness reigns: be this our stay;
A subject for the past of grateful song,
And for the future of undrooping hope.'

"Every thing, it seems, is a subject of contention in this interested world. Let his effects be all given to his cousin, Thomas Turnbull, who so kindly attended him in his illness. Only his great coat, jockey coat, I mean, may be given to David of Minto, since he, I hear, desires it. Very likely he took it amiss that my brother was not lodged with him, but my aunt of Chesters I thought more proper to tend and soften his sickness, she being a very good tender-hearted woman. Let her son Thomas therefore have all his effects, except it be the aforesaid jockey coat. I shall be glad besides to render them all other service.

"Please to let me know to whom I shall pay what is due upon my brother's account. Your goodness on this occasion gives me no new sentiment of satisfaction; it is what I have been long acquainted with. If you would still add to your obligations, lay freely your commands upon me whenever I can be of any service to you. There are no news here. The King is expected this week. A battle likewise is by some expected; we hungered and thirsted after . . . . Seckendorff and Belle-Isle. But the French and Germans seem to have fought enough last campaign in Italy, to excuse them for this. The gallant French this year have made war upon the Germans, I beg their politeness's pardon, like vermin — eat them up. Hang them all. If they make war it is to rob, if peace to cheat one another. Such are the noble dispositions of mankind at present. But before I fall into a bad humour I will take my leave of you, being always, my dear friend, your most affectionate humble servant,

"JAMES THOMSON.

"Pray remember me kindly to all friends."

Thomson published the Fourth and Fifth Parts * of "Liberty" in 1736. Though the most laboured, and in its author's opinion the best of his productions, "Liberty" was never popular; and perhaps most persons have found it as difficult to read to an end as Dr. Johnson did, who eagerly avails himself of the neglect with which it was treated to indulge in one of those sneers with which his account of Thomson abounds. It was inscribed to Frederick Prince of Wales, and probably enabled Mr. Lyttleton to introduce Thomson to the notice of his Royal Highness. However grieved at the coldness of the public towards his favourite work, and that he felt it severely is beyond a doubt, one at least of his friends gave him every consolation that praise can afford. That exquisite flatterer, Aaron Hill, whose taste and judgment added zest to his eulogy, and who is not far behind Thomson himself in the extrava-

* "Britain, being the Fourth Part of Liberty, a Poem," &c. 4to. 1736. — "The Prospect, being the Fifth Part of Liberty," &c. 4to. 1736.

gance of his flattery, thus wrote to him on the 17th of February, 1734, after receiving the First Part of "Liberty;" and it is amusing to compare the opinion of a distinguished contemporary with that of posterity on the same subject:—

"February 17, 1734.

"Dear Sir,

"You have lately given me two pleasures; for one of them I am indebted to fortune, who brought me near you, though not quite near enough, the other night, at the playhouse. The second I owe to a hand, I am infinitely more proud to be obliged by; for I received your beautiful present of 'Liberty' from its author. It will be, in all senses, an ornament to my study. It will, also, be such to my heart and my memory; for I shall never be able to think of a loveliness in moral, a frankness in social, or a penetration in political life, to which you have not, in this inimitable masterpiece, both of language and genius, given a force, and a delicacy, which few shall be born with a capacity to feel, and none ever with a capacity to exceed.

"I do not know a pleasure I should enjoy with more pride than that of filling up the leisure of a well employed year, in exerting the critic, on your poem; in considering it first, with a view to the vastness of its conception, in the general plan; secondly, to the grandeur, the depth, the unleaning, self-supported richness of the sentiments; and thirdly, to the strength, the elegance, the music, the comprehensive living energy, and close propriety of your expression. I look upon this mighty work as the last stretched blaze of our expiring genius. It is the dying effort of despairing and indignant virtue, and will stand, like one of those immortal pyramids, which carry their magnificence through times that wonder to see nothing round them but uncomfortable desert.

"Yet you must give me leave, while I but admire your genius, to love your soul, that has such compass of humanity, your poem is not newer than your mind, nor your expression stronger than your virtue. Whatever school-enthusiasm has misdreamt of Homer, that he knew all arts, and that his works have taught their practice, might be almost said and proved of Mr. Thomson's 'Liberty,' without partiality or flattery; whatever has been suffered, done, or thought, through all the revolutions of forgotten time, your more than magic muse revokes, reacts, and animates, till we become cotemporaries of every busy age, and see, and feel the changes, which they shone or sunk by.

"It is possible that this devoted nation, irrecoverably lost in luxury, may, like your

'—— Little artist, form,
On higher life intent, its silken tomb.'

It may rise to future animation, and, its wealth, its pride, and commerce lost, lose also its corruption, and retriumph, in the strength of undesiring poverty. For, certainly, you have detected the sole root of every English evil you deplore so beautifully:

'Whenever puffed with power, and gorged with wealth,
Nations, like ours, let trade enormous rise,
And east and south their mingled treasure pour;
Then, swelled impetuous, the corrupting flood
Bursts o'er the city, and devours the land.'

"Think, seriously, upon this observation, and try if, in all your acquaintance with past ages, you can find a people long at once retaining public virtue and extended commerce. Search, too, as much in vain for one who is, with warmer truth, and better founded zeal, than I am, dear Sir, your most obedient and most humble servant, A. HILL."

In another letter, dated in the following January, Hill pointed out some slight defects in "Liberty;" and in September, 1735, after referring to a copy of "Zara," which he submitted for Thomson's perusal, he observed:—

"The warmth you express against the corruption and degeneracy of our stage is an indignation both natural and necessary in a breast—

'The bounds of self divinely bursting!'

yet fain would I hope, it is not in the prophetic spirit of the character, that a poet, like you, asserts, 'The root of this evil is too deep to be plucked up.'"

Mr. Hill then approves, with the bitterness of a disappointed author, of the anathema which Thomson had pronounced against the dramatic taste of the time. On the same occasion he suggested the establishment of a Tragic Academy, and asked him if he thought the Prince of Wales would give his support to the plan:—a remark indicative of Thomson's being sufficiently connected with the Prince to be aware of his sentiments.

In 1736 Thomson was one of the committee of managers of the Society for the Encouragement of Learning, his colleagues being either persons of high rank or of considerable literary reputation; and about May in that year he removed to Kew Lane, near Richmond, to which place he requested Mr. Hill to direct his next letter, which shews that, in consequence of the failure of "Liberty" as a speculation, he generously resolved to secure the publisher from loss:—

TO AARON HILL, ESQ.

"May 11, 1736.

"Dear Sir,

"It is far from being the want of a due sense of the honour, your two last letters did me, that has prevented my thanking you for them before now: the truth is, they plunged me so deep into your debt, that I was dispirited, through mere despair, of clearing it. But now I am rather willing to declare myself an irrecoverable bankrupt, than any longer neglect to acknowledge the refined pleasure which your generous approbation of my late performance gives me. I call it generous, that epithet having a peculiar relation to whatever you do; besides, I cannot help being afraid that it must, in a great measure, proceed from so humane a cause. In the mean time, however that be, I will avow, that I am justly proud of, charmed with, and most agreeably rewarded by, your good opinion of my poem. Allow me here, by-the-bye, to remark, that though poets have been long used to this truly spiritual and almost only emolument arising from their works; yet I doubt much, if booksellers have any manner of relish for it: I think, therefore (notwithstanding that the ghosts of many authors walk unrevenged), of annulling the bargain I made with mine, who would else be a considerable loser, by the paper, printing, and publication, of 'Liberty.' As I shall, in this case, be possessed of the entire property of it again, I propose, in a year or two hence, to give a new edition of it; and beg that you would, ere then, enrich me with some criticisms, which I hope I shall have the grace to relish as well as praises.

"Your observations, with regard to political corruption, like natural, when come to a crisis, producing more exalted scenes of animation, is fine, and pleases by the future prospect it opens; but it awakens, at the same time, a sentiment no less mortifying, should we find our lot cast in the times of putrefaction; should we find ourselves devoted, in an anti-heroic manner, for the good of posterity. I wish, heartily, that I could refute what you likewise observe with regard to the cause of this corruption. Certainly the kind exchanger of the superabundance for the sweets and elegancies of life, is itself corrupted, and its gifts abused, from the want of taste: for whence is it, save the want of taste, that the continual tides of riches, poured in upon this nation by commerce, have been lost again in a gulph of ungraceful, inelegant, inglorious luxury? But whence, you will say, this want of taste? Whence this sordid turn to cautious timeserving, money-making, sneaking prudence, instead of regardless, unfettered virtue? To private jobs, instead of public works? To profitable, instead of fine arts? To gain, instead of glory? In a word, to the whole venal system of modern administration? And to those gross perishing luxuries, that reconcile, at once, avarice and profusion, centering all in self, and even in the meanest, the material part of self. This disquisition, I am afraid, would very near lead me back again to your observation. It must be owned, however, that the better genius of this nation has often nobly exerted itself, and will struggle hard before it expire. With regard to arts and learning, one may venture to say, that they might yet stand their ground, were they but merely protected. In lieu of all patrons that have been, are, or will be, in England, I wish we had one good act of parliament for securing to authors the property of their own works; and that the stage were put upon the footing of common sense and humanity. And can it be, that those who impress paper with what constitutes the best and everlasting riches of all civilized nations, and of all ages, should have less property in the paper, so enriched, than those who deal in the rags which make that paper? Can it be, that the great, the delightful school of manners, should be abandoned to common sale, and become the property of any one, who can purchase it, to be, perhaps, the school of folly, and corruption? — A simony this, in virtue; which, if not so wicked, yet is as pernicious as that in religion. What would Athenians have said to this! what laughter, what contempt, what indignation, would it have raised among them!

"Now that I mention the stage, I must still insist upon my copy of that only humane new entertainment I have seen upon it of late. I know not what gothic devil possessed the maid at my lodgings, but my few books must not be so robbed of the honour of boasting Zara among them from its author. Having been tantalized lately by seeing you at a distance, I wish you would be so good as to make me amends some evening, and let me know of it a few days before. Mr. Pope was the other day inquiring kindly after you: I should be glad we could, at the same time, engage him. Poor Mr. Savage would be happy to pass an evening with you; his heart burns towards you with the eternal fire of gratitude: but how to find him, requires more intelligence than is allotted to mortals. Life is too short to lose years without the conversation of those one most loves, and esteems; one of which number you must ever be to, dear Sir, your most affectionate humble servant, JAMES THOMSON.

"P. S. Please to direct to me in Kew Lane, Richmond, Surrey; and order your letter to be put into the General Post."

Hill's reply to this letter:—

"One of the natural growths of such a mind, as we see in your writings, is the generosity of your purpose, in favour of the bookseller. I am in love with the humanity that inspired such a sentiment; but, for the sake of my country, wish it may never be carried into execution, because the beauty of the action would, of necessity, prevent its ever being forgotten; and a kind of national infamy, which must disgrace us to posterity, will, as infallibly, be a consequence of its being remembered. I confess myself sincerely mortified to hear that such a poem as 'Liberty,' in such a nation as Great Britain, can have failed to make a bookseller as rich as an ungrateful people have been made by its invaluable fund of manly sentiments; but there are dispositions, in political as well as natural bodies, which have prevalence to help or hinder the effect of medicines: and I am apprehensive, that republican improvements upon monarchical foundations will but spoil two different orders, either of which, alone, might have had strength and gracefulness."

He then proceeds to comply with Thomson's request, by sending him his criticisms in the event of a second edition; and alluding to his complaint of the want of protection for literary property, Hill says:—

"Would to God you were in the right, in that part of your letter which wishes, in lieu of state patronage, in favour of learning, that we had only some good act of parliament for securing to authors the property of their own works. Methinks if the act would go deep enough to reach the very root of your wish, it should, also, secure to the public the education of her gentlemen as well as the property of her writers; since, where the first are unable to taste, the last must write to no purpose. . . . .

"I am pleased to hear that Mr. Pope was so kind as to make any inquiries concerning me. Your good nature was justly and generously employed in the mention you make of poor Mr. Savage."

The annexed, which is Thomson's last letter to Mr. Hill, alludes apparently to the Part of "Liberty," which was published in 1735:—

TO AARON HILL, ESQ.

"Friday Morning.

"DEAR SIR,

"I AM sorry that my present hurry cannot allow me time to answer your kind and excellent letter, in the manner it deserves. The freedom of your criticism I love, and am more proud of your approbation than it becomes me to say: in one the taste of fame is not more delicious than that of friendship in the other.

You, in the last paragraph of your letter, prescribe me a glorious task; to perform which, would demand the same elegant and powerful pen, that prescribed it. Only to attempt it is my ambition. Please to accept of the Second Part of my Poem, and believe me to be, with the most affectionate esteem, dear Sir, your most obedient humble servant, JAMES THOMSON."

A letter which the Poet wrote to his friend Mr. Ross about this period shews the affection he felt for his relations, and his readiness to contribute to their support. The tragedy to which he alludes was "Agamemnon": —

"London, November 6, 1736.

"DEAR ROSS,

"I OWN I have a good deal of assurance, after asking one favour of you, never to answer your letter till I ask another. But not to mince the matter more to a friend, and all apologies apart, hearken to my request. My sisters have been advised by their friends to set up at Edinburgh a little milliner's shop; and if you can conveniently advance to them twelve pounds, on my account, it will be a particular favour. That will set them a-going, and I design from time to time to send them goods from hence. My whole account I will pay you when you come up here, not in poetical paper credit, but in the solid money of this dirty world. I will not draw upon you, in case you be not prepared to defend yourself; but if your purse be valiant, please to inquire for Jean or Elizabeth Thomson, at the Reverend Mr. Gusthart's; and if this letter be not sufficient testimony of the debt, I will send you whatever you shall desire.

"It is late, and I would not lose this post. Like a laconic man of business, therefore, I must here stop short; though I have several things to impart to you, and, through your canal, to the dearest, truest, heartiest youth that treads on Scottish ground. The next letter I write you shall be washed clean from business in the Castalian fountain.

"I am whipping and spurring to finish a tragedy for you this winter, but am still at some distance from the goal, which makes me fear being distanced. Remember me to all friends, and above them all heartily to Mr. Forbes. Though my affection to him is not fanned by letters, yet it is as high as when I was his brother in the virtu, and played at chess with him in a post-chaise. I am, dear Ross, most sincerely and affectionately yours, JAMES THOMSON."

On the 12th of the following January, he again wrote to Ross:—

"London, January 12, 1737.

"DEAR SIR,

"HAVING been entirely in the country of late, finishing my play, I did not receive yours till some days ago. It was kind in you not to draw rashly upon me, which at present had put me into danger; but very soon, that is to say about two months hence, I shall have a golden buckler, and you may draw boldly. My play is received in Drury Lane playhouse; and will be put into my Lord Chamberlain's or his deputy's hands to-morrow. May we hope to see you this winter, and to have the assistance of your hands in case it is asked? What will become of you if you don't come up? I am afraid the *Creepy* and you will become acquainted.

Forbes, I hope, is cheerful, and in good health. Shall we soon see him? or shall I go to him before he comes to us? I long to see him in order to play out that game of chess which we left unfinished. Remember me kindly to him with all the zealous truth of old friendship. Pettie * came here two or three days ago; I have not yet seen the round man of God to be. He is to be parsonified a few days hence. How a gown and cassock will become him; and with what a holy leer he will edify the devout females! There is no doubt of his having a call, for he is immediately to enter upon a tolerable living. God grant him more, and as fat as himself. It rejoices me to see one worthy, honest, excellent man raised, at least, to any independency. Pray make my compliments to my Lord President,† and all friends. I shall be glad to hear more at large from you. Just now I am with the Alderman, who wishes you all happiness, and desires his services to Joe. Believe me to be ever most affectionately yours, JAMES THOMSON."

His sisters and his forthcoming tragedy appear still to have divided his thoughts, for in February he thus wrote about both to Mr. Gavin Hamilton:—

"I lately heard from my sisters at Edinburgh, that you were so good as to promise to advance to them, on my account, a trifle of money, which I proposed to al-

* "Pettie," thus spoken of, was Dr. Patrick Murdoch, the "oily man of God" of the "Castle of Indolence," and one of Thomson's biographers and editors.

‡ Duncan Forbes.

low them yearly. The sum is sixteen pounds sterling, and which I would have paid them eight pounds sterling at Martinmas, and the other eight pounds at Whitsuntide, the payment to begin from last Martinmas. So that the first year will be completed at Whitsunday next. Your doing this I shall look upon as a particular favour, and the money shall be paid here at your order as you please to direct. Please, upon receipt of this, to send to them at Mr. Gusthart's, and to advance to them the payment for last Martinmas, which place to my account. Had I had time this post, I would have written to them to wait upon you. I have a tragedy, entitled 'Agamemnon,' to be represented here about three weeks hence. Please to let me know how many copies I shall send to you, and you shall have them in full time. I have some thoughts of printing it for myself, but if I do not, I will take care you shall have what copies of it you demand. If I can serve you in any thing else here, I shall be very glad."

Thomson's next work originated in gratitude. His constant and generous patron, Lord Chancellor Talbot, died in February, 1737, and in June the beautiful poem to his memory appeared. Pieces of this nature, however creditable to the feelings which inspired them, must possess extraordinary intrinsic merit to create interest when all remembrance of the individuals whom they celebrate has passed away. This merit is however possessed by the article in question; and the reader who turns from the cold and formal, though elegant versification of "Liberty," if he commence the tribute to Lord Talbot, will be induced to go on; and should he not think himself repaid by any other passage, he will be amply gratified by the description of the delicate species of patronage which it is fit for wealth and greatness to bestow.

The opportunity was also taken to defend Bishop Rundle, his early patron and the confidential friend of the Chancellor, who had incurred the suspicion of heresy; and it is not too much to say, that while this piece does honour to the virtues of its author's heart, it elevates his character as a poet.

His motive for perpetuating the fame of Lord Talbot was wholly disinterested. With the Chancellor he lost the situation which had rendered him independent; and though Lord Hardwicke, Talbot's successor, is stated to have kept the office open in expectation that he would apply for it, he failed to do so, and it was given to another. From what cause this neglect of his interests arose must be left to conjecture. It is said that he was listless and indifferent: but he may perhaps have fancied that his eminence was sufficiently great to have induced the new Chancellor to offer what his lordship imagined would have been sought; and he was possibly deprived of the office from a mistaken pride on both sides. The Poet might, however, without meanness, have asked to retain what he already possessed; and the new Chancellor might have had the urbanity to offer to continue that which it was ungenerous to take away; but he who, trusting to the merits of his works, suffers himself to believe that they will procure him that courtesy from rank which in England is reserved for the possessor of birth, wealth, and political influence, will find himself fatally mistaken, and will, like Thomson, have cause to deplore his error.

The change in his condition did not, however, impair his energies or depress his spirits, nor did he alter his manner of living, trusting probably to the sale of his writings to supply his wants. The loss of his situation as Secretary of Briefs renders it probable that it was about this period that he was arrested for debt, and was rescued from a spunging-house by Quin, the well-known actor. The anecdote is highly creditable to both parties, and is deserving of being recorded, as the origin of a friendship between two distinguished persons, which ended only with their lives; and because it contradicts the aphorism, that a pecuniary obligation is generally repaid by ingratitude.

On learning that Thomson was confined for a debt of about seventy pounds, Quin repaired to the house, and was introduced to him. Thomson was a good deal disconcerted at seeing Quin in such a place, and his embarrassment increased when Quin told him he was come to sup with him, being conscious that all the money he possessed would scarcely procure a good meal, and that credit was out of the question. His anxiety was, however, removed upon Quin's informing him that, as he supposed it would have been inconvenient to have had the supper dressed in the place they were in, he had ordered it from an adjacent tavern, and as a prelude half a dozen of claret was introduced. Supper being over, Quin said, "It is time now, Jemmy Thomson, we should balance accounts." This not a little astonished the Poet, who imagined he had some demand upon him; but Quin, perceiving it, continued, "Sir, the pleasure I have had in perusing your works, I cannot estimate at less than a hundred pounds, and I insist upon taking this opportunity of acquitting myself of the debt." On saying this, he put down a note of that value, and hastily took his leave, without waiting for a reply.

The most valuable acquaintance that Thomson ever formed was with Mr., afterwards the celebrated Lord Lyttelton, whom Pope has described as being

> "Still true to virtue, and as warm as true,"

but the precise time or manner of its commencement is nowhere mentioned. Murdoch says Mr. Lyttelton presented him to the Prince of Wales before he was himself personally known to him; and Johnson states that this occurred after he lost his situation as Secretary of Briefs, which was early in 1737. On being introduced, his Royal Highness inquired into the state of his affairs, and

Thomson having answered that "they were in a more poetical posture than formerly," the Prince granted him a pension of 100*l.* a year, but of which he was afterwards deprived.

Pope's letters to Mr. Hill contain several allusions to Thomson's Tragedy of "Agamemnon." On the 8th of December, 1738, he says, "I have been confirmed by Mr. Thomson as to the retardment of his play, of which he has written but two acts. . . . . I have never once been able to see Mr. Thomson in person; when I do, and it shall be soon, he shall know how much he is obliged to you for that plan of an alteration of his Tragedy, which is too good for me with any honesty to put upon him as my own." On the 12th of February, 1730, Pope wrote again to Hill: — "Mr. Thomson, after many shameful tricks from the manager, is determined to act his play at the other Theatre, where the advantage lies as to the women, and the success of his will depend upon them. I heartily wish you would follow his example that we might not be deprived of 'Cæsar.' I have yet seen but three acts of Mr. Thomson's, but I am told, and believe by what I have seen, that it excels in the pathetic."

The reception of "Agamemnon" was far from favourable; and a ludicrous story is told of Thomson's agony at witnessing the representation on the first night, being so great, as to oblige him to excuse his delay in meeting the friends with whom he had promised to sup, saying that his wig had been so disordered by perspiration that he could not appear until he had submitted to the hands of the hair-dresser. It is said, too, that such was his excitement upon the occasion, that he audibly accompanied the actors in their recitation, until a friend reminded him of the indiscretion. Pope was present at its appearance, and was honoured by the audience with a general clap. "Agamemnon" was inscribed to the Princess of Wales, in a dedication which is good because it is short, and because it is free from the fulsome panegyrics common to such addresses. The prologue was furnished by Mallet; the epilogue, which, from not being assigned to any other author, may in its present form be considered Thomson's own, is remarkable for having been altered after the first representation; and in all the editions of the play a note occurs, stating that the whole, except the six lines with which it commences, "being very justly disliked by the audience, another was substituted in its place." It is doubtful if the original epilogue was written by him, and it would seem from the substituted lines, that those which gave place to it were offensive from their indelicacy. With much tact he hailed their rejection as an indication of a better taste: —

"Thus he began: — and you approved the strain;
Till the next couplet sunk too light and vain.

> You check'd him there. — To you, to reason just,
> He owns he triumph'd in your kind disgust.
> Charm'd by your frown, by your displeasure graced,
> He hails the rising virtue of your taste;"

and he concluded with congratulating them on the improvement.

Shortly before "Agamemnon" was produced, Dr. Rundle thus wrote to Mrs. Sandys, whence it appears that that lady had suggested to Thomson a subject for a play, and which he once intended to adopt: —

"My friend Thomson, the poet, is bringing another untoward hèroine on the stage, and has deferred writing on the subject you chose for him, though he had the whole scheme drawn out into acts and scenes, proper turns of passion and sentiments pointed out to him, and the distress made as touching and important, as new, and interesting, and regular, as any that was ever introduced on the stage at Athens, for the instruction of that polite nation. But perhaps the delicacy of the subject, and the judgment required in saying bold truths, whose boldness should not make them degenerate into offensiveness, deterred him. His present story is the death of Agamemnon. An adulteress, who murders her husband, is but an odd example to be presented before, and admonish the beauties of Great Britain. However, if he will be advised, it shall not be a shocking, though it cannot be a noble story. He will enrich it with a profusion of worthy sentiments and high poetry, but it will be written in a rough, harsh style, and in numbers great, but careless. He wants that neatness and simplicity of diction which is so natural in dialogue. He cannot throw the light of an elegant ease on his thoughts, which will make the sublimest turns of art appear the genuine unpremeditated dictates of the heart of the speaker. But with all his faults, he will have a thousand masterly strokes of a great genius seen in all he writes; and he will be applauded by those who most censure him."

In 1739, his tragedy entitled "Edward and Eleanora" was offered to the stage, but its representation was prohibited. To understand this circumstance, it is necessary to allude to the politics of the period. The heir apparent, Frederick Prince of Wales, lived in open hostility to his father George the Second; his house was the rendezvous of the opposition; and as the advocate of liberal opinions he was the idol of the Whigs and other discontented persons. The plot of "Edward and Eleanora" is derived from the well-known but apocryphal story of Eleanor of Castile, the wife of Prince Edward, afterwards King Edward the First, having preserved her husband's life in the Holy Land by sucking poison from his wound. As Edward was then heir apparent to the crown, he stood in the same position as the Prince of Wales; and Thomson availed himself of the circumstance to introduce some passages calculated to strengthen the Prince's popularity by encouraging the people to hope for his accession. Of these the most striking are:—

"Edward, return; lose not a day, an hour,
Before this city. Though your cause be holy,
Believe me, 'tis a much more pious office,
To save your father's old and broken years,
His mild and easy temper, from the snares
Of low, corrupt, insinuating traitors:
A nobler office far! on the firm base
Of well proportion'd liberty, to build
The common quiet, happiness, and glory
Of King and people, England's rising grandeur.
To you, my Prince, this task, of right, belongs.
Has not the Royal heir a juster claim
To share his father's inmost heart and counsels,
Than aliens to his interest, those, who make
A property, a market of his honour?"

"Edward has great, has amiable virtues;
That virtue chiefly which befits a Prince —
He loves the people he must one day rule;
With fondness loves them, with a noble pride;
Esteems their good, esteems their glory his."

"Amidst his many virtues, youthful Edward
Is lofty, warm, and absolute of temper;
I therefore seek to moderate his heat,
To guide his fiery virtues, that, misled
By dazzling power and flattering sycophants,
Might finish what his father's weaker measures
Have tried in vain. And hence I here attend him.
O save our country, Edward! save a nation,
The chosen land, the last retreat of freedom,
Amidst a world enslaved! — Cast back thy view,
And trace from farthest times her old renown:
Think of the blood that, to maintain her rights,
And guard her sheltering laws, has flow'd in battle,
Or on the patriot's scaffold: think what cares,
What vigilance, what toils, what bright contention,
In councils, camps, and well-disputed senates,
It cost our generous ancestors, to raise

A matchless plan of freedom: whence we shine,
Even in the jealous eye of hostile nations,
The happiest of mankind. — Then see all this,
This virtue, wisdom, toil, and blood of ages,
Behold it ready to be lost for ever.
In this important, this decisive hour,
On thee, and thee alone, our weeping country
Turns her distressful eye; to thee she calls,
And with a helpless parent's piercing voice."

Edward is made to say, in reply,

"O, there is nothing, which for thee, my country,
I, in my proper person, could not suffer!"

Many other political allusions occur, which it was impossible not to understand; hence the suppression of the piece was neither surprising nor unreasonable.* The remark of Johnson that it was difficult to discover why the play was not allowed to be acted, proves that he never read Thomson's works with the attention which was incumbent upon his biographer. It was, however,

* Murdoch says, "This refusal drew after it another; and in a way which, as it is related, was rather ludicrous. Mr. Paterson, a companion of Mr. Thomson, afterwards his deputy and then his successor in the general-surveyorship, used to write out fair copies for his friend, when such were wanted for the press or for the stage. This gentleman likewise courted the tragic muse; and had taken for his subject the story of Arminius the German hero. But his play, guiltless as it was, being presented for a license, no sooner had the censor cast his eyes on the hand-writing in which he had seen 'Edward and Eleanora,' than he cried out, 'Away with it!' and the author's profits were reduced to what his bookseller could afford for a tragedy in distress."

printed, with a dedication to the Princess of Wales, the moderation of which is its chief merit. He says:—

"In the character of Eleanora I have endeavoured to represent, however faintly, a Princess distinguished for all the virtues that render greatness amiable. I have aimed, particularly, to do justice to her inviolable affections and generous tenderness for a Prince, who was the darling of a great and free people. Their descendants, even now, will own with pleasure how properly this address is made to your Royal Highness."

The loss of whatever fame and profit he might have anticipated in consequence of the prohibition of his Tragedy, was more than made up by the sympathy of the public. To the latter he appeared in a light which never fails to render an Englishman attractive, that of an injured patriot suffering for the sake of freedom. Johnson states that he endeavoured to repair his pecuniary loss by a subscription, but he says that he cannot tell its success. Upon the same authority it is related, that "when the public murmured at the unkind treatment of Thomson, one of the Ministerial writers remarked, that he had taken a *Liberty* which was not agreeable to *Britannia* in any *Season*."

In 1740 an edition of Milton's Areopagitica was published, to which Thomson wrote a spirited preface. From this time until 1745 he did little besides writing his "Masque of Alfred," in conjunction with his friend Mallet. It was composed by command of the Prince of Wales for the entertainment of his household at his summer residence, and was performed in the gardens at Clifden on the 1st of August, 1740, before a brilliant audience, consisting of their Royal Highnesses the Prince and Princess of Wales and their whole suite. This piece, which contained "Rule Britannia," was some years after acted at Covent Garden, with alterations and new music.*

Three letters which Thomson wrote in the year 1742, when he was residing at Kew Lane, have been printed. Two of them are addressed to Mrs. Robertson, the sister of Miss Young, to whom he was warmly attached, and whose beauty and merits he repeatedly celebrated under the name of Amanda. Those ladies had gone to Bath for their health, and Thomson laments the

* It was entirely new modelled by Mallet, no part of the original being retained except a few lines, and was acted at Drury Lane, and published in 8vo. in 1751. Though well performed, it was not very successful. The prologue was written by the Earl of Cork. It has been said, that Mallet procured "Alfred" to be performed at Drury Lane, by insinuating to Garrick, that, in his intended Life of the Duke of Marlborough, he should, by an ingenious device, find a niche for the Roscius of the age. "My dear friend," said Garrick, "have you quite left off writing for the stage?" The hint was taken, and Alfred was produced.—*Biographia Dramatica.* Mr. Bolton Corney ascribes "'Rule Britannia' on no slight evidence to Mallet." On a point of so much interest, the evidence should assuredly have been stated.

loss of their society in a lively style: a passage in one of them, in which he speaks of Mrs. Robertson's child, in reference to Miss Young, is worth extracting:—

"I cannot help telling you of a very pleasing scene I lately saw. In the middle of a green field there stands a peaceful lowly habitation; into which having entered, I beheld innocence, sweet innocence, asleep. Your heart would have yearned, your eyes perhaps overflowed with tears of joy, to see how charming he looked; like a young cherub dropped from heaven, if they be so happy as to have young cherubs there.

"When awaked, it is not to be imagined with what complacency and ease, what soft serenity altogether unmixed with the least cloud, he opened his eyes. Dancing with joy in his nurse's arms, his eyes not only smiled, but laughed, which put me in mind of a certain near relation of his, whom I need not name. What delights thee so, thou lovely babe? art thou thinking of thy mother's recovery? does some kind power impress upon thee a presage of thy future happiness under her tender care?—I took the liberty to touch him with unhallowed lips, which restored me to the good opinion of the nurse, who had neither forgot nor forgiven my having slighted that favour once."

This letter contained a Song, which will be found in the second volume. Another letter is here given at length, from its being the only attempt of a humorous nature in prose which Thomson is known to have made, and the manner in which he satirizes travellers and courtiers is amusing:—

"TO A FRIEND, ON HIS TRAVELS.

"December 7, 1742.

"TRUSTY AND WELL-BELOVED DOG,

"HEARING you are gone abroad to see the world, as they call it, I cannot forbear, upon this occasion, transmitting you a few thoughts.

"It may seem presumption in me to pretend to give you any instruction; but you must know, that I am a dog of considerable experience. Indeed, I have not improved so much as I might have done by my justly deserved misfortunes: the case very often of my betters. However, a little I have learned; and sometimes, while I seemed to lie asleep before the fire, I have overheard the conversation of your travellers. In the first place, I will not suppose that you are gone abroad an illiterate cub, just escaped from the lash of your keeper, and running wild about the world like a dog who has lost his master, utterly unacquainted with the proper knowledge, manners, and conversation of dogs.

"These are the public jests of every country through which they run post, and frequently they are avoided as if they were mad dogs. None will converse with them but those who shear, sometimes even skin them, and often they return home like a dog who has lost his tail. In short, these travelling puppies do nothing else but run after foreign bitches, learn to dance, cut capers, play tricks, and admire your fine outlandish howling; though, in my opinion, our vigorous deep mouthed British note is better music. If a timely stop is not put to this, the genuine breed of our ancient sturdy dogs will by degrees dwindle and degenerate into dull Dutch mastiffs, effeminate Italian lapdogs, or tawdry impertinent French harlequins. All our once noble throated guardians of the house and fold will be succeeded by a mean courtly race, that snarl at honest men, flatter rogues, proudly wear badges of slavery, ribands, collars, &c. and fetch and carry sticks at the lion's court. By the by, my dear Marquis, this fetching and carrying of sticks is a diversion you are too much addicted to, and, though a diversion, unbecoming a truc independent country dog. There is another dog vice that greatly prevails among the hungry whelps at court, but you are too well stuffed to fall into that. What I mean is patting, pawing, soliciting, teasing, snapping the morsel out of one another's mouths, being bitterly envious, and insatiably ravenous, nay, sometimes filching when they safely may. Of this vice I have an instance continually before my eyes, in that wretched animal Scrub, whose genius is quite misplaced here in the country. He has, besides, such an admirable talent at scratching at a door, as might well recommend him to the office of a court waiter. A word in your ear — I wish a certain two-legged friend of mine had a little of his assiduity. These canine courtiers are also extremely given to bark at merit and virtue, if ill clad and poor: they have likewise a nice discernment with regard to those whom their master distinguishes; to such you shall see them go up immediately, and fawning in the most abject manner — *baiser leur cul.* For me, it is always a maxim

> 'To honour humble worth; and scorning state,
> P— on the proud inhospitable gate.'

For which reason I go scattering my water every where about Richmond. And now that I am upon this topic, I must cite you two lines of a letter from Bounce, of celebrated memory, to Fop, a dog in the country to a dog at court. She is giving an account of her generous offspring, among which she mentions two, far above the vice I now censure:

'One ushers friends to Bathurst's door,
One fawns at Oxford's on the poor.'

Charming dogs! I have little more to say; but only, considering the great mart of scandal you are at, to warn you against flattering those you converse with, and the moment they turn to go away, backbiting them — a vice with which the dogs of old ladies are much infected; and you must have been most furiously affected with it here at Richmond, had you not happened into a good family; therefore I might have spared this caution. One thing I had almost forgot. You have a base custom, when you chance upon a certain fragrant exuvium, of perfuming your carcass with it. Fie! fie! leave that nasty custom to your little, foppish, crop-eared dogs, who do it to conceal their own stink.

"My letter, I fear, grows tedious. I will detain you from your slumbers no longer, but conclude by wishing that the waters and exercise may bring down your fat sides, and that you may return a genteel accomplished dog. Play lick for me, you happy dog you, the hands of the fair ladies you have the honour to attend. I remember to have had that happiness once, when one who shall be nameless looked with an envious eye upon me.

"Farewell, my dear Marquis. Return, I beg it of you, soon to Richmond; when I will treat you with some choice fragments, a marrow-bone, which I will crack for you myself, and a dessert of high toasted cheese. I am, without further ceremony, yours sincerely, BUFF.

"Mi Dewti to Marki. X, Scrub's mark."

In a letter which Thomson wrote to Mr. Lyttelton, in July, 1743, he says he was employed in correcting "The Seasons." At that time he had never seen Hagley, his friend's seat, in Worcestershire:—

"London, July 14, 1743.

"DEAR SIR,

"I HAVE the pleasure of yours some posts ago, and have delayed answering it hitherto that I might be able to determine when I could have the happiness of waiting upon you. Hagley is the place in England I most desire to see; I imagine it to be greatly delightful in itself, and I know it to be so to the highest degree by the company it is animated with. Some reasons prevent my waiting upon you immediately, but, if you will be so good as let me know how long you design to stay in the country, nothing shall hinder me from passing three weeks or a month with you before you leave it. As this will fall in Autumn I shall like it the better, for I think that season of the year the most pleasing and the most poetical. The spirits are not then dissipated with the gaiety of Spring, and the glaring light of Summer, but composed into a serious and tempered joy. The year is perfect. In the mean time I will go on with correcting 'The Seasons,' and hope to carry down more than one of them with me. The Muses, whom you obligingly say I shall bring along with me, I shall find with you — the muses of the great simple country, not the little, fine-lady muses of Richmond Hill.

"I have lived so long in the noise, or at least its distant din of the town, that I begin to forget what retirement is: with you I shall enjoy it in its highest elegance, and purest simplicity. The mind will not only be soothed into peace, but enlivened into harmony. My compliments attend all at Hagley, and particularly her * who gives it charms to you it never had before.

"Believe me to be ever, with the greatest respect,

"Most affectionately yours,

"JAMES THOMSON."

In August Thomson visited Mr. Lyttelton at Hagley, and from thence wrote a letter to Miss Young, which shews that he was warmly attached to her:—

TO MISS YOUNG.

"Hagley, August 29, 1743.

"AFTER a disagreeable stage-coach journey, disagreeable in itself, and infinitely so as it carried me from you, I am come to the most agreeable place and company in the world. The park, where we pass a great part of our time, is thoroughly delightful, quite enchanting. It consists of several little hills, finely tufted with wood, and rising softly one above another; from which are seen a great variety of at once beautiful and grand extensive prospects: but I am most charmed with its sweet embowered retirements, and particularly with a winding dale that runs through the middle of it. This dale is overhung with deep woods, and enlivened by a stream, that, now gushing from mossy

* Lucy, daughter of Hugh Fortescue, Esq., Mr. Lyttelton's first wife, whom he married in June, 1742.

rocks, now falling in cascades, and now spreading into a calm length of water, forms the most natural and pleasing scene imaginable. At the source of this water, composed of some pretty rills, that purl from beneath the roots of oaks, there is as fine a retired seat as lover's heart could wish. There I often sit, and with a dear exquisite mixture of pleasure and pain of all that love can boast of excellent and tender, think of you. But what do I talk of sitting and thinking of you there? wherever I am, and however employed, I never cease to think of my loveliest Miss Young. You are part of my being; you mix with all my thoughts, even the most studious, and instead of disturbing give them greater harmony and spirit. Ah tell me, do I not now and then steal a tender thought from you? I may claim that distinction from the merit of my love. Yes, I love you to that degree as must inspire into the coldest breast a mutual passion. So look to your heart, for you will scarce be able to defend it against my tenderness. Nor is the society here inferior to the scene. It is gentle, animated, pleasing. Nothing passes but what either tends to amuse the imagination, improve the head, or better the heart. This is the truly happy life, this union of retirement and choice society; it gives an idea of that which the patriarchal or golden age is supposed to have been; when every family was a little state of itself, governed by the mild laws of reason, benevolence and love. Don't however imagine me so madly rural as not to think those who have the powers of happiness in their own minds happy every where. The mind is its own place, the genuine source of its own happiness; and, amidst all my raptures with regard to the country, I would rather live in the most

London corner of London with you, than in the finest country retirement, and that too enlivened by the best society, without you. You so fill my mind with all ideas of beauty, so satisfy my soul with the purest and most sincere delight, I should feel the want of little else. Yet still the country life with you, diversified now and then by the contrast of the town, is the wish of my heart. May heaven grant me that favourite happiness, and I shall be the happiest of men, and so much the happier as the possession of you will excite me to deserve my happiness, by whatever is virtuous and praiseworthy.

"Let me now, my dearest Miss Young, bespeak your goodness. I shall soon, I am afraid, have occasion for all your friendship; and I would fain flatter myself that you will generously in my absence speak of me more than you ever owned to me. If I am so happy as to have your heart, I know you have spirit to maintain your choice; and it shall be the most earnest study and purpose of my life not only to justify but to do you credit by it. Believe me, though happy here as the most beautiful scenes of nature, elegant society and friendship can make me, I languish to see you, and to draw every thing that is good and amiable from your lovely eyes. Without you there is a blank in my happiness, which nothing else can fill up. I will not be so extravagant as to hope to hear from you, but I will hope to hear of you or rather from you by the means of our friend. Think with friendship and tenderness of him, who is with friendship and tenderness inexpressible all yours, JAMES THOMSON."

During the year 1744 Mr. Lyttelton came into

office; and the earliest exercise of his patronage was to bestow on Thomson the situation of Surveyor General of the Leeward Islands,* the duties of which he performed by deputy, and of which the profits were 300*l.* a year. He was thus placed above want; and this piece of good fortune must have been the more grateful since he was indebted for it to a friendship produced by his own merits.

In 1745 his "Tancred and Sigismunda" was performed at Drury Lane with considerable applause; and he again found a patron in the Prince of Wales, to whom he says, in the dedication,—

> "Allow me only to wish, that what I have now the honour to offer to your Royal Highness may be judged not unworthy of your protection, at least in the sentiments which it inculcates. A warm and grateful sense of your goodness to me makes me desirous to seize every occasion of declaring in public my profound respect and dutiful attachment."

Part of the Summer of 1745, and of the Autumn of 1746, were passed at Hagley. In 1746, the best of all the editions of "The Seasons" ap-

* It is very remarkable that the Records of the Custom House should not contain any notice of Thomson's appointment as Surveyor General of the Leeward Islands, or to any other employment in the Customs at any of the Plantations. On the 29th of May, 1746, Thomson's friend, Mr. William Paterson, was appointed to that situation.—Letters from Mr. Hume, of the Custom House, to Mr. George Chalmers, 16th and 20th July, 1793.

peared.* Living so close to the Gardens of Richmond Park, Thomson naturally wished to walk in them, and had obtained his friend Mr. Lyttelton's private key, but was obliged to give it up. In a letter written to him Mr. Lyttelton says on the 21st of May, 1747:—

"Dear Thomson,

"I entirely agree with you, that you have the same natural right as the nightingales have to the garden of Richmond, but as those iniquitous gardeners will dispute it, and might overcomes right, I doubt you will not be able to keep the key: nor can I refuse to give it up if demanded, therefore I have disposed of it to the Duchess of Bridgewater, who will be better able to maintain her possession than either you or I, at this time. She is very desirous of it, and I could not deny it her, as she knows I don't use it myself."

This letter contains a remarkable passage, which with two other letters from Mr. Lyttelton after Thomson's death, shew but too plainly that the poet was a better Christian in heart and practice, than in faith; and that Lyttelton's "Observations on the Conversion and Apostleship of St. Paul," were written mainly with a view to the poet's conviction. After noticing the death of many of his relations he says:—

* The copy of the impression of 1744, with Thomson's manuscript corrections, is now the property of the Reverend John Mitford, of Benhall.

"My refuge and consolation is in philosophy—Christian philosophy, which I heartily wish you may be a disciple of, as well as myself. Indeed, my dear friend, it is far above the platonic. I have sent you a pamphlet upon a subject relative to it, which we have formerly talked of. I writ it in Kew Lane last year, and I writ it with a particular view to your satisfaction. You have therefore a double right to it, and I wish to God it may appear to you as convincing as it does to me, and bring you to add the faith to the heart of a Christian." *

The interest which Mr. Lyttelton felt in Thomson's happiness extended to his temporal as well as to his spiritual welfare; and it appears from the following curious letter, that he had, through Mr. Gray, recommended some lady to the poet as worthy of becoming his wife; but that she did not "pique his imagination":—

"Kew Lane, Dec. 14, 1747.

"Dear Sir,

"I should have answered your kind, and truly friendly letter some time ago. My not having answered it hitherto proceeded from my giving it mature and deep consideration. I have considered it in all lights and in all humours, by night, by day, and even during these long evenings. But the result of my consideration is not such as you would wish. My judgment agrees with you, and you know I first impressed yours in her favour. She deserves a better than me, and

* Phillimore's Memoirs and Correspondence of George Lord Lyttelton, vol. i. p. 307.

has as many good and worthy qualities as any woman: nay, to others, and I hope too men of taste, she has charming and piquant ones: but every man has a singular and uncontrollable imagination of his own: now, as I have told you before, she does not pique mine. I wonder you should treat that objection so lightly, as you seem to do in your last. To strike one's fancy is the same in love that charity is in religion. Though a woman had the form, and spoke with the tongue of angels; though all divine gifts and graces were hers; yet, without striking the fancy she does nothing. I am too much advanced in life to venture to marry, without feeling myself invigorated, and made as it were young again, with a great flame of imagination. But we shall discuss this matter more fully when I have the happiness of seeing you at full leisure. What betwixt judgment and fancy, I shall run a great risk of never entering into the holy state, in the mean time I wish to see you once more happy in it. Forgive me if I say, it would be an ungrateful frowardness, to refuse the bounty of providence, because you have been deprived of former enjoyments. If you cannot again love so exquisitely as you have done, so much the better; you will not then risque being so miserable. To say that one cannot love twice, is utterly unphilosophical, and give me leave to say contrary to my own experience. Can there not be more objects than one for the same passion? If so, why cannot the passion be renewed, when it finds a new object? The flame of any love was never so strong yet, as to burn out the heart. So far from that, the powers of the mind rather grow by exercise. The truth is, it is not a former passion that prevents a second: it is only the hardening of the heart from years and harsh untender business. If you could get so much master of your just grief as to think of a second match, I may be tempted also to try to be happy along with you. I wish you joy of the sun's now turning his all-enlivening and beautiful face towards us. May the genial spirit of the returning year animate and cheer you, and yet again make you happy! than which nothing can give greater pleasure to yours,

"J. THOMSON."

"P. S. Mr. Gray discharged his commission faithfully, and with very decent gravity; to whom I gave the same answer I send you. The inclosed I received from the consul of Tunis, Mr. Gordon, whose memorial I troubled you with some time ago. It will give you further light in the matter. Do favour poor Dinwiddie against that old serpent, who would sting him to death for having done his duty." *

While at Hagley, Mr. Lyttelton's seat, in October, 1747, he wrote to his sister, Mrs. Thomson, and, as it is the last letter to his family which has been preserved, it will be read with interest. Dr. Johnson received it from Boswell to whom that lady had given it:—

TO MRS. THOMSON IN LANARK.

"Hagley, in Worcestershire,
October the 4th, 1747.

"MY DEAR SISTER,

'I THOUGHT you had known me better than to interpret

* Phillimore's Life and Correspondence of George Lord Lyttelton, vol. i. p. 307.

my silence into a decay of affection, especially as your behaviour has always been such as rather to increase than diminish it. Do not imagine, because I am a bad correspondent, that I can ever prove an unkind friend and brother. I must do myself the justice to tell you, that my affections are naturally very fixed and constant; and if I had ever reason of complaint against you, of which, by the by, I have not the least shadow, I am conscious of so many defects in myself, as dispose me to be not a little charitable and forgiving.

"It gives me the truest heartfelt satisfaction to hear you have a good, kind husband, and are in easy, contented circumstances; but were they otherwise, that would only awaken and heighten my tenderness towards you. As our good and tender-hearted parents did not live to receive any material testimonies of that highest human gratitude I owed them, than which nothing could have given me equal pleasure, the only return I can make them now is, by kindness to those they left behind them. Would to God poor Lizy had lived longer, to have been a farther witness of the truth of what I say; and that I might have had the pleasure of seeing once more a sister, who so truly deserved my esteem and love. But she is happy, while we must toil a little longer here below: let us, however, do it cheerfully and gratefully, supported by the pleasing hope of meeting yet again on a safer shore, where to recollect the storms and difficulties of life will not, perhaps, be inconsistent with that blissful state.

"You did right to call your daughter by her name; for you must needs have had a particular tender friendship for one another, endeared as you were by nature, by having passed the affectionate years of your youth together, and by that great softener and engager of hearts, mutual hardship. That it was in my power to ease it a little, I account one of the most exquisite pleasures of my life. But enough of this melancholy though not unpleasing strain.

"I esteem you for your sensible and disinterested advice to Mr. Bell, as you will see by my letter to him. As I approve, entirely, of his marrying again, you may readily ask me why I do not marry at all. My circumstances have hitherto been so variable and uncertain in this fluctuating world, as induce me to keep from engaging in such a state; and now, though they are more settled, and of late, which you will be glad to hear, considerably improved, I begin to think myself too far advanced in life for such youthful undertakings, not to mention some other petty reasons that are apt to startle the delicacy of difficult old bachelors. I am, however, not a little suspicious, that was I to pay a visit to Scotland, of which I have some thoughts of doing soon, I might possibly be tempted to think of a thing not easily repaired if done amiss. I have always been of opinion, that none make better wives than the ladies of Scotland; and yet, who more forsaken than they, while the gentlemen are continually running abroad all the world over? Some of them, it is true, are wise enough to return for a wife. You see I am beginning to make interest already with the Scotch ladies. But no more of this infectious subject. Pray let me hear from you now and then; and though I am not a regular correspondent, yet, perhaps I may mend in that respect. Remember me kindly to your husband, and believe me to be your most affectionate brother, JAMES THOMSON."

It was during this visit to Hagley that he was met by Shenstone, who says, in a letter dated on the 20th of September, 1747:—

"As I was returning from church, on Sunday last, whom should I meet in a chaise, with two horses lengthways, but that right friendly bard, Mr. Thomson? I complimented him upon his arrival in this country, and asked him to accompany Mr. Lyttelton to the Leasowes, which he said he would do with abundance of pleasure, and so we parted."

Thomson did not fail to go to the Leasowes, and Shenstone commemorated the circumstance by placing the following inscription in Virgil's grove:—

"Celeberrimo Poetæ
JACOBO THOMSON,
Prope fontes ille non fastiditos
G. S.
Sedem hanc ornavit.
Quæ tibi, quæ tali reddam pro carmine dona?
Nam neque me tantum venientis sibilus austri,
Nec percussa juvant fluctu tam littora, nec quæ
Saxosas inter decurrunt flumina valles." *

* To the much celebrated Poet,
JAMES THOMSON,
This seat was placed
near his favourite springs
by
W. S.
How shall I thank thy Muse, so formed to please?
For not the whisperings of the southern breeze,
Nor banks still beaten by the breaking wave,
Nor limpid rills that pebbly valleys lave,
Yield such delight.

The "Castle of Indolence" and "Coriolanus" next occupied his attention; and the former, which had been in progress for nearly fifteen years, and was originally intended to consist of a few stanzas ridiculing his own want of energy and that of some of his friends, appeared about May, 1748, and was reprinted in the same year. This was the last production of his pen which he lived to print. The sketch of himself is extremely interesting; though he says all, except the first line, was written by a friend, who is supposed to have been Mr. Lyttelton:—

> "A Bard here dwelt, more fat than Bard beseems;
> Who, void of envy, guile, and lust of gain,
> On virtue still, and nature's pleasing themes,
> Pour'd forth his unpremeditated strain;
> The world forsaking with a calm disdain,
> Here laugh'd he careless in his easy seat;
> Here quaff'd encircled with the joyous train,
> Oft moralizing sage: his ditty sweet
> He loathed much to write, ne cared to repeat."

Of the other portraits a few only have been identified. The sixty-sixth stanza alludes to Mr. Lyttelton; the sixty-seventh to Mr. Quin; the sixty-ninth has been supposed to describe Dr. Ayscough, Mr. Lyttelton's brother-in-law, but it was clearly a picture of Dr. Murdoch, as he applies nearly the same words to him in a letter printed in this Memoir. Another was, he says, intended for his friend, Mr. Paterson, the translator of Paterculus, and who was appointed

Surveyor General of the Leeward Islands in 1746.

About 1748 Thomson again experienced the uncertainty of patronage by the loss of the pension of 100*l.* a year, which the Prince of Wales had granted him. This it would seem, from a passage in the following letter to his friend Paterson, arose from Mr. Lyttelton, whose influence had obtained it, having incurred the Prince's displeasure. West and Mallet, two other friends of Mr. Lyttelton, and who were similarly favoured with pensions, were deprived of them on the same day and for the same reason. This letter is proved to have been written about April, 1748, by his saying that the "Castle of Indolence" would be published in a fortnight.

"Dear Paterson,

"In the first place, and previous to my letter, I must recommend to your favour and protection Mr. James Smith, Searcher in St. Christopher's: and I beg of you, as occasion shall serve, and as you find he merits it, to advance him in the business of the Customs. He is warmly recommended to me by Sargent, who, in verity, turns out one of the best men of our youthful acquaintance, — honest, honourable, friendly, and generous. If we are not to oblige one another, life becomes a paltry, selfish affair, — a pitiful morsel in a corner. Sargent is so happily married, that I could almost say, — the same case happen to us all.

"That I have not answered several letters of yours, is not owing to the want of friendship and the sincerest regard for you, but you know me well enough to account for my silence, without my saying any more upon that head; besides, I have very little to say that is worthy to be transmitted over the great ocean. The world either futilises so much, or we grow so dead to it, that its transactions make but feeble impressions on us. Retirement and nature are more and more my passion every day; and now, even now, the charming time comes on: Heaven is just on the point, or rather in the very act, of giving earth a green gown. The voice of the nightingale is heard in our lane.

"You must know that I have enlarged my rural domain much to the same dimensions you have done yours. The two fields next to me, from the first of which I have walled — no, no — paled in about as much as my garden consisted of before, so that the walk runs round the hedge, where you may figure *me* walking any time of the day, and sometimes of the night. For *you*, I imagine you reclining under cedars, and there enjoying more magnificent slumbers than are known to the pale climates of the north; slumbers rendered awful and divine by the solemn stillness and deep fervours of the torrid noon. At other times I image you drinking punch in groves of lime or orange trees, gathering pineapples from hedges, as commonly as we may blackberries, poetising under lofty laurels, or making love under full spread myrtles. But, to lower my style a little, as I am such a genuine lover of gardening, why do not you remember me in that instance, and send me some seeds of things that might succeed here during the summer, though they cannot perfect their seed sufficiently in this, to them, uncongenial climate to propagate? in which case is the caliloo, which, from the seed it bore here, came up puny, rickety, and good for nothing. There are other things certainly with you, not yet brought over hither, that might flourish here in the summer time, and live tolerably well, provided they be sheltered in a hospitable stove, or greenhouse during the winter. You will give me no small pleasure by sending me, from time to time, some of these seeds, if it were no more but to amuse me in making the trial. With regard to the brother gardeners, you ought to know that, as they are half vegetables, the animal part of them will never have spirit enough to consent to the transplanting of the vegetable into distant, dangerous climates. They, happily for themselves, have no other idea but to dig on here, eat, drink, sleep, and kiss their wives.

"As to more important business, I have nothing to write to you. You know best. Be, as you always must be, just and honest: but if you are, unhappily, romantic, you shall come home without money, and write a tragedy on yourself. Mr. Lyttelton told me that the Grenvilles and he had strongly recommended the person the governor and you proposed for that considerable office, lately fallen vacant in your department, and that there was good hopes of succeeding. He told me also that Mr. Pitt had said that it was not to be expected that offices such as that is, for which the greatest interest is made here at home, could be accorded to your recommendation, but that as to the middling or inferior offices, if there was not some particular reason to the contrary, regard would be had thereto. This is all that can be reasonably desired; and if you are not infected with a certain Creolian distemper, whereof I am persuaded that your soul will utterly resist the contagion, as I hope your body will that of the natural ones, there are few men so capable of that unperishable happiness, that peace and satisfaction of mind, at least that proceeds from being reasonable and moderate in our desires, as you. These are the treasures dug from an inexhaustible mine in our own breasts, which, like those in the kingdom of heaven, the rust of time cannot corrupt, nor thieves break through and steal. I must learn to work this mine a little more, being struck off from a certain hundred pounds a year which you know I had. West, Mallet, and I, were all routed in one day; if you would know why — out of resentment to our friend in Argyll Street. Yet I have hopes given me of having it restored with interest some time or other. Oh, that 'some time or other' is a great deceiver.

"Coriolanus has not yet appeared on the stage, from the little, dirty jealousy of Tullus* towards him who alone can act Coriolanus.† Indeed, the first has entirely jockeyed the last off the stage, for this season, like a giant in his wrath. Let us have a little more patience, Paterson; nay, let us be cheerful; at last all will be well, at least all will be over, — here I mean: God forbid it should be so hereafter! But, as sure as there is a God, that will not be so.

"Now that I am prating of myself, know that, after fourteen or fifteen years, the 'Castle of Indolence' comes abroad in a fortnight. It will certainly travel as far as Barbadoes. You have an apartment in it as a night pensioner; which, you may remember, I filled up for you during our delightful party at North Haw. Will ever these days return again? Do not you re-

* Garrick. † Quin.

member eating the raw fish that were never caught? All our friends are pretty much in *statu quo*, except it be poor Mr. Lyttelton. He has had the severest trial a human tender heart can have; * but the old physician, Time, will at last close up his wounds, though there must always remain an inward smarting. Mitchell † is in the house for Aberdeenshire, and has spoke modestly well; I hope he will be something else soon; none deserves better: true friendship and humanity dwell in his heart. Gray is working hard at passing his accounts; I spoke to him about that affair. If he gave you any trouble about it, even that of dunning, I shall think strangely, but I dare say he is too friendly to his old friends, and you are among the oldest.

"Symmer is at last tired of gaiety, and is going to take a semi-country house at Hammersmith. I am sorry that honest, sensible Warrender, who is in town, seems to be stunted in church preferment. He ought to be a tall cedar in the house of the Lord. If he is not so at last it will add more fuel to my indignation, that burns already too intensely, and throbs towards an eruption. Peter Murdoch is in town, tutor to Admiral Vernon's son, and is in good hope of another living in Suffolk, that country of tranquillity, where he will then burrow himself in a wife and be happy. Good-natured, obliging Millar, is as usual. Though the Doctor ‡ increases in business he does not decrease in spleen, but there is a certain kind of spleen that is both humane and agreeable, like Jacques in the play: I sometimes, too, have a touch of it.

* Mrs. Lyttelton died on the 19th of January, 1746–7.

† Afterwards Envoy to Berlin and a Knight of the Bath.

‡ Dr. Armstrong.

"But I must break off this chat with you about your friends, which, were I to indulge in, would be endless. As for politics, we are, I believe, on the brink of a peace. The French are vapouring at present in the siege of Maestricht, at the same time they are mortally sick in their marine, and through all the vitals of France. It is a pity we cannot continue the war a little longer, and put their agonizing trade quite to death. This siege, I take it, they mean as their last flourish in the war.

"May your health, which never failed you yet, still continue, till you have scraped together enough to return home and live in some snug corner, as happy as the corycius senex, in Virgil's fourth Georgic, whom I recommend both to you and myself as a perfect model of the truest happy life. Believe me to be ever, most sincerely and affectionately yours,

"JAMES THOMSON." *

This letter discloses the reason of "Coriolanus" being delayed, and the same or some other cause continuing to prevent its appearance, its author never witnessed its reception.

It was Thomson's habit to walk to London from his residence in Kew Lane, near Richmond, whenever the weather made it inconvenient to go by water. In one of these journeys from London, he found himself, on reaching Hammersmith, tired and heated, and he imprudently took a boat to convey him to Kew. The walk from the landing place to his house did not remove the chill which

* Autograph in the possession of John Wild, Esq.

the air on the river had produced, and the next day he found himself in a high fever, a state which his plethoric habit rendered alarming. His disorder yielded, however, to care and medicine, and he was soon out of danger; but being tempted by a fine evening to expose himself to the dew before he was perfectly restored, a relapse took place, and he was speedily beyond human aid. The moment his situation became known in town, his friends, Mr. Mitchell, Mr. Reid, and Dr. Armstrong hastened to him at midnight; but their presence availed nothing, and they had only the melancholy satisfaction of witnessing his last moments. He expired on the 27th of August, 1748, having within a few days completed his forty-eighth year. Of his illness all that is known is stated in the following letter from Mr. Mitchell:—

TO THE REVEREND MR. GUSTHART, MINISTER AT EDINBURGH.

"Richmond, August 27th, 1748.

"Dear Sir,

"It is with the most sincere and unaffected concern that I must acquaint you with the death of our worthy friend Mr. Thomson. He expired this morning about 4 o'clock, after a short illness: his distemper appeared first in the shape of tertian, but soon turned to a continued fever. I came here on the first notice I had of his illness, and shall see the last duties paid to my deceased friend. I have ordered every thing to be sealed up, and you will take the most proper method to acquaint his relations with what has happened, as I do not know how to direct to them. At present I see no occasion for any of them coming to London, as it will only occasion expense, and they shall have notice how affairs stand. I am, dear Sir, your most humble servant, ANDREW MITCHELL."

The sincerity and warmth of Mr. Lyttelton's affection for Thomson are strikingly shewn in two letters to Dr. Doddridge. On the 30th of September, 1748, a month after the Poet's death, he says:—

"I HEARTILY thank you for your last letter and the picture you give me in it of Mrs. Doddridge, in which I see so strong a resemblance to my dear Lucy that I don't wonder you think your whole earthly happiness wrapt as in her life. I pray God to preserve her to you, and save your heart from the pangs which mine has felt and still feels! I could hardly bear to read the letter you was so kind to send me a copy of, or the story you tell me, so much did I find in both to put me in mind of what I have lost. But God's will be done! it has pleased his providence to afflict me lately with a new stroke in the sudden death of poor Mr. Thomson, one of the best and most beloved of my friends. He loved my Lucy too, and was loved by her; I hope and trust in the Divine Goodness that they are now together in a much happier state: that is my consolation, that is my support." *

On the 7th of November following, Mr. Lyttelton wrote again to Dr. Doddridge, and gave the

* Phillimore's Memoirs of Lord Lyttelton, vol. i. p. 406.

following satisfactory account of Thomson's religious sentiments on his death-bed: —

"I HAVE not read the sermons you mention, but will upon your recommendation. Thomson I hope and believe died a Christian. Had he lived longer I don't doubt but he would have openly profest his faith; for he wanted no courage in what he thought right, but his mind had been much perplexed with doubts which I have the pleasure to think my book on St. Paul had almost entirely removed. He told me so himself, and in his sickness declared so to others. This is my best consolation in the loss of him, for as to the heart of a Christian he always had that, in a degree of perfection beyond most men I have known." *

Mr. Mitchell and Mr. Lyttelton charged themselves with the care of his effects; and on the 25th of October, 1748, letters of administration were granted to them as attorneys of his sister, and next of kin, Mary Craig, of Edinburgh, formerly Thomson, wife of William Craig, for her use.

It was the next object of these generous friends to bring Thomson's posthumous tragedy before the public, and in 1749, "Coriolanus" was acted for the benefit of his relations. The Prologue, which was written by Mr. Lyttelton, and was spoken by Quin, is peculiarly entitled to notice from the affecting manner in which the writer speaks of the author: —

* Ibid. 409.

"I come not here your candour to implore
For scenes, whose author is, alas! no more;
He wants no advocate his cause to plead;
You will yourselves be patrons of the dead.
No party his benevolence confined,
No sect — alike it flow'd to all mankind.
He loved his friends, — forgive this gushing tear,
Alas! I feel I am no actor here, —
He loved his friends with such a warmth of heart,
So clear of interest, so devoid of art,
Such generous friendship, such unshaken zeal,
No words can speak it, but our tears may tell.
Oh candid truth, O faith without a stain,
Oh manners gently firm, and nobly plain,
Oh sympathizing love of others' bliss,
Where will you find another breast like his?
Such was the Man — the Poet well you know:
Oft has he touched your hearts with tender woe:
Oft in this crowded house, with just applause
You heard him teach fair Virtue's purest laws;
For his chaste Muse employ'd her heaven-taught lyre
None but the noblest passions to inspire,
Not one immoral, one corrupted thought,
One line, which dying he could wish to blot.
Oh, may to-night your favourable doom
Another laurel add to grace his tomb:
Whilst he, superior now to praise or blame,
Hears not the feeble voice of human fame.
Yet if to those, whom most on earth he loved,
From whom his pious care is now removed,
With whom his liberal hand, and bounteous heart,
Shared all his little fortune could impart;
If to those friends your kind regard shall give
What they no longer can from his receive,
That, that, even now, above yon starry pole,
May touch with pleasure his immortal soul."

Truly was the speaker made to say he was no actor on that occasion; and the feeling which he evinced, in reciting these verses, gave increased effect to their touching eloquence.

Within a few months of his death, his old patroness, the Countess of Hertford, stated in a letter to Lady Luxborough, that Shenstone had shown her his Poem on Autumn, and the honour he had done Thomson's memory in it; adding, that he told her he purposed erecting an urn to him in Virgil's Grove. In a letter to Shenstone in November, 1753, that lady, then Duchess of Somerset, requested him to allow Dodsley to add to his collection his poem called "Damon's Bower," addressed to William Lyttelton, Esq., and offered to lend him a copy if he had lost the original. These passages prove her grace's respect for his memory, and render Johnson's remark, that he had displeased her, unlikely. Shenstone speaks feelingly of Thomson's death in a letter written on the 3d of September following:—

"Poor Mr. Thomson, Mr. Pitt tells me, is dead. He was to have been at Hagley this week, and then I should probably have seen him here. As it is, I will erect an urn in Virgil's Grove to his memory. I was really as much shocked to hear of his death, as if I had known and loved him for a number of years. God knows I lean on a very few friends, and if they drop me, I become a wretched misanthrope."

The author of The Seasons is thus alluded to

in Shenstone's Poem, mentioned by the Duchess of Somerset:—

"Though Thomson, sweet descriptive bard!
Inspiring Autumn sung;
Yet how should we the months regard
That stopp'd his flowing tongue?

"Ah! luckless months, of all the rest,
To whose hard share it fell!
For sure he was the gentlest breast
That ever sung so well.

"He! he is gone, whose moral strain
Could wit and mirth refine;
He! he is gone, whose social vein
Surpass'd the power of wine.

"Fast by the streams he deign'd to praise
In yon sequester'd grove,
To him a votive urn I raise,
To him and friendly Love.

"Yes, there, my Friend! forlorn and sad,
I grave your Thomson's name,
And there his lyre, which Fate forbade
To sound your growing fame.

"There shall my plaintive song recount
Dark themes of hopeless woe,
And faster than the dropping fount
I'll teach mine eyes to flow.

"There leaves, in spite of Autumn green,
Shall shade the hallow'd ground,
And Spring will there again be seen
To call forth flowers around.

"But no kind suns will bid me share,
Once more, his social hour;
Ah! Spring! thou never canst repair
This loss to Damon's bower."

Thomson's funeral was attended by Quin, Mallet, Mr. Robertson, (the brother-in-law of his Amanda,) and another friend, probably either Mr. Lyttelton or Mr. Mitchell. He was buried in Richmond Church, under a plain stone without any inscription, and his works formed his only memorial until the erection of the monument in Westminster Abbey, which was opened to public view on the 10th of May, 1762. The cost of it was defrayed by an edition of his works printed in that year in two quarto volumes, and published by subscription. It is situated between those of Shakespeare and Rowe, and Thomson appears sitting, leaning his left arm upon a pedestal, and holding a book with the cap of liberty in his right hand. Upon the pedestal is carved a bas-relief of "The Seasons," to which a boy points, offering him a laurel crown as the reward of his genius. At the feet of the figure is a tragic mask and ancient harp. The whole is supported by a projecting pedestal; and on a panel is inscribed his name, age, and the date of his death, with the lines which are inserted at the commencement of this Memoir, taken from his "Summer." The monument was designed by Adam, and executed by Michael Henry Spang.

Lord Buchan afterwards placed a small brass tablet in Richmond Church with the following inscription:—

In the earth, below this tablet,
are the remains of
JAMES THOMSON,
Author of the beautiful Poems, entituled
"The Seasons," the "Castle of Indolence," &c.
who died at Richmond
on the 27th of August,
and was buried
on the 29th O. S. 1748.
The Earl of Buchan,
unwilling that
so good a Man, and sweet a Poet,
should be without a memorial,
has denoted the place of his interment,
for the satisfaction of his Admirers,
in the year of our Lord,
M.DCC.XCII.

Beneath this inscription, his lordship added this beautiful passage from Winter: —

"Father of Light and Life! thou Good Supreme!
O teach me what is good! teach me thyself!
Save me from folly, vanity, and vice,
From every low pursuit! and feed my soul
With knowledge, conscious peace, and virtue pure;
Sacred, substantial, never fading bliss!"

By the sale of an edition of his works, undertaken for the purpose of aiding his relations, and the profits of his last Tragedy, a sufficient sum was raised to liquidate all his debts and to leave a handsome residue.*

* A correspondent in the European Magazine, for 1819, has afforded very satisfactory information about the sums which Thomson obtained for several of his works, and of the dates

There is reason to believe that a fragment of a poem was found amongst Thomson's papers, as Dr. Bell remarks, in his letter to Lord Buchan, in September, 1791:—

"I remember to have heard my aunt, Mrs. Thomson, say, that the outlines of a fine poem were found among her brother's papers after his death. If this was the case, Mr. Gray, of Richmond Hill, got possession of them. The heirs of that gentleman will be able to ascertain the fact; and to put it in my power, if they are worthy of Thomson's character, to give

of the agreements respecting them, derived from an appeal against a decision of the Court of Chancery, many years since, on a question of literary property.

It appears that Thomson sold "Sophonisba," a Tragedy, and "Spring," a Poem, to Andrew Millar, on the 16th of January, 1729, for 137*l.* 10*s.* On the 28th of July, in the same year, he sold to John Millan, "Summer," "Winter," "Autumn," "Britannia," Poem to Newton, the Hymn, and an Essay on Descriptive Poetry, for 105*l.* On the 16th of June, 1738, Andrew Millar purchased these Poems of John Millan at the original price. On the 13th of June, 1769, Andrew Millar's executors sold the copyright of the whole by auction to fifteen London booksellers, for the sum of 505*l.* Soon after Davis, the Bookseller, sold half his twelfth, for the shares were unequal, to Becket and Dehondt, not of the original list of purchasers, for 21*l.*, being the price he had paid for that proportion.

This was a close sale; and Alexander Donaldson, the Edinburgh Bookseller, who wished to attend, was not admitted. He then published a copy of "The Seasons" at Edinburgh, stated in the title to be printed in 1768, the sale of which was said, however, to have begun, before the auction of the copyright took place.

them to the public. Your lordship has taken so much trouble in this little plan of mine, that I am ashamed to throw out this hint."

An original picture of Thomson, by Slaughter, is preserved at Dryburgh Abbey, the seat of Lord Buchan, and has been engraved. It belonged to the Poet, and hung in the room he used at Slaughter's Coffee-house. On the back is this inscription, in his Lordship's hand-writing:—

"Procured for the Earl of Buchan by his friend, Richard Cooper, Esq., engraver. Thomson and his friends, Dr. Anderson, Peter Murdoch, &c. used to frequent Old Slaughter's

A singular anecdote was related in the Edinburgh Star, dated from Logan House, G. D. October, 1821, and signed "An Old Shepherd," which tends to fix the authorship of "The Gentle Shepherd," attributed to Allan Ramsay, on Thomson. To what degree of credit it is entitled is left to the reader to determine. The following is the statement on the subject, which was copied into the Gentleman's Magazine, vol. xci. part ii. p. 351.

"About thirty years ago, there was a respectable old man, of the name of John Steel, who was well acquainted with Allan Ramsay; and he told John Steel himself, that when Mr. Thomson, the author of 'The Seasons,' was in his shop at Edinburgh, getting himself shaven, Ramsay was repeating some of his poems. Mr. Thomson says to him, 'I have something to emit to the world, but I do not wish to father it.' Ramsay asked what he would give him, and he would father it. Mr. Thomson replied, all the profit that arose from the publication. 'A bargain be it,' said Ramsay. Mr. Thomson delivered him the manuscript. So, from what is said above, Mr. Thomson, the author of 'The Seasons,' is the author of 'The Gentle Shepherd,' and Allan Ramsay is the father of it. This, I believe, is the truth."

Coffee-house, London, and his portrait was painted at that time by Slaughter, a kinsman of old Slaughter.

"Dec. 3, 1812. BUCHAN."

A monument to Thomson has been erected on an eminence, about half-way between Kelso and Ednam, but the only admiration which it is likely to excite is for the motives of those to whom it owes its existence. Taste is rarer even than money; and it is lamentable to reflect that, however calculated the monuments in this country, to departed greatness, may be to exalt the fame of the deceased, they have often a contrary effect upon the reputation of the persons who superintended their erection.

In the whole range of British poetry Thomson's "Seasons" are, perhaps, the earliest read, and most generally admired. He was the Poet of Nature, and studying her deeply, his mind acquired that placidity of thought and feeling which an abstraction from public life is sure to produce. She was to him, as he has himself said, a source of happiness of which Fortune could not deprive him:—

"I care not, Fortune, what you me deny;
You cannot rob me of free Nature's grace;
You cannot shut the windows of the sky,
Through which Aurora shows her brightening face;
You cannot bar my constant feet to trace
The woods and lawns, by living stream at eve:
Let health my nerves and finer fibres leave;
Of fancy, reason, virtue, nought can me bereave."

His pictures of scenery and of rural life are the productions of a master, and render him the Claude of Poets. "The Seasons" are the first book from which we are taught to worship the goddess to whose service the bard of Ednam devoted himself; and who is there that has reflected on the magnificence of an extended landscape, viewed the sun as he emerges from the horizon, or witnessed the setting of that glorious orb when he leaves the world to reflection and repose, and does not feel his descriptions rush upon the mind, and heighten the enjoyment?

It has been said that the style of that work is pompous, and that it contains many faults. The remark is partially true. Thomson's style is, in some places, monotonous, from its unvaried elevation; but to him Nature was a subject of the profoundest reverence; and he, doubtless, considered that she ought to be spoken of with solemnity. It is evident, however, from one of his verses, which is often cited, that he was aware simplicity is the most becoming garb of beauty. Another objection to "The Seasons" is, that they contain frequent digressions; and, though it is made by an authority from which it may be presumptuous to dissent, the justice of the observation cannot, perhaps, be established. Every one who has read them will admit that the History of Celedon and Amelia, and of Lavinia, for example, have afforded as much pleasure as any other parts;

and a poem descriptive of scenery, and of changes in the weather, requires the introduction of human beings to give it life and animation. A painter is not censured for adding figures to a landscape, and he is only required to render them graceful, and to make them harmonize with his subject. The characters in "The Seasons" are all in keeping; a gleaner is as necessary to a harvest field as a lover to a romance; and it seems hypercritical to say that there should be nothing to interest the feeling in the lives of the inhabitants of the villages or hamlets which are described.

Another test of the soundness of this criticism is, to inquire, whether "The Seasons" do not owe their chief popularity to those very digressions. Few persons will read a volume, however beautiful the descriptions which it contains, unless they are relieved by incidents of human life; and, if it were possible to strip "The Seasons" of every passage not strictly relevant, they would probably lose their chief attractions, and soon be thrown aside.

One charm of poetry is, that it often represents the idiosyncrasy of the Poet's mind, and which is most conspicuous in the episodes to the immediate subject of his labours. The thoughts which led him astray may not unfrequently be discovered; and it is on such occasions, chiefly, that those beautiful passages which become aphorisms to future ages occur. Genius seems then to cast aside all the fetters that art imposes; and the mistress who has cheered his hopes, or the coquette who has abandoned him, his friend, or his enemy, as they present themselves to his imagination, are sure to be commemorated in words glowing with the fervour of inspiration. While he pursues the thread of his tale, we are reminded of the Poet only; and though we admire his artistical skill, it is not until he breaks upon us in some burst of passion that we sympathise with the Man, and are excited to kindred enthusiasm.

To the power of painting scenery, and delineating the softer and more pleasing traits of character, Thomson's genius seems to have been confined. Truly has he said of himself,

> "I solitary court
> The inspiring breeze, and meditate the book
> Of Nature, ever open; aiming thence,
> Warm from the heart, to pour the moral song:"

but he was incapable of describing the heart when assailed by boisterous passions; and his representations of ambition, patriotism, or revenge, are feeble. His tragedies, though not without merit as compositions, are declamatory, cold and vapid. His heroes and heroines relate their woes in good verse; but we remain unmoved, and follow them to their fate with the indifference of stoics. No man was animated by a stronger or more disinterested love of Public freedom than Thomson, but his "Liberty" is read only because it is one of his works; and it is not likely that it will ever become popular. His patriotism has however found its noblest reward, by his "Rule Britannia" having become the second National, and first War-song of his Country.

The "Castle of Indolence" displays greater poetical invention than any other of his pieces; and, little as allegory is suited to the existing taste, it must still be read with pleasure. Of his Odes and minor articles there is little that need be said; and part of them have already been sufficiently noticed. His "Hymn" is destined to be as permanent a favourite as "The Seasons," to which, indeed, it is an appropriate conclusion, and, like every other production of its author, displays the highest veneration for the Deity.

Thomson's only prose work is an Essay on Descriptive Poetry, which was advertised as a separate production, in 1730, but which formed the Preface to the second edition of "Winter," and in this edition it is prefixed to "The Seasons." That Essay is remarkable, not so much for ingenuity or original conceptions as for the arguments used to show that poetry ought to be devoted to loftier subjects than those to which it is sometimes applied. It was Thomson's especial merit that he founded a new school in his art; and that disdaining to follow in the path which conducted most of his contemporaries to fame, he, with the daring of genius, struck out a course for himself.

To these remarks will be added a letter from Voltaire to Mr. Lyttelton on receiving a copy of Thomson's works:—

"A Paris, 17th May, 1790. N. St.

"SIR,

"You was beneficent to Mr. Thomson, when he lived, and you is so to me in favouring me with his works. I was acquainted with the author when I stayed in England. I discovered in him a great genius, and a great simplicity, I liked in him the poet and the true philosopher, I mean the lover of mankind. I think that without a good stock of such a philosophy a poet is just above a fidler, who amuses our ears and cannot go to our soul.

"I am not surprised your nation has done more justice to Mr. Thomson's Seasons than to his dramatic performances; there is one kind of poetry of which the judicious readers and the men of taste are *the* proper judges; there is another that depends upon the vulgar, great or small, tragedy and comedy are of these . . . . they must be suited to the turn of mind and to the ability of the multitude and proportioned to their taste: your nation two hundred years since, is used to a wild scene, to a crowd of tumultuous events, to an emphatical poetry mixed with loose and comical expressions, to murthers, to a lively representation of bloody deeds, to a kind of horrour which seems often barbarous and childish, all faults which never sullied the Greek, the Roman, or the French stage, and, give me leave to say, that the taste of your politest countrymen differs not much in point of tragedy from the taste of the mob at bear garden; 'tis true we have too much of words if you have too much of action, and perhaps the perfection of the art should consist in a due mixture of the French taste and English energy. Mr. Addison, who would have reached to that pitch of perfection had he succeeded in the amorous part of his tragedy as well as in the part of Cato, warned often your nation against the corrupted taste of the stage, and since he could not reform the genius of the country, I am afraid the contagious distemper is past curing.

"Mr. Thomson's tragedies seem to me wisely intricated, and elegantly writ; they want perhaps some fire, and it may be that his heroes are neither moving nor busy enough, but taking him all in all, methinks he has the highest claim to the greatest esteem; your friendship, Sir, is a good vouchsafer for his merit. I know what reputation you have acquired; if I am not mistaken you have writ for your own sport many a thing that could raise a great fame to one who had in view that vain reward called glory. I have by me some verses that pass under your name, and which you are supposed to have writ in a journey to Paris. They reflect very justly on our [country] and they run thus:—

"'A nation here I pity and admire
Whom noblest sentiments of glory fire,
Yet taught by custom's force and bigot fear
To serve with pride and boast the yoke they bear,
Whose noble born to cringe and to command
In courts a mean, in camps a gen'rous, band;
From priests and tax-jobbers content receive
Those laws their dreaded arms to Europe give;
Whose people vain in want in bondage blest,
The plundered, gay, industrious, though oppressed,' &c.

These verses deserve a good translator, and they should be learned by every Frenchman. Give me leave to send you a little performance of mine, 'tis but a pebble

I do offer to you for your precious stones. I am with the highest respect, Sir, your most humble, obedient servant, VOLTAIRE."

It must be evident, from the Letters in this Memoir, that Thomson did not excel in correspondence; and his dislike to writing letters, which was very great, may have been either the cause or effect of his being inferior in this respect to other Poets of the last century.

Thomson's character was in every respect consistent with what his writings lead us to expect. He was high-minded, amiable, generous, and humane. Equable in his temper, and affable in his deportment, he was rarely ruffled except by some act of cruelty or injustice; and as he magnanimously forgave the petty assaults which envy or malignity levelled at him, and stood aloof from the Poetical warfare which raged with great heat during some part of his career, he was soon, as if by common consent, respected by all the belligerents. His society was select and distinguished. Pope, Hill, Dr. Armstrong, the Bishop of Derry, Mr. afterwards Sir Andrew Mitchell, Mendez, Dr. De la Cour, Mallet, Hammond whom he eulogises in "The Seasons," Quin, and above all Mr. Lyttelton, were his most intimate friends. With Pope he lived on terms of great friendship; and, according to Dr. Johnson, he displayed his regard for him in a Poetical epistle addressed to Thomson, while he was in Italy in 1731, but of which

Pope "abated the value by transplanting some of the lines into his Epistle to Arbuthnot." Mr. Robertson stated, in reply to Mr. Park's question,* whether Pope did not often visit Thomson, "Yes, frequently. Pope has sometimes said, 'Thomson, I'll walk to the end of your garden, and then set off to the bottom of Kew Foot Lane, and back.' Pope courted Thomson, and Thomson was always admitted to Pope, whether he had company or not."

Next to poetry Thomson was most fond of civil and natural history, voyages and travels, and in his leisure hours he found amusement in gardening. Of the fine arts, music was his chief delight; but he was an admirer of painting and sculpture, and formed a valuable collection of prints and drawings from the antique.

The besetting sin of Thomson's character was indolence; and of this he was himself fully aware, as he alludes to the failing in himself as well as in some of his friends, in the "Castle of Indolence." He seldom rose before noon, and his time for composition was generally about midnight. His manners are sometimes represented as having been coarse; but his zealous defender,

* In October, 1791, Thomas Park, Esq., the poet, called on Mr. Robertson, who was surgeon to the Royal Household at Kew, the intimate friend of Thomson, with the view of gaining information about him. He committed to paper all he gleaned, and it has since been printed.

Lord Buchan, asserts, on the contrary, that Lord Chatham, Lord Temple, Lord Lyttelton, Sir Andrew Mitchell, Dr. Armstrong, and Dr. Murdoch, agreed in declaring that he was "a gentleman at all points." His intimate friend, Mr. Robertson, told Mr. Park, that "Thomson was neither a petit maître nor a boor; he had simplicity without rudeness, and a cultivated manner without being courtly;" and this may, perhaps, be considered the most accurate account of his deportment.

Much light is often thrown on a man's character by anecdotes. Of Thomson, however, very few are remembered, and the following are introduced because his previous biographers have thought them worthy of notice, rather than from any particular claims which they possess to attention.

It is said that he was so careless about money, that once, when paying a brewer, he gave him two bank-notes rolled together instead of one, and, when told of his mistake, he appeared perfectly indifferent, saying, "he had enough to go on without it." On one occasion he was robbed of his watch between London and Richmond, and when Mr. Robertson expressed regret for his loss, he replied, "Pshaw, I am glad they took it from me, it was never good for any thing." Having invited some friends to dinner, one of them informed him that there was a general stipulation there should be no hard drinking. Thomson acquiesced, only requiring that each man should drink his bottle. The terms were accepted unconditionally, and, when the cloth was removed, a three quart bottle was set before each of his guests.

In person Thomson was rather stout and above the middle size; his countenance was not remarkable for expression, though, in his youth, he was considered handsome, but in conversation his face became animated and his eye fiery and intellectual. Silent in mixed company, his wit and vivacity seemed reserved for his friends, and in their society he was communicative, playful, and entertaining. Few men possessed in a greater degree the art of creating firm and affectionate friendships. Those with whom he became acquainted at the commencement of his career loved him till its close; and the individuals who had given to his life its sweetest enjoyments watched over his death-bed, and became the guardians of his fame, by superintending the only monuments of which genius ought to be ambitious, a complete edition of his works, and a tablet in Westminster Abbey.

It has been remarked that the Poets of the day did not commemorate Thomson's genius by exerting their own in honour of his memory; and an epigram appeared in consequence. There is not, however, much justice in the remark. Not only did Collins, Shenstone, Lyttelton, Mendez, and others, sing his praises in appropriate strains, but immediately after his decease, "Musidorus, a Poem sacred to his Memory," appeared; and since that time Burns, Pye, the Honourable Mrs. Boscawen, and others, have imitated their example. That lady became possessed of his house near Richmond, and showed her respect for the Poet, by preserving every memorial of him which could be found.

In a retired part of the gardens she replaced Thomson's favourite little rural seat, and hung votive tablets or inscriptions round it, in honour of her admired Poet, whose bust on a pediment of the seat on entering it, had the following sentence: —

> "Here Thomson sung
> The Seasons, and their change."

Within the alcove Mrs. Boscawen placed the little antique table, on which it is said the Poet penned many of his lines. The inside was further adorned with well adapted citations from other writers, who have eulogized his talents; and in the centre, was the following inscription: —

> "Within this pleasing retirement,
> allured by the music of the nightingale,
> which warbled in soft unison
> to the melody of his soul,
> in unaffected cheerfulness,
> and genial, though simple elegance,
> lived
> James Thomson!

Sensibly alive to all the beauties of nature,
he painted their images as they rose in review;
and poured the whole profusion of them
into his inimitable
SEASONS!
Warmed with intense devotion
to the Sovereign of the Universe,
its flame glowed through all his compositions.
Animated with unbounded benevolence,
with the tenderest social sensibility,
he never gave one moment's pain
to any of his fellow creatures;
save, only, by his death,
which happened at this place,
on the
27th day of August, 1748."

Thomson was never married, and in his letter to his sister, in 1747, he says he was too poor to form a domestic establishment. The only woman to whom he was known to be attached, was Miss Young, daughter of Captain Gilbert Young, of that name, in Gulyhill, in Dumfriesshire. She was a very fine young woman of superior endowments, and married Vice-Admiral John Campbell. Her lover has celebrated her in several poems by the name of "Amanda," and so deep was his passion, that his friend, Mr. Robertson, who married her sister, considers that his disappointment in obtaining her rendered him indifferent to life. One, if not the only impediment to their union, was his straitened circumstances.

Thomson was, as has been before stated, one of nine children. Of his sisters, only three are known to have married. Jean, the eldest, was the wife of Mr. Robert Thomson, Master of the Grammar School at Lanark, with whom Boswell says, in July, 1777, he had placed two of his nephews. She was then an old woman, but having retained her memory, gave that writer many particulars of the Poet, together with the letter which Johnson has printed. Her son Robert, who was a student of medicine in Edinburgh, died in his father's lifetime at Lanark; and of her daughters, Elizabeth was born before 1747, and Beatrix married Mr. Thomas Prentice of Jerviswood. Mrs. Thomson died at Lanark, on the 3d of September, 1781.

Elizabeth, his second and favourite sister, was the wife of the Reverend Robert Bell, Minister of Strathaven in Clydesdale, and died some time before 1747. In reply to Mr. Bell's request that he would consent to their marriage he wrote her the following letter: —

"My dear Sister,

"I received a letter from Mr. Robert Bell, Minister of Strathaven, in which he asks my consent to his marriage with you. Mr. Gusthart acquainted me with this some time ago; to whose letter I have returned an answer, which he tells me he has showed you both. I entirely agree to this marriage, as I find it to be a marriage of inclination, and founded upon long acquaintance and mutual esteem. Your behaviour hitherto has been such as gives me very great satisfaction, in the small assistance I have been able to afford you. Now you are going to enter upon a new state of life, charged with higher cares and duties, I need not advise you how to behave in it, since you are so near Mr. Gusthart, who, by his good counsel and friendly assistance, has been so kind to you all along; only I must chiefly recommend to you to cultivate, by every method, that union of hearts, that agreement and sympathy of tempers, in which consists the true happiness of the marriage state. The economy and gentle management of a family is a woman's natural province, and from that her best praise arises. You will apply yourself thereto as it becomes a good and virtuous wife. I dare say I need not put you in mind of having a just and grateful sense of, and future confidence in, the goodness of God, who has been to you a 'Father to the fatherless.' Though you will hereafter be more immediately under the protection of another, yet you may always depend upon the sincere friendship, and tenderest good offices of your most affectionate brother,

"James Thomson.

"By last post I wrote to Jeany about the affairs she mentioned to me. Remember me kindly to all friends."

Mrs. Bell had two sons, Dr. James Bell, Minister of Coldstream, who printed a volume of sermons, and who intended to publish an edition of his uncle's works, and Thomas Bell, who died a merchant at Jamaica.

Mary, the poet's youngest sister, married Mr. William Craig, merchant of Edinburgh; and dying on the 11th of September, 1790, was buried in the Grey Friars Churchyard, beside the remains of her mother, on the 22d of that month. She had only one son, James Craig, an ingenious architect, who planned the new Town of Edinburgh, and died in that city on the 23d of June, 1795. He intended to erect a pillar to his uncle in the village of Ednam, and wished Dr. Beattie to write an appropriate inscription. The intention was not carried into effect, but Beattie's sensible letter in reply to the request, in which he ridicules inscriptions in Latin to an English poet, and states what ought to be said on these occasions, might have been read with advantage by those who superintended Burns' monument. Lord Buchan's exuberant zeal, in honour of Thomson, in crowning his bust, and other fooleries, approaches so nearly to the ridiculous, that his motive did not prevent his being laughed at. The annual commemoration of the Poet's birth is in better taste; and proves the generous pride with which

"——— Scotia, with exulting tear,
Proclaims that Thomson was her son."

Lord Lyttelton has justly said of Thomson's writings, that they contain

"No line which dying he could wish to blot";

and, considering the taste of the age in which he lived, this praise is perhaps the highest which could be pronounced. With a slight alteration the same eulogy may be passed on his whole life;

for it was free from a single act which could create remorse. To his relations he was liberal and affectionate; to his friends faithful and devoted: viewing all mankind with beneficence and love, he performed with exemplary but unostentatious piety that first of Christian virtues, to teach the world to reverence the Creator in his works, and to learn from them veneration for his wisdom and confidence in his mercy. Secure from the revolutions of taste or time, Thomson's labours are destined to descend with undiminished admiration to the latest posterity; and it may be predicted with confidence, that future generations, like the last and present, will have their reverence for the God of Nature excited, and their earliest attachment to Nature herself strengthened, by the Poet who has sung her in all her "Seasons."

PREFACE.*

I AM neither ignorant nor concerned how much one may suffer in the opinion of several persons of great gravity and character by the study and pursuit of poetry.

Although there may seem to be some appearance of reason for the present contempt of it, as managed by the most part of our modern writers, yet that any man should, seriously, declare against that divine art is really amazing. It is declaring against the most charming power of imagination, the most exalting force of thought, the most affecting touch of sentiment; in a word, against the very soul of all learning and politeness. It is affronting the universal taste of mankind, and declaring against what has charmed the listening world from Moses down to Milton. In fine, it is even declaring against the sublimest passages of the inspired writings themselves, and what seems to be the peculiar language of Heaven.

The truth of the case is this: these weak-sighted gentlemen cannot bear the strong light of poetry, and the finer and more amusing scene of things it displays; but must those, therefore, whom Heaven has blessed with the discerning eye, shut it to keep them company?

It is pleasant enough, however, to observe, frequently, in these enemies of poetry, an awkward imitation of it. They sometimes have their little brightnesses, when the opening glooms will permit. Nay, I have seen their heaviness, on some occasions, deign to turn friskish and witty, in which they make just such another figure as Æsop's Ass, when he began to fawn. To complete the absurdity, they would, even in their efforts against poetry, fain be poetical; like those gen-

* By Thomson, prefixed to the second edition of Winter, 1726.

tlemen that reason with a great deal of zeal and severity against reason.

That there are frequent and notorious abuses of poetry is as true as that the best things are most liable to that misfortune; but is there no end of that clamorous argument against the use of things from the abuse of them? And yet I hope that no man, who has the least sense of shame in him, will fall into it after the present sulphureous attacker of the stage.

To insist no further on this head, let poetry once more be restored to her ancient truth and purity; let her be inspired from heaven; and, in return, her incense ascend thither: let her exchange her low, venal, trifling subjects for such as are fair, useful, and magnificent; and let her execute these so as at once to please, instruct, surprise, and astonish; and then, of necessity, the most inveterate ignorance and prejudice shall be struck dumb, and poets yet become the delight and wonder of mankind.

But this happy period is not to be expected till some long-wished illustrious man, of equal power and beneficence, rise on the wintry world of letters; one of a genuine and unbounded greatness and generosity of mind; who, far above all the pomp and pride of fortune, scorns the little, addressful flatterer, pierces through the disguised designing villain, discountenances all the reigning fopperies of a tasteless age, and who, stretching his views into late futurity, has the true interest of virtue, learning, and mankind entirely at heart. A character, so nobly desirable! that, to an honest heart, it is almost incredible so few should have the ambition to deserve it.

Nothing can have a better influence towards the revival of poetry than the choosing of great and serious subjects, such as at once amuse the fancy, enlighten the head, and warm the heart. These give a weight and dignity to the poem, nor is the pleasure, I should say rapture, both the writer and the reader feel, unwarranted by reason, or followed by repentant disgust. To be able to write on a dry, barren theme, is looked upon by some as the sign of a happy, fruitful genius — fruitful indeed! like one of the pendent gardens in

Cheapside, watered every morning by the hand of the alderman himself. And what are we commonly entertained with on these occasions, save forced, unaffecting fancies, little, glittering prettinesses, mixed turns of wit and expression, which are as widely different from native poetry as buffoonery is from the perfection of human thinking. A genius fired with the charms of truth and nature is tuned to a sublimer pitch, and scorns to associate with such subjects.

I cannot more emphatically recommend this poetical ambition than by the four following lines from Mr. Hill's poem, called The Judgment Day, which is so singular an instance of it.

For me, suffice it to have taught my muse
The tuneful triflings of her tribe to shun;
And raised her warmth such heavenly themes to choose,
As, in past ages, the best garlands won.

I know no subject more elevating, more amusing, more ready to awake the poetical enthusiasm, the philosophical reflection, and the moral sentiment, than the works of Nature. Where can we meet with such variety, such beauty, such magnificence? All that enlarges and transports the soul? What more inspiring than a calm, wide survey of them? In every dress nature is greatly charming! whether she puts on the crimson robes of the morning! the strong effulgence of noon! the sober suit of the evening! or the deep sables of blackness and tempest! How gay looks the Spring! how glorious the Summer! how pleasing the Autumn! and how venerable the Winter! — But there is no thinking of these things without breaking out into poetry, which is, by the by, a plain and undeniable argument of their superior excellence.

For this reason the best, both ancient and modern, poets have been passionately fond of retirement and solitude. The wild romantic country was their delight. And they seem never to have been more happy than when, lost in unfrequented fields, far from the little busy world, they were at leisure to meditate, and sing the works of nature.

The Book of Job, that noble and ancient poem, which even

strikes so forcibly through a mangling translation, is crowned with a description of the grand works of nature, and that, too, from the mouth of their Almighty Author.

It was this devotion to the works of nature, that, in his Georgics, inspired the rural Virgil to write so inimitably; and who can forbear joining with him in this declaration of his, which has been the rapture of ages?

Me vero primum dulces ante omnia Musæ,
Quarum sacra fero ingenti perculsus amore,
Accipiant; Cœlique vias et sidera monstrent,
Defectus solis varios, lunæque labores;
Unde tremor terris: qua vi maria alta tumescant
Objicibus ruptis, rursusque in seipsa residant:
Quid tantum oceano properent se tingere soles
Hyberni: vel quæ tardis mora noctibus obstet.
Sin, has ne possim naturæ accedere partes,
Frigidus obstiterit circum præcordia sanguis;
Rura mihi et rigui placeant in vallibus amnes;
Flumina amem silvasque inglorius.

Which may be Englished thus:—

Me may the Muses, my supreme delight!
Whose priest I am, smit with immense desire,
Snatch to their care; the starry tracts disclose,
The sun's distress, the labors of the moon;
Whence the earth quakes; and by what force the deeps
Heave at the rocks, then on themselves reflow.
Why winter-suns to plunge in ocean speed;
And what retards the lazy summer-night.
But, lest I should these mystic truths attain,
If the cold current freezes round my heart,
The country me, the brooky vales may please
Mid woods and streams unknown.

I cannot put an end to this Preface without taking the freedom to offer my most sincere and grateful acknowledgments to all those gentlemen who have given my first performance so favourable a reception.

It is with the best pleasure, and a rising ambition, that I

reflect on the honour Mr. Hill has done me in recommending my poem to the world after a manner so peculiar to himself, than whom none approves and obliges with a nobler and more unreserving promptitude of soul. His favours are the very smiles of humanity, graceful and easy, flowing from and to the heart. This agreeable train of thought awakens naturally in my mind all the other parts of his great and amiable character, which I know not well how to quit, and yet dare not here pursue.

Every Reader, who has a heart to be moved, must feel the most gentle power of poetry in the lines with which Mira has graced my poem.

It perhaps might be reckoned vanity in me, to say how richly I value the approbation of a gentleman of Mr. Malloch's fine and exact taste, so justly dear and valuable to all those that have the happiness of knowing him; and who, to say no more of him, will abundantly make good to the world the early promise his admired piece of William and Margaret has given.

I only wish my description of the various appearance of Nature in Winter, and, as I purpose, in the other Seasons, may have the good fortune to give the Reader some of that true pleasure which they, in their agreeable succession, are always sure to inspire into my heart.

TO MR. THOMSON,

DOUBTFUL TO WHAT PATRON HE SHOULD ADDRESS HIS POEM CALLED WINTER.

Some peers, perhaps, have skill to judge, 'tis true;
Yet no mean prospect bounds the Muse's view.
Firm in your native strength, thus nobly shown,
Slight such delusive props, and stand alone;
Fruitless dependance oft has found too late
That greatness rarely dwells among the great.
Patrons are Nature's nobles, not the state's,
And wit 's a title no broad seal creates;
E'en kings, from whose high source all honours flow,
Are poor in power when they would souls bestow.

Heedless of fortune then look down on state,
Balanced within by reason's conscious weight:
Divinely proud of independent will,
Prince of your passions, live their sovereign still.
He who stoops safe beneath a patron's shade
Shines, like the moon, but by another's aid;
Free Truth should open and unbias'd steer,
Strong as heaven's heat, and as its brightness clear.

O, swell not then the bosoms of the vain
With false conceit that you protection gain;
Poets, like you, their own protectors stand,
Placed above aid from pride's inferior hand.
Time, that devours the lord's unlasting name,
Shall lend her soundless depth to float your fame.

On verse like yours no smiles from power expect,
Born with a worth that doom'd you to neglect;
Yet, would your wit be noised, reflect no more,
Let the smooth veil of flattery silk you o'er,
Aptly attach'd, the court's soft climate try,
Learn your pen's duty from your patron's eye.

Ductile of soul, each pliant purpose wind,
And tracing interest close, leave doubt behind:
Then shall your name strike loud the public ear;
For through good fortune virtue's self shines clear.

But, in defiance of our taste, to charm!
And fancy's force with judgment's caution arm!
Disturb, with busy thought, so lull'd an age!
And plant strong meanings o'er the peaceful page!
Impregnate sound with sense! teach nature art!
And warm e'en Winter till it thaws the heart!
How could you thus your country's rules transgress,
Yet think of patrons, and presume success!

A. Hill.

TO MR. THOMSON,

ON HIS BLOOMING WINTER.

Oh gaudy Summer, veil thy blushing head,
Dull is thy sun, and all thy beauties dead:
From thy short nights, and noisy mirthful day,
My kindling thoughts, disdainful, turn away.

Majestic Winter with his floods appears,
And o'er the world his awful terrors rears:
From north to south his train dispreading slow,
Blue frost, bleak rain, and fleecy-footed snow.

In thee, sad Winter, I a kindred find,
Far more related to poor human kind;
To thee my gently drooping head I bend,
Thy sigh my sister, and thy tear my friend!
On thee I muse, and in thy hastening sun,
See life expiring ere 'tis well begun.

Thy sickening ray and venerable gloom
Show life's last scene, the solitary tomb;
But thou art safe, so shaded by the bays,
Immortal in the noblest poet's praise;

From time and death he will thy beauties save;
Oh may such numbers weep o'er Mira's grave!
Secure and glorious would her ashes lie,
Till Nature fade — and all the Seasons die.

MIRA.

TO MR. THOMSON,

ON HIS PUBLISHING THE SECOND EDITION OF HIS POEM, CALLED WINTER.

CHARM'D and instructed by thy powerful song,
I have, unjust, withheld my thanks too long;
This debt of gratitude at length receive,
Warmly sincere, 'tis all a friend can give.

Thy worth new lights the poet's darken'd name,
And shows it, blazing, in the brightest fame.
Through all thy various Winter full are found,
Magnificence of thought and pomp of sound,
Clear depth of sense, expression's heightening grace,
And goodness, eminent in power and place!
For this, the wise, the knowing few commend
With zealous joy — for thou art virtue's friend:
Even age and truth severe, in reading thee,
That Heaven inspires the muse, convinced agree.

Thus I dare sing of merit faintly known,
Friendless — supported by itself alone:
For those whose aided will could lift thee high
In fortune, see not with discernment's eye.
Nor place nor power bestows the sight refined,
And wealth enlarges not the narrow mind.

How couldst thou think of such and write so well?
Or hope reward by daring to excel!
Unskilful of the age! untaught to gain
Those favours which the fawning base obtain!

A thousand shameful arts to thee unknown,
Falsehood and flattery must be first thy own.
If thy loved country lingers in thy breast,
Thou must drive out the unprofitable guest;
Extinguish each bright aim that kindles there,
And centre in thyself thy every care.

But hence that vileness — pleased to charm mankind,
Cast each low thought of interest far behind:
Neglected into noble scorn — away
From that worn path where vulgar poets stray;
Inglorious herd! profuse of venal lays!
And by the pride despised they stoop to praise!
Thou, careless of the statesman's smile or frown,
Tread that straight way that leads to fair renown.
By virtue guided, and by glory fired,
And by reluctant envy slow admired,
Dare to do well, and in thy boundless mind
Embrace the general welfare of thy kind;
Enrich them with the treasures of thy thought,
What Heaven approves and what the Muse has taught,
Where thy power fails, unable to go on,
Ambitious, greatly will the good undone.
So shall thy name, through ages, brightening shine,
And distant praise from worth unborn be thine:
So shalt thou, happy! merit Heaven's regard,
And find a glorious, though a late reward.

D. Malloch.

ODE ON THE DEATH OF THOMSON.

By Collins.

THE SCENE ON THE THAMES NEAR RICHMOND.

In yonder grave a Druid lies,
Where slowly winds the stealing wave;
The year's best sweets shall duteous rise
To deck its poet's sylvan grave.

In yon deep bed of whispering reeds
  His airy harp * shall now be laid,
That he, whose heart in sorrow bleeds,
  May love through life the soothing shade.

Then maids and youths shall linger here,
  And while its sounds at distance swell,
Shall sadly seem in pity's ear
  To hear the woodland pilgrim's knell.

Remembrance oft shall haunt the shore
  Where Thames in summer-wreaths is drest,
And oft suspend the dashing oar,
  To bid his gentle spirit rest!

And oft, as ease and health retire
  To breezy lawn, or forest deep,
The friend shall view yon whitening spire,†
  And 'mid the varied landscape weep.

But thou, who own'st that earthy bed,
  Ah! what will every dirge avail;
Or tears, which love and pity shed,
  That mourn beneath the gliding sail?

Yet lives there one, whose heedless eye
  Shall scorn thy pale shrine glimmering near?
With him, sweet bard, may fancy die,
  And joy desert the blooming year.

But thou, lorn stream, whose sullen tide
  No sedge-crown'd sisters now attend,
Now waft me from the green hill's side,
  Whose cold turf hides the buried friend!

* The Æolian harp.

† Richmond Church, where Thomson lies buried in the north-west corner of it, below the christening pew, without a tablet or memorial to say — Here Thomson lies.

And see, the fairy valleys fade,
  Dun night has veiled the solemn view:
Yet once again, dear parted shade,
  Meek Nature's child, again adieu!

The genial meads, assign'd to bless
  Thy life, shall mourn thy early doom:
Their hinds and shepherd-girls shall dress,
  With simple hands, thy rural tomb.

Long, long, thy stone and pointed clay
  Shall melt the musing Briton's eyes:
O! vales and wild woods, shall he say,
  In yonder grave your Druid lies.

ADDRESS TO THE SHADE OF THOMSON.*

By Robert Burns.

While virgin Spring, by Eden's flood,
  Unfolds her tender mantle green;
Or pranks the sod in frolic mood,
  Or tunes the Eolian strains between;

While Summer with a matron grace
  Retreats to Dryburgh's cooling shade,
Yet oft delighted stops to trace
  The progress of the spiky blade;

* This was written at the request of Lord Buchan, and sent with the following modest remark: 'Your lordship hints at an Ode for the occasion: but who would write after Collins? I read over his Verses to the Memory of Thomson, and despaired. I attempted three or four stanzas in the way of Address to the Shade of the Bard, on crowning his bust. I trouble your lordship with the enclosed copy of them, which I am afraid will be but too convincing a proof how unequal I am to the task you would obligingly assign me.'

While Autumn, benefactor kind,
  By Tweed erects her aged head,
And sees, with self-approving mind,
  Each creature on her bounty fed;

While maniac Winter rages o'er
  The hills whence classic Yarrow flows,
Rousing the turbid torrent's roar,
  Or sweeping wild a waste of snows;

So long, sweet poet of the year,
  Shall bloom that wreath thou well hast won.
While Scotia, with exulting tear,
  Proclaims that Thomson was her son.

POEMS.

POEMS.

THE HAPPY MAN.

[First printed 1729.]

He 's not the happy man, to whom is given
A plenteous fortune by indulgent Heaven;
Whose gilded roofs on shining columns rise,
And painted walls enchant the gazer's eyes;
Whose table flows with hospitable cheer,
And all the various bounty of the year;
Whose valleys smile, whose gardens breathe the spring,
Whose carved mountains bleat, and forests sing;
For whom the cooling shade in summer twines,
While his full cellars give their generous wines;
From whose wide fields unbounded autumn pours
A golden tide into his swelling stores;
Whose winter laughs; for whom the liberal gales
Stretch the big sheet, and toiling commerce sails;
When yielding crowds attend, and pleasure serves;
While youth, and health, and vigour string his nerves.
E'en not all these, in one rich lot combined,

Can make the happy man, without the mind;
Where judgment sits clear-sighted, and surveys
The chain of reason with unerring gaze;
Where fancy lives, and to the brightening eyes,
His fairer scenes, and bolder figures rise;
Where social love exerts her soft command,
And lays the passions with a tender hand,
Whence every virtue flows, in rival strife,
And all the moral harmony of life.
  Nor canst thou, Dodington, this truth decline,
Thine is the fortune, and the mind is thine.

ON HAPPINESS.

[First printed 1720.]

WARM'D by the summer sun's meridian ray,
As underneath a spreading oak I lay
Contemplating the mighty load of woe,
In search of bliss that mortals undergo,
Who, while they think they happiness enjoy,
Embrace a curse wrapt in delusive joy,
I reason'd thus: Since the Creator, God,
Who in eternal love has his abode,
Hath blended with the essence of the soul
An appetite as fixed as the pole,
That 's always eager in pursuit of bliss,
And always veering till it point to this,

There is some object adequate to fill
This boundless wish of our extended will.
Now, while my thought round nature's circle runs
(A bolder journey than the furious sun's)
This chief and satiating good to find
The attracting centre of the human mind,
My ears they deafen'd, to my swimming eyes
His magic wand the drowsy god applies,
Bound all my senses in a silken sleep,
While mimic fancy did her vigils keep;
Yet still methinks some condescending power
Ranged the ideas in my mind that hour.
Methought I wandering was, with thousands more,
Beneath a high prodigious hill, before,
Above the clouds whose towering summit rose,
With utmost labor only gain'd by those
Who grovelling prejudices throw away,
And with incessant straining climb'd their way;
Where all who stood their failing breath to gain,
With headlong ruin tumbled down amain.
This mountain is through every nation famed,
And, as I learned, Contemplation named.
O happy me! when I had reach'd its top
Unto my sight a boundless scene did ope.
First, sadly I survey'd, with downward eye,
Of restless men below the busy fry,
Who hunted trifles in an endless maze,
Like foolish boys, on sunny summer days,
Pursuing butterflies with all their might,

Who can't their troubles in the chase requite.
The painted insect, he who most admires,
Grieves most when it in his rude hand expires;
Or should it live, with endless fears is toss'd,
Lest it take wing and be for ever lost.
Some men I saw their utmost art employ
How to attain a false deceitful joy,
Which from afar conspicuously did blaze,
And at a distance fix'd their ravish'd gaze,
But nigh at hand it mock'd their fond embrace.
When lo! again it flashed in their eyes,
But still, as they drew near, the fond illusion dies.
Just so I 've seen a water-dog pursue
An unflown duck within his greedy view,
When he has, panting, at his prey arrived,
The coxcomb fooling — suddenly it dived;
He, gripping, is almost with water choked,
And grief, that all his towering hopes are mock'd.
Then it emerges, he renews his toil,
And o'er and o'er again he gets the foil.
Yea, all the joys beneath the conscious sun,
And softer ones that his inspection shun,
Much of their pleasures in fruition fade.
Enjoyment o'er them throws a sullen shade.
The reason is, we promise vaster things
And sweeter joys than from their nature springs:
When they are lost, weep the apparent bliss,
And not what really in Fruition is;
So that our griefs are greater than our joys,
And real pain springs from fantastic toys.

Though all terrene delights of men below
Are almost nothing but a glaring show;
Yet if there always were a virgin joy
When t' other fades to soothe the wanton boy,
He somewhat might excuse his heedless course,
Some show of reason for the same enforce:
But frugal nature wisely does deny
To mankind such profuse variety;
Has only what is needful to us given,
To feed and cheer us in the way to Heaven;
And more would but the traveller delay,
Impede and clog him in his upward way.
I from the mount all mortal pleasures saw
Themselves within a narrow compass draw:
The libertine a nauseous circle run,
And dully acted what he 'd often done.
Just so when Luna darts her silver ray,
And pours on silent earth a paler day:
From Stygian caves the flitting fairies scud,
And on the margent of some limpid flood,
Which by reflected moonlight darts a glance,
In midnight circles range themselves and dance.
To-morrow, cries he, will us entertain:
Pray what 's to-morrow but to-day again?
Deluded youth, no more the chase pursue,
So oft deceived, no more the toil renew.
Though in a constant and a fix'd design
Of acting well there is a lasting mine
Of solid satisfaction, purest joy,
For virtue's pleasures never, never cloy:

Yet hither come, climb up the steep ascent,
Your painful labor you will ne'er repent,
From Heaven itself here you 're but one remove,
Here 's the præludium of the joys above,
Here you 'll behold the awful Godhead shine,
And all perfections in the same combine;
You 'll see that God, who, by his powerful call,
From empty nothing drew this spacious all,
Made beauteous order the rude mass control,
And every part subservient to the whole;
Here you 'll behold upon the fatal tree
The God of nature bleed, expire, and die,
For such as 'gainst his holy laws rebel,
And such as bid defiance to his hell.
Through the dark gulf, here you may clearly pry
'Twixt narrow Time and vast Eternity.
Behold the Godhead just, as well as good,
And vengeance pour'd on tramplers on his blood:
But all the tears wiped from his people's eyes,
And, for their entrance, cleave the parting skies.
Then sure you will with holy ardours burn,
And to seraphic heats your passion turn;
Then in your eyes all mortal fair will fade,
And leave of mortal beauties but the shade;
Yourself to him you 'll solemnly devote,
To him, without whose providence you 're not;
You 'll of his service relish the delight,
And to his praises all your powers excite;
You 'll celebrate his name in heavenly sound,
Which well pleased skies in echoes will rebound;

This is the greatest happiness that can
Possessed be in this short life by man.
  But darkly here the Godhead we survey,
Confined and cramped in this cage of clay.
What cruel band is this to earth that ties
Our souls from soaring to their native skies?
Upon the bright eternal face to gaze,
And there drink in the beatific rays:
There to behold the good one and the fair,
A ray from whom all mortal beauties are?
In beauteous nature all the harmony
Is but the echo of the Deity,
Of all perfection who the centre is,
And boundless ocean of untainted bliss;
For ever open to the ravish'd view,
And full enjoyment of the radiant crew
Who live in raptures of eternal joy,
Whose flaming love their tuneful harps employ
In solemn hymns Jehovah's praise to sing,
And make all heaven with hallelujahs ring.
  These realms of light no further I 'll explore,
And in these heights I will no longer soar:
Not like our grosser atmosphere beneath,
The ether here 's too thin for me to breathe.
The region is unsufferable bright,
And flashes on me with too strong a light.
Then from the mountain, lo! I now descend,
And to my vision put a hasty end.

LISY'S PARTING WITH HER CAT.

(THOMSON'S SISTER.)

THE dreadful hour with leaden pace approach'd,
Lash'd fiercely on by unrelenting fate,
When Lisy and her bosom Cat must part:
For now, to school and pensive needle doom'd,
She 's banish'd from her childhood's undash'd joy,
And all the pleasing intercourse she kept
With her gray comrade, which has often soothed
Her tender moments, while the world around
Glow'd with ambition, business, and vice,
Or lay dissolved in sleep's delicious arms;
And from their dewy orbs the conscious stars
Shed on their friendship influence benign.
  But see where mournful Puss, advancing, stood
With outstretch'd tail, cast looks of anxious woe
On melting Lisy, in whose eye the tear
Stood tremulous, and thus would fain have said,
If nature had not tied her struggling tongue:
'Unkind, O! who shall now with fattening milk,
With flesh, with bread, and fish beloved, and meat,
Regale my taste? and at the cheerful fire,
Ah, who shall bask me in their downy lap?
Who shall invite me to the bed, and throw
The bedclothes o'er me in the winter night,
When Eurus roars? Beneath whose soothing hand
Soft shall I purr? But now, when Lisy 's gone,

What is the dull officious world to me?
I loathe the thoughts of life:' thus plain'd the Cat,
While Lisy felt, by sympathetic touch,
These anxious thoughts that in her mind revolved,
And casting on her a desponding look,
She snatch'd her in her arms with eager grief,
And mewing, thus began:—'O Cat beloved!
Thou dear companion of my tender years!
Joy of my youth! that oft hast lick'd my hands
With velvet tongue ne'er stain'd by mouse's blood.
Oh, gentle Cat! how shall I part with thee?
How dead and heavy will the moments pass
When you are not in my delighted eye,
With Cubi playing, or your flying tail.
How harshly will the softest muslin feel.
And all the silk of schools, while I no more
Have your sleek skin to soothe my soften'd sense?
How shall I eat while you are not beside
To share the bit? How shall I ever sleep
While I no more your lulling murmurs hear?
Yet we must part—so rigid fate decrees—
But never shall your loved idea, dear,
Part from my soul, and when I first can mark
The embroider'd figure on the snowy lawn,
Your image shall my needle keen employ.
Hark! now I 'm call'd away! O direful sound!
I come—I come, but first I charge you all—
You—you—and you, particularly you,
O, Mary, Mary, feed her with the best,
Repose her nightly in the warmest couch,

And be a Lisy to her!' — Having said,
She sat her down, and with her head across,
Rush'd to the evil which she could not shun,
While a sad mew went knelling to her heart!

ON MAY.

Among the changing months, May stands confest
The sweetest, and in fairest colours drest!
Soft as the breeze that fans the smiling field;
Sweet as the breath that opening roses yield;
Fair as the colour lavish Nature paints
On virgin flowers free from unodorous taints! —
To rural scenes thou tempt'st the busy crowd,
Who, in each grove, thy praises sing aloud!
The blooming belles and shallow beaux, strange sight,
Turn nymphs and swains, and in their sports delight.

THE MORNING IN THE COUNTRY.

When from the opening chambers of the east
The morning springs, in thousand liveries drest,

The early larks their morning tribute pay,
And, in shrill notes, salute the blooming day.
Refreshed fields with pearly dew do shine,
And tender blades therewith their tops incline.
Their painted leaves the unblown flowers expand,
And with their odorous breath perfume the land.
The crowing cock and chattering hen awakes
Dull sleepy clowns, who know the morning breaks.
The herd his plaid around his shoulders throws,
Grasps his dear crook, calls on his dog, and goes
Around the fold :, he walks with careful pace,
And fallen clods sets in their wonted place;
Then opes the door, unfolds his fleecy care,
And gladly sees them crop their morning fare!
Down upon easy moss he lays,
And sings some charming shepherdess's praise.

ON A COUNTRY LIFE.

[First printed 1720.]

I HATE the clamours of the smoky towns,
But much admire the bliss of rural clowns;
Where some remains of innocence appear,
Where no rude noise insults the listening ear;
Nought but soft zephyrs whispering through the
trees,
Or the still humming of the painful bees;

The gentle murmurs of a purling rill,
Or the unwearied chirping of the drill;
The charming harmony of warbling birds,
Or hollow lowings of the grazing herds;
The murmuring stockdoves' melancholy coo,
When they their loved mates lament or woo;
The pleasing bleatings of the tender lambs,
Or the indistinct mum'ling of their dams;
The musical discord of chiding hounds,
Whereto the echoing hill or rock resounds;
The rural mournful songs of lovesick swains,
Whereby they soothe their raging amorous pains;
The whistling music of the lagging plough,
Which does the strength of drooping beasts renew.
  And as the country rings with pleasant sounds,
So with delightful prospects it abounds:
Through every season of the sliding year,
Unto the ravish'd sight new scenes appear.
  In the sweet Spring the sun's prolific ray
Does painted flowers to the mild air display;
Then opening buds, then tender herbs, are seen,
And the bare fields are all array'd in green.
  In ripening Summer, the full laden vales
Gives prospect of employment for the flails;
Each breath of wind the bearded groves makes bend,
Which seems the fatal sickle to portend.
  In Autumn, that repays the labourer's pains,
Reapers sweep down the honours of the plains.
  Anon black Winter, from the frozen north,

Its treasuries of snow and hail pours forth;
Then stormy winds blow through the hazy sky,
In desolation nature seems to lie;
The unstain'd snow from the full clouds descends,
Whose sparkling lustre open eyes offends.
In maiden white the glittering fields do shine;
Then bleating flocks for want of food repine,
With wither'd eyes they see all snow around,
And with their fore feet paw and scrape the ground:
They cheerfully crop the insipid grass,
The shepherds sighing, cry, Alas! alas!
Then pinching want the wildest beast does tame;
Then huntsmen on the snow do trace their game;
Keen frost then turns the liquid lakes to glass,
Arrests the dancing rivulets as they pass.
  How sweet and innocent are country sports,
And, as men's tempers, various are their sorts.
  You, on the banks of soft meandering Tweed,
May in your toils ensnare the watery breed,
And nicely lead the artificial flee,*
Which, when the nimble, watchful trout does see,
He at the bearded hook will briskly spring;
Then in that instant twieth your hairy string,
And, when he 's hook'd, you, with a constant hand,
May draw him struggling to the fatal land.
  Then at fit seasons you may clothe your hook
With a sweet bait, dress'd by a faithless cook;
The greedy pike darts to 't with eager haste,

* *Anglice*, fly.

And being struck, in vain he flies at last;
He rages, storms, and flounces through the stream,
But all, alas! his life cannot redeem.
  At other times you may pursue the chase,
And hunt the nimble hare from place to place.
See, when the dog is just upon the grip,
Out at a side she 'll make a handsome skip,
And ere he can divert his furious course,
She, far before him, scours with all her force:
She 'll shift, and many times run the same ground;
At last, outwearied by the stronger hound,
She falls a sacrifice unto his hate,
And with sad piteous screams laments her fate.
  See how the hawk doth take his towering flight,
And in his course outflies our very sight,
Bears down the fluttering fowl with all his might.
  See how the wary gunner casts about,
Watching the fittest posture when to shoot:
Quick as the fatal lightning blasts the oak,
He gives the springing fowl a sudden stroke;
He pours upon 't a shower of mortal lead,
And ere the noise is heard the fowl is dead.
  Sometimes he spreads his hidden subtile snare,
Of which the entangled fowl was not aware;
Through pathless wastes he doth pursue his sport,
Where nought but moor-fowl and wild beasts resort.
  When the noon sun directly darts his beams
Upon your giddy heads, with fiery gleams,
Then you may bathe yourself in cooling streams;
Or to the sweet adjoining grove retire,

Where trees with interwoven boughs conspire
To form a grateful shade; — there rural swains
Do tune their oaten reeds to rural strains;
The silent birds sit listening on the sprays,
And in soft charming notes do imitate their lays.
There you may stretch yourself upon the grass,
And, lull'd with music, to kind slumbers pass:
No meagre cares your fancy will distract,
And on that scene no tragic fears will act;
Save the dear image of a charming she,
Nought will the object of your vision be.
Away the vicious pleasures of the town;
Let empty partial fortune on me frown;
But grant, ye powers, that it may be my lot
To live in peace from noisy towns remote.

ON ÆOLUS'S HARP.

Ethereal race, inhabitants of air,
Who hymn your God amid the secret grove;
Ye unseen beings, to my harp repair,
And raise majestic strains, or melt in love.

Those tender notes, how kindly they upbraid,
With what soft woe they thrill the lover's heart!
Sure from the hand of some unhappy maid,
Who died for love, these sweet complainings part.

But hark! that strain was of a graver tone,
  On the deep strings his hand some hermit throws;
Or he, the sacred Bard,* who sat alone
  In the drear waste, and wept his people's woes.

Such was the song which Zion's children sung,
  When by Euphrates' stream they made their
    plaint;
And to such sadly solemn notes are strung
  Angelic harps, to soothe a dying saint.

Methinks I hear the full celestial choir,
  Through heaven's high dome their awful an-
    them raise;
Now chanting clear, and now they all conspire
  To swell the lofty hymn from praise to praise.

Let me, ye wandering spirits of the wind,
  Who, as wild fancy prompts you, touch the string;
Smit with your theme, be in your chorus join'd,
  For till you cease, my Muse forgets to sing.

* Jeremiah.

HYMN ON SOLITUDE.

[First printed 1729.]

Hail, mildly pleasing Solitude,
Companion of the wise and good;
But, from whose holy, piercing eye,
The herd of fools and villains fly.
Oh! how I love with thee to walk,
And listen to thy whisper'd talk,
Which innocence and truth imparts,
And melts the most obdurate hearts.

A thousand shapes you wear with ease,
And still in every shape you please.
Now wrapt in some mysterious dream,
A lone philosopher you seem;
Now quick from hill to vale you fly,
And now you sweep the vaulted sky;
A shepherd next, you haunt the plain,
And warble forth your oaten strain.
A lover now, with all the grace
Of that sweet passion in your face;
Then, calm'd to friendship, you assume
The gentle looking Hertford's bloom,
As, with her Musidora, she
(Her Musidora fond of thee)
Amid the long-withdrawing vale,
Awakes the rival'd nightingale.

Thine is the balmy breath of morn,
Just as the dew-bent rose is born;
And while meridian fervors beat,
Thine is the woodland dumb retreat;
But chief, when evening scenes decay,
And the faint landscape swims away,
Thine is the doubtful soft decline,
And that best hour of musing thine.

Descending angels bless thy train,
The virtues of the sage, and swain;
Plain Innocence in white array'd
Before thee lifts her fearless head;
Religion's beams around thee shine,
And cheer thy glooms with light divine:
About thee sports sweet Liberty;
And wrapt Urania sings to thee.

Oh, let me pierce thy secret cell!
And in thy deep recesses dwell;
Perhaps from Norwood's oak-clad hill,
When meditation has her fill,
I just may cast my careless eyes,
Where London's spiry turrets rise,
Think of its crimes, its cares, its pain,
Then shield me in the woods again.

HYMN TO GOD'S POWER.

HAIL! Power Divine, who by thy sole command,
From the dark empty space,
Made the broad sea and solid land
Smile with a heavenly grace.

Made the high mountain and firm rock,
Where bleating cattle stray;
And the strong, stately, spreading oak,
That intercepts the day.

The rolling planets thou madest move,
By thy effective will;
And the revolving globes above
Their destined course fulfil.

His mighty power, ye thunders, praise,
As through the heavens you roll;
And his great name, ye lightnings, blaze,
Unto the distant pole.

Ye seas, in your eternal roar,
His sacred praise proclaim;
While the inactive sluggish shore
Reechoes to the same.

Ye howling winds, howl out his praise,
And make the forests bow;

While through the air, the earth, and seas,
His solemn praise ye blow.

O yon high harmonious spheres,
Your powerful mover sing;
To him your circling course that steers,
Your tuneful praises bring.

Ungrateful mortals, catch the sound,
And in your numerous lays,
To all the listening world around,
The God of nature praise.

A PARAPHRASE ON THE LATTER PART OF THE SIXTH CHAPTER OF ST. MATTHEW.

[First printed 1729.]

When my breast labours with oppressive care,
And o'er my cheek descends the falling tear;
While all my warring passions are at strife,
O, let me listen to the words of life!
Raptures deep-felt His doctrine did impart,
And thus He raised from earth the drooping heart.
'Think not, when all, your scanty stores afford,
Is spread at once upon the sparing board;
Think not, when worn the homely robe appears,
While, on the roof, the howling tempest bears;

What further shall this feeble life sustain,
And what shall clothe these shivering limbs again!
Say, does not life its nourishment exceed?
And the fair body its investing weed?
'Behold! and look away your low despair—
See the light tenants of the barren air:
To them, nor stores, nor granaries belong,
Nought, but the woodland, and the pleasing song;
Yet, your kind Heavenly Father bends his eye
On the least wing that flits along the sky,
To him they sing, when Spring renews the plain,
To him they cry, in Winter's pinching reign;
Nor is their music, nor their plaint in vain;
He hears the gay and the distressful call,
And with unsparing bounty fills them all.
'Observe the rising lily's snowy grace,
Observe the various vegetable race;
They neither toil, nor spin, but careless grow,
Yet see how warm they blush! how bright they glow!
What regal vestments can with them compare!
What king so shining! or what queen so fair!
If ceaseless thus the fowls of heaven he feeds,
If o'er the fields such lucid robes he spreads:
Will he not care for you, ye faithless, say?
Is he unwise? or are ye less than they?'

PSALM CIV. PARAPHRASED.*

To praise thy Author, Soul, do not forget;
Canst thou, in gratitude, deny the debt?
Lord, thou art great, how great we cannot know;
Honour and majesty do round thee flow.
The purest rays of primogenial light
Compose thy robes, and make them dazzling bright;
The heavens and all the wide spread orbs on high
Thou like a curtain stretch'd of curious dye;
On the devouring flood thy chambers are
Establish'd; a lofty cloud 's thy car;
Which quick through the ethereal road doth fly,
On swift wing'd winds, that shake the troubled sky.
Of spiritual substance angels thou didst frame,
Active and bright, piercing and quick as flame.
Thou 'st firmly founded this unwieldy earth;
Stand fast for aye, thou saidst, at nature's birth.
The swelling flood thou o'er the earth madest creep,
And coveredst it with the vast hoary deep:
Then hills and vales did no distinction know,
But levell'd nature lay oppress'd below.
With speed they, at thy awful thunder's roar,
Shrinked within the limits of their shore.
Through secret tracts they up the mountains creep,
And rocky caverns fruitful moisture weep,

* This was one of Thomson's earliest pieces. See the MEMOIR, p. xiii. and the ADDENDA.

Which sweetly through the verdant vales doth glide,
Till 'tis devoured by the greedy tide.
The feeble sands thou 'st made the ocean's mounds,
Its foaming waves shall ne'er repass these bounds,
Again to triumph over the dry grounds.
Between the hills, grazed by the bleating kind,
Soft warbling rills their mazy way do find;
By him appointed fully to supply,
When the hot dogstar fires the realms on high,
The raging thirst of every sickening beast,
Of the wild ass that roams the dreary waste:
The feather'd nation, by their smiling sides,
In lowly brambles, or in trees abides;
By nature taught, on them they rear their nests,
That with inimitable art are dress'd.
They for the shade and safety of the wood
With natural music cheer the neighbourhood.
He doth the clouds with genial moisture fill,
Which on the [shr]ivell'd ground they bounteously distil,
And nature's lap with various blessings crowd:
The giver, God! all creatures cry aloud.
With freshest green he clothes the fragrant mead,
Whereon the grazing herds wanton and feed.
With vital juice he makes the plants abound,
And herbs securely spring above the ground,
That man may be sustain'd beneath the toil
Of manuring the ill producing soil;
Which with a plenteous harvest does at last
Cancel the memory of labors past;

Yields him the product of the generous vine,
And balmy oil that makes his face to shine:
Fills all his granaries with a loaden crop,
Against the bare barren winter his great prop.
The trees of God with kindly sap do swell,
E'en cedars tall in Lebanon that dwell,
Upon whose lofty tops the birds erect
Their nests, as careful nature does direct.
The long neck'd storks unto the fir trees fly,
And with their crackling cries disturb the sky.
To unfrequented hills wild goats resort,
And on bleak rocks the nimble conies sport.
The changing moon he clad with silver light,
To check the black dominion of the night:
High through the skies in silent state she rides,
And by her rounds the fleeting time divides.
The circling sun doth in due time decline,
And unto shades the murmuring world resign.
Dark night thou makest succeed the cheerful day,
Which forest beasts from their lone caves survey:
They rouse themselves, creep out, and search their prey.
Young hungry lions from their dens come out,
And, mad on blood, stalk fearfully about:
They break night's silence with their hideous roar,
And from kind heaven their nightly prey implore.
Just as the lark begins to stretch her wing,
And, flickering on her nest, makes short essays to sing,
And the sweet dawn, with a faint glimmering light,

Unveils the face of nature to the sight,
To their dark dens they take their hasty flight.
Not so the husbandman, — for with the sun
He does his pleasant course of labours run:
Home with content in the cool e'en returns,
And his sweet toils until the morn adjourns.
How many are thy wondrous works, O Lord!
They of thy wisdom solid proofs afford:
Out of thy boundless goodness thou didst fill,
With riches and delights, both vale and hill:
E'en the broad ocean, wherein do abide
Monsters that flounce upon the boiling tide,
And swarms of lesser beasts and fish beside:
'Tis there that daring ships before the wind
Do send amain, and make the port assign'd:
'Tis there that Leviathan sports and plays,
And spouts his water in the face of day;
For food with gaping mouth they wait on thee,
If thou withhold'st, they pine, they faint, they die.
Thou bountifully opest thy liberal hand,
And scatter'st plenty both on sea and land.
Thy vital spirit makes all things live below,
The face of nature with new beauties glow.
God's awful glory ne'er will have an end,
To vast eternity it will extend.
When he surveys his works, at the wide sight
He doth rejoice, and take divine delight.
His looks the earth into its centre shakes;
A touch of his to smoke the mountains makes.
I'll to God's honour consecrate my lays,

And when I cease to be I'll cease to praise.
Upon the Lord, a sublime lofty theme,
My meditations sweet, my joys supreme.
Let daring sinners feel thy vengeful rod,
May they no more be known by their abode.
My soul and all my powers, O bless the Lord,
And the whole race of men with one accord.

A COMPLAINT ON THE MISERIES OF LIFE.

I LOATHE, O Lord, this life below,
And all its fading, fleeting joys;
'Tis a short space that's filled with woe,
Which all our bliss by far outweighs.
When will the everlasting morn
With dawning light the skies adorn?

Fitly this life's compared to night,
When gloomy darkness shades the sky;
Just like the morn's our glimmering light
Reflected from the Deity.
When will celestial morn dispel
These dark surrounding shades of hell?

I'm sick of this vexatious state,
Where cares invade my peaceful hours;

Strike the last blow, O courteous fate,
  I 'll smiling fall like mowed flowers;
I 'll gladly spurn this clogging clay,
And, sweetly singing, soar away.

What 's money but refined dust?
  What 's honour but an empty name?
And what is soft enticing lust,
  But a consuming idle flame?
Yea, what is all beneath the sky
But emptiness and vanity?

With thousand ills our life 's oppress'd,
  There 's nothing here worth living for,
In the lone grave I long to rest,
  And be harass'd here no more:
Where joy 's fantastic, grief 's sincere,
And where there 's nought for which I care.

Thy word, O Lord, shall be my guide,
  Heaven, where thou dwellest is my goal;
Through corrupt life grant I may glide
  With an untainted upward soul.
Then may this life, this dreary night,
Dispelled be by morning light.

A PASTORAL BETWIXT DAVID, THIRSIS, AND THE ANGEL GABRIEL,

UPON THE BIRTH OF OUR SAVIOUR.

DAVID.

WHAT means yon apparition in the sky,
Thirsis, that dazzles every shepherd's eye?
I slumbering was when from yon glorious cloud
Came gliding music heavenly, sweet, and loud,
With sacred raptures which my bosom fires,
And with celestial joy my soul inspires;
It soothes the native horrors of the night,
And gladdens nature more than dawning light.

THIRSIS.

But hold, see hither through the yielding air
An angel comes: for mighty news prepare.

ANGEL GABRIEL.

Rejoice, ye swains, anticipate the morn
With songs of praise; for lo! a Saviour 's born.
With joyful haste to Bethlehem repair,
And you will find the almighty infant there;
Wrapp'd in a swaddling band you 'll find your king,
And in a manger laid, to him your praises bring.

CHORUS OF ANGELS.

To God who in the highest dwells,
Immortal glory be ;
Let peace be in the humble cells
Of Adam's progeny.

DAVID.

No more the year shall wintry horrors bring ;
Fix'd in the indulgence of eternal spring,
Immortal green shall clothe the hills and vales,
And odorous sweets shall load the balmy gales ;
The silver brooks shall in soft murmurs tell
The joy that shall their oozy channels swell.
Feed on, my flocks, and crop the tender grass,
Let blooming joy appear on every face ;
For lo ! this blessed, this propitious morn,
The saviour of lost mankind is born.

THIRSIS.

Thou fairest morn that ever sprang from night,
Or deck'd the opening skies with rosy light,
Well mayst thou shine with a distinguish'd ray,
Since here Emmanuel condescends to stay,
Our fears, our guilt, our darkness to dispel,
And save us from the horrid jaws of hell.
Who from his throne descended, matchless love !
To guide poor mortals to bless'd seats above :
But come without delay, let us be gone,
Shepherd, let 's go, and humbly kiss the Son.

A PASTORAL

BETWEEN THIRSIS AND CORYDON, UPON THE DEATH OF DAMON,

BY WHOM IS MEANT MR. W. RIDDELL.

THIRSIS.

SAY, tell me true, what is the doleful cause
That Corydon is not the man he was?
Your cheerful presence used to lighten cares,
And from the plains to banish gloomy fears.
Whene'er unto the circling swains you sung,
Our ravish'd souls upon the music hung;
The gazing, listening flocks forgot their meat,
While vocal grottoes did your lays repeat:
But now your gravity our mirth rebukes,
And in your downcast and desponding looks
Appears some fatal and impending woe;
I fear to ask, and yet desire to know.

CORYDON.

The doleful news, how shall I, Thirsis, tell!
In blooming youth the hapless Damon fell:
He 's dead, he 's dead, and with him all my joy;
The mournful thought does all gay forms destroy:
This is the cause of my unusual grief,
Which sullenly admits of no relief.

THIRSIS.

Begone all mirth! begone all sports and play,
To a deluge of grief and tears give way.
Damon the just, the generous, and the young,
Must Damon's worth and merit be unsung?
No, Corydon, the wondrous youth you knew
How as in years so he in virtue grew;
Embalm his fame in never dying verse,
As a just tribute to his doleful hearse.

CORYDON.

Assist me, mighty grief, my breast inspire
With generous heats and with thy wildest fire,
While in a solemn and a mournful strain
Of Damon gone for ever I complain.
Ye muses, weep; your mirth and songs forbear,
And for him sigh and shed a friendly tear;
He was your favourite, and by your aid
In charming verse his witty thoughts array'd;
He had of knowledge, learning, wit, a store,
To it denied he still press'd after more.
He was a pious and a virtuous soul,
And still press'd forward to the heavenly goal;
He was a faithful, true, and constant friend,
Faithful, and true, and constant to the end.
Ye flowers, hang down and droop your heads,
No more around your grateful odour spreads;
Ye leafy trees, your blooming honours shed,
Damon for ever from your shade is fled;

Fled to the mansions of eternal light,
Where endless wonders strike his happy sight.
Ye birds, be mute, as through the trees you fly,
Mute as the grave wherein my friend does lie.
Ye winds, breathe sighs as through the air you rove,
And in sad pomp the trembling branches move.
Ye gliding brooks, O weep your channels dry,
My flowing tears them fully shall supply;
You in soft murmurs may your grief express,
And yours, you swains, in mournful songs confess.
I to some dark and gloomy shade will fly,
Dark as the grave wherein my friend does lie;
And for his death to lonely rocks complain
In mournful accents and a dying strain,
While pining echo answers me again.

A PASTORAL ENTERTAINMENT.

While in heroic numbers some relate
The amazing turns of wise eternal fate;
Exploits of heroes in the dusty field,
That to their name immortal honour yield;
Grant me, ye powers, fast by the limpid spring
The harmless revels of the plain to sing.
At a rich feast, kept each revolving year,
Their fleecy care when joyful shepherds shear,

A wreath of flowers cull'd from the neighbouring
lands
Is all the prize my humble muse demands.
Now blithsome shepherds, by the early dawn,
Their new shorn flocks drive to the dewy lawn;
While, in a bleating language, each salutes
The welcome morning and their fellow brutes:
Then all prepared for the rural feast,
And in their finest Sunday habits drest;
The crystal brook supplied the mirror's place,
. . . they bathed and viewed their cleanly face,
. . . . . and nymphs resorted to the fields
. . . . pomp the country yields.
The place appointed was a spacious vale,
Fann'd always by a cooling western gale,
Which in soft breezes through the meadows stray,
And steals the ripen'd fragrancies away;
With native incense all the air perfumes,
Renewing with its genial breath the blooms,
Here every shepherd might his flocks survey,
Securely roam and take his harmless play;
And here were flowers each shepherdess to grace,
On her fair bosom courting but a place.
How in this vale, beneath a grateful shade,
By twining boughs of spreading beeches made,
On seats of homely turf themselves they place,
And cheerfully enjoy'd their rural feast,
Consisting of the product of the fields,
And all the luxury the country yields.
No maddening liquors spoil'd their harmless mirth,

But an untainted spring their thirst allay'd,
Which in meanders through the valley stray'd.
Thrice happy swains who spend your golden days
In country pastime; and when night displays
Her sable shade, to peaceful huts retire;
Can any man a sweeter bliss desire?
In ancient times so pass'd the smiling hour,
When our first parents lived in Eden's bower,
Ere care and trouble were pronounced ou . . .
Or sin had blasted the creation's blo . . . .

LINES ON MARLEFIELD.*

WHAT is the task that to the muse belongs?
What but to deck in her harmonious songs
The beauteous works of nature and of art,
Rural retreats that cheer the heavy heart?
Then Marlefield begin, my muse, and sing;
With Marlefield the hills and vales shall ring.
O! what delight and pleasure 'tis to rove
Through all the walks and alleys of this grove,
Where spreading trees a checker'd scene display,
Partly admitting and excluding day;
Where cheerful green and odorous sweets conspire
The drooping soul with pleasure to inspire;

* The seat of Sir William Burnet of Grubit, Bart.

Where little birds employ their narrow throats
To sing its praises in unlabour'd notes.
To it adjoin'd a rising fabric stands,
Which with its state our silent awe commands.
Its endless beauties mock the poet's pen;
So to the garden I'll return again.
Pomona makes the trees with fruit abound,
And blushing Flora paints the enamel'd ground.
Here lavish nature does her stores disclose,
Flowers of all hue, their queen the bashful rose,
With their sweet breath the ambient air's perfumed,
Nor is thereby their fragrant stores consumed.
O'er the fair landscape sportive zephyrs scud,
And by kind force display the infant bud.
The vegetable kind here rear their head,
By kindly showers and heaven's indulgence fed:
Of fabled nymphs such were the sacred haunts,
But real nymphs this charming dwelling vaunts.
Now to the greenhouse let's awhile retire,
To shun the heat of Sol's infectious fire:
Immortal authors grace this cool retreat,
Of ancient times, and of a modern date.
Here would my praises and my fancy dwell;
But it, alas, description does excel.
O may this sweet, this beautiful abode
Remain the charge of the eternal God.

ON BEAUTY.

Beauty deserves the homage of the muse:
Shall mine, rebellious, the dear theme refuse?
No; while my breast respires the vital air,
Wholly I am devoted to the fair.
Beauty I'll sing in my sublimest lays,
I burn to give her just immortal praise.
The heavenly maid with transport I'll pursue
To her abode, and all her graces view.
This happy place with all delights abounds,
And plenty broods upon the fertile grounds.
Here verdant grass their waving . . . . . .
And hills and vales in sweet confusion lie:
The nibbling flock stray o'er the rising hills,
And all around with bleating music fills:
High on their fronts tall blooming forests nod,
Of sylvan deities the blest abode:
The feather'd minstrels hop from spray to spray,
And chant their gladsome carols all the day;
Till dusky night, advancing in her car,
Makes with declining light successful war.
Then Philomel her mournful lay repeats,
And through her throat breathes melancholy sweets.
Still higher yet wild rugged rocks arise,
That all ascent to human foot denies,
And strike beholders with a dread surprise.
This paradise these towering hills surround,

That thither is one only passage found.
Increasing brooks roll down the mountain's side,
And as they pass the opposing pebbles chide.

. . . .

. . . .

But vernal showers refresh the blooming year.
Their only season is eternal spring,
Which hovers o'er them with a downy wing:
Blossoms and fruits at once the trees adorn
With glowing blushes, like the rosy morn.
The way that to this stately palace goes
Of myrtle trees, lies 'twixt two even rows,
Which, towering high, with outstretch'd arms display'd,
Over our heads a living arch have made.
To sing, my muse, the bold attempt begin,
Of awful beauties you behold within:
The Goddess sat upon a throne of gold,
Emboss'd with figures charming to behold;
Here new made Eve stood in her early bloom,
Not yet obscured with sin's sullen gloom;
Her naked beauties do the soul confound,
From every part is given a fatal wound;
There other beauties of a meaner fame
Oblige the sight, whom here I shall not name.
In her right hand she did a sceptre sway,
O'er all mankind ambitious to obey:
Her lovely forehead and her killing eye,
Her blushing cheeks of a vermilion dye,

Her lip's soft pulp, her heaving snowy breast,
Her well turn'd arm, her handsome slender waist,
And all below veil'd from the curious eye;
Oh! heavenly maid! makes all beholders cry.
  Her dress was plain, not pompous as a bride,
Which would her sweeter native beauties hide.
One thing I mind, a spreading hoop she wore,
Than nothing which adorns a lady more.
With equal rage, could I its beauties sing,
I 'd with the hoop make all Parnassus ring.
Around her shoulders, dangling on her throne,
A bright Tartana carelessly was thrown,
Which has already won immortal praise,
Most sweetly sung in Allan Ramsay's lays;
The wanton Cupids did around her play,
And smiling loves upon her bosom stray;
With purple wings they round about her flew,
And her sweet lips tinged with ambrosial dew:
  Her air was easy, graceful was her mien,
Her presence banish'd the ungrateful spleen;
In short, her divine influence refined
Our corrupt hearts, and polished mankind.
  Of lovely nymphs she had a smiling train,
Fairer than those e'er graced Arcadia's plain.
The British ladies next to her took place,
Who chiefly did the fair assembly grace.
What blooming virgins can Britannia boast,
Their praises would all eloquence exhaust.
With ladies there my ravish'd eyes did meet,
That oft I 've seen grace fair Edina's street,

With their broad hoops cut through the willing air,
Pleased to give place unto the lovely fair:
  Sure this is like those blissful seats above,
Here is peace, transporting joy, and love.
  Should I be doom'd by cruel angry fate
In some lone isle my lingering end to wait,
Yet happy I! still happy should I be!
While bless'd with virtue and a charming she;
With full content I 'd fortune's pride despise,
And die still gazing on her lovely eyes.
  May all the blessings mortals need below,
May all the blessings heaven can bestow,
May every thing that 's pleasant, good, or rare,
Be the eternal portion of the Fair.

ON THE DEATH OF HIS MOTHER.*

Ye fabled Muses, I your aid disclaim,
Your airy raptures, and your fancied flame:
True genuine woe my throbbing breast inspires,
Love prompts my lays, and filial duty fires;
My soul springs instant at the warm design,
And the heart dictates every flowing line.
See! where the kindest, best of mothers lies,
And death has closed her ever watching eyes;

* See the Memoir.

Has lodged at last in peace her weary breast,
And lull'd her many piercing cares to rest.
No more the orphan train around her stands,
While her full heart upbraids her needy hands!
No more the widow's lonely fate she feels,
The shock severe that modest want conceals,
The oppressor's scourge, the scorn of wealthy pride,
And poverty's unnumber'd ills beside.
For see! attended by the angelic throng,
Through yonder worlds of light she glides along,
And claims the well earn'd raptures of the sky:
Yet fond concern recalls the mother's eye;
She seeks the helpless orphans left behind:
So hardly left! so bitterly resign'd!
Still, still! is she my soul's diurnal theme,
The waking vision, and the wailing dream:
Amid the ruddy sun's enlivening blaze
O'er my dark eyes her dewy image plays,
And in the dread dominion of the night
Shines out again the sadly pleasing sight.
Triumphant virtue all around her darts,
And more than volumes every look imparts —
Looks, soft, yet awful; melting, yet serene;
Where both the mother and the saint are seen.
But ah! that night — that torturing night remains;
May darkness dye it with the deepest stains,
May joy on it forsake her rosy bowers,
And streaming sorrow blast its baleful hours,
When on the margin of the briny flood,
Chill'd with a sad presaging damp I stood,

Took the last look, ne'er to behold her more,
And mix'd our murmurs with the wavy roar;
Heard the last words fall from her pious tongue,
Then, wild into the bulging vessel flung,
Which soon, too soon, convey'd me from her sight,
Dearer than life, and liberty, and light!
Why was I then, ye powers, reserved for this?
Nor sunk that moment in the vast abyss?
Devour'd at once by the relentless wave,
And whelm'd for ever in a watery grave?—
Down, ye wild wishes of unruly woe!—
I see her with immortal beauty glow;
The early wrinkle, care-contracted, gone,
Her tears all wiped, and all her sorrows flown;
The exalting voice of Heaven I hear her breathe,
To soothe her soul in agonies of death.
I see her through the mansions blest above,
And now she meets her dear expecting Love.
Heart-cheering sight! but yet, alas! o'erspread
By the dark gloom of Grief's uncheerful shade.
Come then, of reason the reflecting hour,
And let me trust the kind o'erruling Power,
Who from the right commands the shining day,
The poor man's portion, and the orphan's stay.

EPITAPH ON MISS STANLEY,*

IN HOLYROOD CHURCH, SOUTHAMPTON.

E. S.

Once a lively image of human nature,
Such as God made it
When he pronounced every work of his to be good.
To the memory of Elizabeth Stanley,
Daughter of George and Sarah Stanley;
Who to all the beauty, modesty,
And gentleness of nature,
That ever adorned the most amiable woman,
Joined all the fortitude, elevation,
And vigour of mind,
That ever exalted the most heroical man;
Who having lived the pride and delight of her parents,
The joy, the consolation, and pattern of her friends,
A mistress not only of the English and French,
But in a high degree of the Greek and Roman learning,
Without vanity or pedantry,
At the age of eighteen,
After a tedious, painful, desperate illness,
Which, with a Roman spirit,
And a Christian resignation,

* See an allusion to this Lady in "Summer," p. 78.

She endured so calmly, that she seemed insensible
To all pain and suffering, except that of her friends,
Gave up her innocent soul to her Creator,
And left to her mother, who erected this monument,
The memory of her virtues for her greatest support;
Virtues which, in her sex and station of life,
Were all that could be practised,
And more than will be believed,
Except by those who know what this inscription relates.

Here, Stanley, rest! escaped this mortal strife,
Above the joys, beyond the woes of life,
Fierce pangs no more thy lively beauties stain,
And sternly try thee with a year of pain;
No more sweet patience, feigning oft relief,
Lights thy sick eye, to cheat a parent's grief:
With tender art to save her anxious groan,
No more thy bosom presses down its own:
Now well earn'd peace is thine, and bliss sincere:
Ours be the lenient, not unpleasing tear!
O born to bloom, then sink beneath the storm;
To show us virtue in her fairest form;
To show us artless reason's moral reign,
What boastful science arrogates in vain;
The obedient passions knowing each their part;
Calm light the head, and harmony the heart!
Yes, we must follow soon, will glad obey;
When a few suns have roll'd their cares away,
Tired with vain life, will close the willing eye:

'Tis the great birthright of mankind to die.
Bless'd be the bark! that wafts us to the shore,
Where death-divided friends shall part no more:
To join thee there, here with thy dust repose,
Is all the hope thy hapless mother knows.

ON THE DEATH OF MR. AIKMAN.*

Oh, could I draw, my friend, thy genuine mind,
Just as the living forms by thee design'd;
Of Raphael's figures none should fairer shine,
Nor Titian's colours longer last than mine.
A mind in wisdom old, in lenience young,
From fervent truth where every virtue sprung;
Where all was real, modest, plain, sincere:
Worth above show, and goodness unsevere:
View'd round and round, as lucid diamonds throw
Still as you turn them a revolving glow,
So did his mind reflect with secret ray,
In various virtues, Heaven's internal day;

* Mr. Aikman was born in Scotland, and was designed for the profession of the law; but went to Italy, and returned a painter. He was patronized in Scotland by the Duke of Argyle, and afterwards met with encouragement to settle in London; but falling into a long and languishing disease, he died at his house in Leicester Fields, June, 1731, aged 50. Boyse wrote a panegyric upon him, and Mallet an epitaph. See Walpole's Anecdotes, vol. iv. p. 41.

Whether in high discourse it soar'd sublime
And sprung impatient o'er the bounds of Time,
Or wandering nature through with raptured eye,
Adored the hand that turn'd yon azure sky:
Whether to social life he bent his thought,
And the right poise of mingling passions sought,
Gay converse bless'd; or in the thoughtful grove
Bid the heart open every source of love:
New varying lights still set before your eyes
The just, the good, the social, or the wise.
For such a death who can, who would refuse
The friend a tear, a verse the mournful muse?
Yet pay we just acknowledgment to heaven,
Though snatch'd so soon, that Aikman e'er was given.
A friend, when dead, is but removed from sight,
Hid in the lustre of eternal light:
Oft with the mind he wonted converse keeps
In the lone walk, or when the body sleeps
Lets in a wandering ray, and all elate
Wings and attracts her to another state;
And, when the parting storms of life are o'er,
May yet rejoin him in a happier shore.
As those we love decay, we die in part,
String after string is sever'd from the heart;
Till loosen'd life at last — but breathing clay,
Without one pang, is glad to fall away.
Unhappy he who latest feels the blow,
Whose eyes have wept o'er every friend laid low,
Dragg'd lingering on from partial death to death;
And dying, all he can resign is breath.

ON THE REPORT THAT A WOODEN BRIDGE

WAS TO BE BUILT AT WESTMINSTER.

By Rufus' hall, where Thames polluted flows,
Provoked, the Genius of the river rose,
And thus exclaim'd: 'Have I, ye British swains,
Have I for ages laved your fertile plains?
Given herds, and flocks, and villages increase,
And fed a richer than a golden fleece?
Have I, ye merchants, with each swelling tide,
Pour'd Afric's treasure in, and India's pride?
Lent you the fruit of every nation's toil?
Made every climate yours, and every soil?
Yet, pilfer'd from the poor, by gaming base,
Yet must a wooden bridge my waves disgrace?
Tell not to foreign streams the shameful tale,
And be it publish'd in no Gallic vale.'
He said; and plunging to his crystal dome,
While o'er his head the circling waters foam.

THE INCOMPARABLE SOPORIFIC DOCTOR.

[First printed 1729.]

Sweet, sleeky Doctor! dear pacific soul!
Lay at the beef, and suck the vital bowl!

* Dr. Patrick Murdoch.

Still let the involving smoke around thee fly,
And broad-look'd dulness settle in thine eye.
Ah! soft in down these dainty limbs repose,
And in the very lap of slumber doze;
But chiefly on the lazy day of grace,
Call forth the lambent glories of thy face;
If aught the thoughts of dinner can prevail,
And sure the Sunday's dinner cannot fail.
To the thin church in sleepy pomp proceed,
And lean on the lethargic book thy head.
These eyes wipe often with the hallow'd lawn,
Profoundly nod, immeasurably yawn.
Slow let the prayers by thy meek lips be sung,
Now let thy thoughts be distanced by thy tongue;
If ere the lingerers are within a call,
Or if on prayers thou deign'st to think at all.
Yet — only yet — the swimming head we bend;
But when, serene, the pulpit you ascend,
Through every joint a gentle horror creeps,
And round you the consenting audience sleeps.
So when an ass with sluggish front appears,
The horses start, and prick their quivering ears;
But soon as e'er the sage is heard to bray,
The fields all thunder, and they bound away.

ON THE HOOP.

THE hoop, the darling justly of the fair,
Of every generous swain deserves the care.
It is unmanly to desert the weak,
'Twould urge a stone, if possible to speak;
To hear stanch hypocrites bawl out, and cry,
'This hoop 's a whorish garb, fie! ladies, fie!'
O cruel and audacious men, to blast
The fame of ladies more than vestals chaste;
Should you go search the globe throughout,
You 'll find none so pious and devout;
So modest, chaste, so handsome, and so fair,
As our dear Caledonian ladies are.
When awful beauty puts on all her charms,
Nought gives our sex such terrible alarms,
As when the hoop and tartan both combine
To make a virgin like a goddess shine.
Let quakers cut their clothes unto the quick,
And with severities themselves afflict;
But may the hoop adorn Edina's street,
Till the south pole shall with the northern meet.

TO SERAPHINA.

The wanton's charms, however bright,
Are like the false illusive light,
Whose flattering unauspicious blaze
To precipices oft betrays:
But that sweet ray your beauties dart,
Which clears the mind, and cleans the heart,
Is like the sacred queen of night,
Who pours a lovely gentle light
Wide o'er the dark, by wanderers blest,
Conducting them to peace and rest.
 A vicious love depraves the mind,
'Tis anguish, guilt, and folly join'd;
But Seraphina's eyes dispense
A mild and gracious influence;
Such as in visions angels shed
Around the heaven-illumined head.
To love thee, Seraphina, sure
Is to be tender, happy, pure;
'Tis from low passions to escape,
And woo bright virtue's fairest shape;
'Tis ecstacy with wisdom join'd;
And heaven infused into the mind.

VERSES ON RECEIVING A FLOWER FROM HIS MISTRESS.

[First printed 1720.]

MADAM, the flower that I received from you,
Ere I came home, had lost its lovely hue:
As flowers deprived of the genial day,
Its sprightly bloom did wither and decay;
Dear, fading flower, I know full well, said I,
The reason that you shed your sweets and die;
You want the influence of her enlivening eye.
Your case is mine—Absence, that plague of love!
With heavy pace makes every minute move:
It of my being is an empty blank,
And hinders me myself with men to rank;
Your cheering presence quickens me again,
And new-sprung life exults in every vein.

VERSES ADDRESSED TO AMANDA.*

AH, urged too late! from beauty's bondage free,
Why did I trust my liberty with thee?

* Amanda, as is stated in the Memoir, was a Miss Young, who married Vice Admiral Campbell.

And thou, why didst thou, with inhuman heart,
If not resolved to take, seduce my heart?
Yes, yes, you said, for lovers' eyes speak true;
You must have seen how fast my passion grew:
And, when your glances chanced on me to shine,
How my fond soul ecstatic sprung to thine!
But mark me, fair one — what I now declare
Thy deep attention claims and serious care:
It is no common passion fires my breast;
I must be wretched, or I must be blest!
My woes all other remedy deny;
Or, pitying, give me hope, or bid me die!

TO THE SAME,

WITH A COPY OF THE 'SEASONS.'

Accept, loved Nymph, this tribute due
To tender friendship, love, and you: *
But with it take what breathed the whole,
O take to thine the poet's soul.
If Fancy here her powers displays,
And if a heart exalts these lays —
You, fairest, in that fancy shine,
And all that heart is fondly thine.

* In another MS. the first two lines read:
Accept, dear Nymph! a tribute due
To sacred friendship and to you.

STANZAS*

SENT TO GEORGE LYTTELTON, ESQ. SOON AFTER THE DEATH OF HIS WIFE,

WRITTEN IN A COPY OF THE 'SEASONS.'

Go, little book, and find our Friend,
  Who nature and the Muses loves,
Whose cares the public virtues blend
  With all the softness of the groves.

A fitter time thou canst not choose,
  His fostering friendship to repay;
Go then, and try, my rural muse,
  To steal his widow'd hours away.

AN ELEGY ON PARTING.

It was a sad, ay 'twas a sad farewell,
I still afresh the pangs of parting feel;
Against my breast my heart impatient beat,
And in deep sighs bemoan'd its cruel fate;
Thus with the object of my love to part,
My life! my joy! 'twould rend a rocky heart.

* Now in the collection of George Daniel, Esq. of Canonbury Square, Islington.

Where'er I turn myself, where'er I go,
I meet the image of my lovely foe;
With witching charms the phantom still appears,
And with her wanton smiles insults my tears;
Still haunts the places where we used to walk,
And where with raptures oft I heard her talk:
Those scenes I now with deepest sorrow view,
And sighing bid to all delight adieu.
While I my head upon this turf recline,
Officious sun, in vain on me you shine;
In vain unto the smiling fields I hie;
In vain the flowery meads salute my eye;
In vain the cheerful birds and shepherds sing,
And with their carols make the valleys ring;
Yea, all the pleasure that the country yield
Can't me from sorrow for her absence shield:
With divine pleasure books which one inspire,
Yea, books themselves I do not now admire.
But hark! methinks some pitying power I hear,
This welcome message whisper in my ear:
'Forget thy groundless griefs, dejected swain,
You and the nymph you love shall meet again;
No more your muse shall sing such mournful lays,
But bounteous heaven and your kind mistress praise.'

SONGS.

A NUPTIAL SONG.

COME, gentle Venus! and assuage
A warring world, a bleeding age.
For nature lives beneath thy ray,
The wintry tempests haste away,
A lucid calm invests the sea,
Thy native deep is full of thee:
The flowering earth where'er you fly,
Is all o'er spring, all sun the sky.
A genial spirit warms the breeze;
Unseen among the blooming trees,
The feather'd lovers tune their throat,
The desert growls a soften'd note,
Glad o'er the meads the cattle bound,
And love and harmony go round.
But chief into the human heart
You strike the dear delicious dart;
You teach us pleasing pangs to know,
To languish in luxurious woe,
To feel the generous passions rise,
Grow good by gazing, mild by sighs;

Each happy moment to improve,
And fill the perfect year with love.
  Come, thou delight of heaven and earth!
To whom all creatures owe their birth;
Oh, come, sweet smiling! tender, come!
And yet prevent our final doom.
For long the furious god of war
Has crush'd us with his iron car,
Has raged along our ruin'd plains,
Has foil'd them with his cruel stains,
Has sunk our youth in endless sleep,
And made the widow'd virgin weep.
Now let him feel thy wonted charms,
Oh, take him to thy twining arms!
And, while thy bosom heaves on his,
While deep he prints the humid kiss,
Ah, then! his stormy heart control,
And sigh thyself into his soul.

TO AMANDA.*

Come, dear Amanda, quit the town,
  And to the rural hamlets fly;
Behold! the wintry storms are gone;
  A gentle radiance glads the sky.

* This song was obligingly contributed to this edition by William Henry, present Lord Lyttelton, from a copy in Thomson's own hand, and is printed for the first time.

The birds awake, the flowers appear,
  Earth spreads a verdant couch for thee;
'Tis joy and music all we hear,
  'Tis love and beauty all we see.

Come, let us mark the gradual spring,
  How peeps the bud, the blossom blows;
Till Philomel begins to sing,
  And perfect May to swell the rose.

E'en so thy rising charms improve,
  As life's warm season grows more bright;
And opening to the sighs of love,
  Thy beauties glow with full delight.

TO AMANDA.

Unless with my Amanda bless'd,
  In vain I twine the woodbine bower;
Unless to deck her sweeter breast,
  In vain I rear the breathing flower.

Awaken'd by the genial year,
  In vain the birds around me sing;
In vain the freshening fields appear:—
  Without my love there is no Spring.

TO FORTUNE.

For ever, Fortune, wilt thou prove
An unrelenting foe to love,
And when we meet a mutual heart,
Come in between, and bid us part:

Bid us sigh on from day to day,
And wish, and wish the soul away;
Till youth and genial years are flown,
And all the love of life is gone?

But busy, busy still art thou,
To bind the loveless joyless vow,
The heart from pleasure to delude,
And join the gentle to the rude.

For pomp, and noise, and senseless show,
To make us Nature's joys forego,
Beneath a gay dominion groan,
And put the golden fetter on!

For once, O Fortune, hear my prayer,
And I absolve thy future care;
All other blessings I resign,
Make but the dear Amanda mine.

COME, GENTLE GOD.

Come, gentle God of soft desire,
Come and possess my happy breast,
Not fury-like in flames and fire,
Or frantic folly's wildness drest; *

But come in friendship's angel-guise;
Yet dearer thou than friendship art,
More tender spirit in thy eyes,
More sweet emotions at thy heart.

O, come with goodness in thy train,
With peace and pleasure void of storm,
And wouldst thou me for ever gain,
Put on Amanda's winning form.

* A MS. copy of this song has the following variations:—

In rapture, rage, and nonsense drest.
These are the vain disguise of love,
And, or bespeak dissembled pains;
Or else a fleeting fever prove,
The frantic passion of the veins.

TO HER I LOVE.

Tell me, thou soul of her I love,
  Ah! tell me, whither art thou fled;
To what delightful world above,
  Appointed for the happy dead?

Or dost thou, free, at pleasure, roam,
  And sometimes share thy lover's woe;
Where, void of thee, his cheerless home
  Can now, alas! no comfort know?

Oh! if thou hover'st round my walk,
  While, under every well known tree,
I to thy fancied shadow talk,
  And every tear is full of thee:

Should then the weary eye of grief,
  Beside some sympathetic stream,
In slumber find a short relief,
  Oh, visit thou my soothing dream!

TO THE GOD OF FOND DESIRE.

ONE day the God of fond desire,
  On mischief bent, to Damon said,
'Why not disclose your tender fire,
  Not own it to the lovely maid?'

The shepherd mark'd his treacherous art,
  And, softly sighing, thus replied:
''Tis true, you have subdued my heart,
  But shall not triumph o'er my pride.

'The slave, in private only bears
  Your bondage, who his love conceals;
But when his passion he declares,
  You drag him at your chariot-wheels.'

THE LOVER'S FATE.

HARD is the fate of him who loves,
  Yet dares not tell his trembling pain,
But to the sympathetic groves,
  But to the lonely listening plain.

Oh! when she blesses next your shade,
  Oh! when her footsteps next are seen

In flowery tracts along the mead,
  In fresher mazes o'er the green:

Ye gentle spirits of the vale,
  To whom the tears of love are dear,
From dying lilies waft a gale,
  And sigh my sorrows in her ear.

Oh! tell her what she cannot blame,
  Though fear my tongue must ever bind;
Oh, tell her, that my virtuous flame
  Is, as her spotless soul, refined.

Not her own guardian-angel eyes
  With chaster tenderness his care,
Not purer her own wishes rise,
  Not holier her own sighs in prayer.

But if, at first, her virgin fear
  Should start at love's suspected name,
With that of friendship soothe her ear —
  True love and friendship are the same.

TO THE NIGHTINGALE.

O NIGHTINGALE, best poet of the grove,
  That plaintive strain can ne'er belong to thee,

Bless'd in the full possession of thy love:
O lend that strain, sweet Nightingale, to me!

'Tis mine, alas! to mourn my wretched fate:
I love a maid who all my bosom charms,
Yet lose my days without this lovely mate;
Inhuman fortune keeps her from my arms.

You, happy birds! by nature's simple laws
Lead your soft lives, sustain'd by nature's fare;
You dwell wherever roving fancy draws.
And love and song is all your pleasing care:

But we, vain slaves of interest and pride,
Dare not be bless'd, lest envious tongues should blame:
And hence, in vain, I languish for my bride!
O mourn with me, sweet bird, my hapless flame!

TO MYRA.

O THOU, whose tender serious eyes
Expressive speak the mind I love;
The gentle azure of the skies,
The pensive shadows of the grove:

O mix their beauteous beams with mine,
And let us interchange our hearts;

Let all their sweetness on me shine,
  Pour'd through my soul be all their darts.

Ah! 'tis too much! I cannot bear
  At once so soft, so keen a ray:
In pity then, my lovely fair,
  O turn those killing eyes away!

But what avails it to conceal
  One charm, where nought but charms I see?
Their lustre then again reveal,
  And let me, Myra, die of thee!

SONGS IN THE MASQUE OF 'ALFRED.'*

TO PEACE.

O PEACE! the fairest child of Heaven,
To whom the sylvan reign was given,
The vale, the fountain, and the grove,
With every softer scene of love:
Return, sweet Peace! and cheer the weeping swain!
Return, with Ease and Pleasure in thy train.

* The Masque of Alfred was the joint composition of Thomson and Mallet; hence the authorship of the following songs is somewhat doubtful.

TO ALFRED.

FIRST SPIRIT.

HEAR, Alfred, father of the state,
  Thy genius Heaven's high will declare!
What proves the hero truly great,
  Is never, never to despair:
    Is never to despair.

SECOND SPIRIT.

Thy hope awake, thy heart expand,
  With all its vigour, all its fires.
Arise! and save a sinking land!
  Thy country calls, and Heaven inspires.

BOTH SPIRITS.

Earth calls, and Heaven inspires.

"SWEET VALLEY, SAY."

SWEET valley, say, where, pensive lying,
For me, our children, England, sighing,
    The best of mortals leans his head.
Ye fountains, dimpled by my sorrow,
Ye brooks that my complainings borrow,

O lead me to his lonely bed:
Or if my lover,
Deep woods, you cover,
Ah whisper where your shadows o'er him spread.
'Tis not the loss of pomp and pleasure,
Of empire or of tinsel treasure,
That drops this tear, that swells this groan:
No; from a nobler cause proceeding,
A heart with love and fondness bleeding,
I breathe my sadly pleasing moan.
With other anguish,
I scorn to languish,
For love will feel no sorrows but his own.

"FROM THOSE ETERNAL REGIONS."

From those eternal regions bright,
Where suns, that never set in night,
Diffuse the golden day:
Where Spring, unfading, pours around,
O'er all the dew-impearled ground,
Her thousand colors gay:
O whether on the fountain's flowery side,
Whence living waters glide,
Or in the fragrant grove,
Whose shade embosoms peace and love,
New pleasures all our hours employ,

And ravish every sense with every joy!
Great heirs of empire! yet unborn,
Who shall this island late adorn;
A monarch's drooping thought to cheer,
Appear! appear! appear!

CONTENTMENT.

If those, who live in shepherd's bower,
Press not the rich and stately bed:
The new-mown hay and breathing flower
A softer couch beneath them spread.

If those, who sit at shepherd's board,
Soothe not their taste by wanton art;
They take what Nature's gift afford,
And take it with a cheerful heart.

If those who drain the shepherd's bowl,
No high and sparkling wines can boast,
With wholesome cups they cheer the soul,
And crown them with the village toast.

If those who join in shepherd's sport,
Gay dancing on the daisied ground,
Have not the splendour of a court;
Yet love adorns the merry round.

RULE, BRITANNIA!

WITH VARIATIONS.

When Britain first, at Heaven's command,
Arose from out the azure main,
This was the charter of the land,
And guardian angels sung this strain:
'Rule, Britannia, rule the waves;
Britons never will be slaves.'

The nations, not so bless'd as thee,
Must, in their turns, to tyrants fall;
While thou shalt flourish great and free,,
The dread and envy of them all.
'Rule,' &c.

Still more majestic shalt thou rise,
More dreadful from each foreign stroke;
As the loud blast that tears the skies
Serves but to root thy native oak.
'Rule,' &c.

Thee haughty tyrants ne'er shall tame:
All their attempts to bend thee down
Will but arouse thy generous flame,
But work their woe, and thy renown.
'Rule,' &c.

To thee belongs the rural reign;
  Thy cities shall with commerce shine:
All thine shall be the subject main:
  And every shore it circles thine.
    'Rule,' &c.

The Muses, still with freedom found,
  Shall to thy happy coast repair:
Bless'd isle! with matchless beauty crown'd,
  And manly hearts to guard the fair:
    'Rule, Britannia, rule the waves;
    Britons never will be slaves.'

SONG.

When blooming spring
Arrays the laughing fields in green,
Then flowers in open air are seen,
And warbling birds are heard to sing,
    Almighty love
    Doth sweetly move
    All nature through;
Then tell me, Chloe, why are you
      Averse thereto;
      When blooming charms
    Invite your lover's circling arms?
      O be no longer coy
. . . . . . to love and share of joy.

PROLOGUE TO TANCRED AND SIGISMUNDA.

Bold is the man! who, in this nicer age,
Presumes to tread the chaste corrected stage.
Now, with gay tinsel arts, we can no more
Conceal the want of Nature's sterling ore.
Our spells are vanish'd, broke our magic wand,
That used to waft you over sea and land.
Before your light the fairy people fade,
The demons fly — the ghost itself is laid.
In vain of martial scenes the loud alarms,
The mighty prompter thundering out to arms,
The playhouse posse clattering from afar,
The close-wedged battle, and the din of war.
Now, e'en the senate seldom we convene:
The yawning fathers nod behind the scene.
Your taste rejects the glittering false sublime,
To sigh in metaphor, and die in rhyme.
High rant is tumbled from his gallery throne:
Description dreams — nay, similes are gone.

What shall we then? to please you how devise,
Whose judgment sits not in your ears and eyes?
Thrice happy! could we catch great Shakespeare's art,
To trace the deep recesses of the heart;
His simple plain sublime, to which is given
To strike the soul with darted flame from heaven;

Could we awake soft Otway's tender woe,
The pomp of verse and golden lines of Rowe.

We to your hearts apply; let them attend;
Before their silent candid bar we bend.
If warm'd, they listen, 'tis our noblest praise;
If cold, they wither all the Muse's bays.

EPILOGUE TO TANCRED AND SIGISMUNDA.

Cramm'd to the throat with wholesome moral stuff,
Alas! poor audience! you have had enough.
Was ever hapless heroine of a play
In such a piteous plight as ours to-day?
Was ever woman so by love betray'd?
Match'd with two husbands, and yet — die a maid.
But bless me! — hold — What sounds are these I
hear! —
I see the Tragic Muse herself appear.

The back scene opens, and discovers a romantic sylvan landscape; from which Mrs. Cibber, in the character of the Tragic Muse, advances slowly to music, and speaks the following lines: —

Hence with your flippant epilogue, that tries
To wipe the virtuous tear from British eyes;
That dares my moral, tragic scene profane,
With strains — at best, unsuiting, light and vain.
Hence from the pure unsullied beams that play
In yon fair eyes where virtue shines — Away!

Britons, to you from chaste Castalian groves,
Where dwell the tender, oft unhappy loves!
Where shades of heroes roam, each mighty name,
And court my aid to rise again to fame;
To you I come, to Freedom's noblest seat,
And in Britannia fix my last retreat.
In Greece and Rome, I watch'd the public weal,
The purple tyrant trembled at my steel:
Nor did I less o'er private sorrows reign,
And mend the melting heart with softer pain.
On France and you then rose my brightening star,
With social ray — The arts are ne'er at war.
O, as your fire and genius stronger blaze,
As yours are generous Freedom's bolder lays,
Let not the Gallic taste leave yours behind,
In decent manners and in life refined;
Banish the motley mode to tag low verse,
The laughing ballad to the mournful hearse.
When through five acts your hearts have learnt to glow,
Touch'd with the sacred force of honest woe;
O keep the dear impression on your breast,
Nor idly lose it for a wretched jest.

EPILOGUE TO AGAMEMNON.

Our bard, to modern epilogue a foe,
Thinks such mean mirth but deadens generous woe;

Dispels in idle air the moral sigh,
And wipes the tender tear from Pity's eye:
No more with social warmth the bosom burns;
But all the unfeeling selfish man returns.*
  Thus he began: — And you approved the strain;
Till the next couplet sunk to light and vain.
You check'd him there. — To you, to reason just,
He owns he triumph'd in your kind disgust.
Charm'd by your frown, by your displeasure graced,
He hails the rising virtue of your taste.
Wide will its influence spread as soon as known:
Truth, to be loved, needs only to be shown.
Confirm it, once, the fashion to be good:
(Since fashion leads the fool, and awes the rude)
No petulance shall wound the public ear;
No hand applaud what honour shuns to hear:
No painful blush the modest cheek shall stain;
The worthy breast shall heave with no disdain.
Chastised to decency, the British stage
Shall oft invite the fair, invite the sage:
Both shall attend well pleased, well pleased depart;
Or if they doom the verse, absolve the heart.

* Thomson observes, "Another epilogue was spoken after the first representation of the play, which began with the first six lines of this; but the rest of that epilogue having been very justly disliked by the audience, this was substituted in its place."

PROLOGUE TO MALLET'S MUSTAPHA.

SINCE Athens first began to draw mankind,
To picture life, and show the impassion'd mind;
The truly wise have ever deem'd the stage
The moral school of each enlighten'd age.
There, in full pomp, the tragic Muse appears,
Queen of soft sorrows, and of useful fears.
Faint is the lesson reason's rules impart:
She pours it strong, and instant through the heart.
If virtue is her theme, we sudden glow
With generous flame; and what we feel, we grow.
If vice she paints, indignant passions rise;
The villain sees himself with loathing eyes.
His soul starts, conscious, at another's groan,
And the pale tyrant trembles on his throne.
To-night, our meaning scene attempts to show
What fell events from dark suspicion flow;
Chief when it taints a lawless monarch's mind,
To the false herd of flattering slaves confined,
The soul sinks gradual to so dire a state;
E'en excellence but serves to feed its hate:
To hate remorseless cruelty succeeds,
And every worth, and every virtue bleeds.
Behold, our author at your bar appears,
His modest hopes depress'd by conscious fears.
Faults he has many — but to balance those,
His verse with heart-felt love of virtue glows:

All slighter errors let indulgence spare,
And be his equal trial full and fair.
For this best British privilege we call,
Then, as he merits, let him stand or fall.

TO THE REVEREND PATRICK MURDOCH.

RECTOR OF STRADISHALL, IN SUFFOLK. 1738.

THUS safely low, my friend, thou canst not fall:
Here reigns a deep tranquillity o'er all;
No noise, no care, no vanity, no strife;
Men, woods, and fields, all breathe untroubled life.
Then keep each passion down, however dear;
Trust me, the tender are the most severe.
Guard, while 'tis thine, thy philosophic ease,
And ask no joy but that of virtuous peace;
That bids defiance to the storms of fate:
High bliss is only for a higher state!

TO HIS ROYAL HIGHNESS THE PRINCE OF WALES.

WHILE secret-leaguing nations frown around,
  Ready to pour the long-expected storm;
While she, who wont the restless Gaul to bound,
  Britannia, drooping, grows an empty form;

While on our vitals selfish parties prey,
And deep corruption eats our soul away:

Yet in the Goddess of the Main appears
  A gleam of joy, gay-flushing every grace,
As she the cordial voice of millions hears,
  Rejoicing, zealous, o'er thy rising race:
Straight her rekindling eyes resume their fire,
The Virtues smile, the Muses tune the lyre.

But more enchanting than the Muse's song,
  United Britons thy dear offspring hail:
The city triumphs through her glowing throng,
  The shepherd tells his transport to the dale
The sons of roughest toil forget their pain,
And the glad sailor cheers the midnight main.

Can aught from fair Augusta's gentle blood,
  And thine, thou friend of liberty! be born:
Can aught save what is lovely, generous, good;
  What will, at once, defend us, and adorn?
From thence prophetic joy new Edwards eyes,
New Henries, Annas, and Elizas rise.

May fate my fond devoted days extend,
  To sing the promised glories of thy reign!
What though, by years depress'd, my Muse might
    bend;
  My heart will teach her still a nobler strain:
How, with recover'd Britain, will she soar,
When France insults, and Spain shall rob no more.

TO DR. DE LA COUR, IN IRELAND.

ON HIS "PROSPECT OF POETRY."

Hail, gently warbling De la Cour, whose fame,
Spurning Hibernia's solitary coast,
Where small rewards attend the tuneful throng,
Pervades Britannia's well discerning isle:
In spite of all the gloomy-minded tribe
That would eclipse thy fame, still shall the Muse,
High soaring o'er the tall Parnassian mount
With spreading pinions—sing thy wondrous praise,
In strains attuned to the seraphic lyre.
Sing unappall'd, though mighty be the theme!
O! could she in thy own harmonious strain,
Where softest numbers smoothly flowing glide
In trickling cadence; where the milky maze
Devolves in silence; by the harsher sound
Of hoarser periods still unruffled, could
Her lines but like thine own Euphrates flow—
Then might she sing in numbers worthy thee.
But what can language do, when fancy finds
Herself unequal to the lovely task?
Can feeble words thy vivid colours paint,
Or show the sweets which inexhaustive flow?
Hearken, ye woods, and long-resounding groves;
Listen, ye streams, soft purling through the meads;
And hymning horrid, all ye tempests, roar.
Awake, ye woodlands! sing, ye warbling larks,

In wildly luscious notes! But most of all,
Attend, ye grateful fair, attend the youth
Who sweetly sings of nature and of you:
From you alone his conscious breast expects
Its soft rewards, by sordid love of gain
Unbias'd, undebased; to meaner minds
Belong such narrow views; his nobler soul,
Transported with a generous thirst of fame,
Sublimely rises with expanded wings,
And through the lucid empyrean soars.
So the young eagle wings its rapid way
Through heaven's broad azure; sometimes springs aloft,
Now drops, now cleaves with even-waving wings
The yielding air, nor seas nor mountains stop
Its flight impetuous, gazing at the sun
With irretorted eye, whilst he pervades
A trackless void, and unexplored before.
Long had the curious traveller strove to find
The ruins of aspiring Babylon —
In vain — for nought the nicest eye could trace
Save one wide, watery, undistinguish'd waste:
But you with more than magic art have raised
Semiramis's city from its grave;
You have reversed the scripture curse, which said,
Dragons shall here inhabit; in your page
We view the rising spires; the hurried eye
Distracted wanders through the verdant maze;
In middle air the pendant gardens hang,
Tremendous ceiling! — whilst no solar beam

Falls on the lengthen'd gloom beneath; the woods
Project above a steep-alluring shade;
The finish'd garden opens to the view
Wide stretching vistas, while the whispering wind
Dimples along the breezy-ruffled lake.
Now every tree irregular and bush
Are prodigal of harmony: the birds
Frequent the aerial wood, and nature blushes,
Ashamed to find herself outdone by art:
These and a thousand beauties could I sing,
Collecting like the ever-toiling bee
From yonder mingled wilderness of flowers
The aromatic sweets; while you, great youth!
O'er thy decaying country chief preside;
Be thou her genius call'd, inspire her youth
With noble emulation to arrive
At Helicon's fair font, which few, alas!
Save you, have tasted of Hibernian youth.
Thy country, though corrupted, brought thee forth,
And deem'd her greatest ornament; and now
Regards thee as her brightest northern star.
Long may you reign as such; and should grim Time,
With iron teeth, deprive us of our Pope,
Then we'll transplant thy blooming laurels fresh
From your bleak shore to Albion's happier coast.

A POETICAL EPISTLE TO SIR WILLIAM BENNET, BART. OF GRUBBAT.*

My trembling muse your honour does address,
That it 's a bold attempt most humbly I confess;
If you 'll encourage her young fagging flight,
She 'll upward soar and mount Parnassus' height.
If little things with great may be compared,
In Rome it so with the divine Virgil fared;
The tuneful bard Augustus did inspire,
Made his great genius flash poetic fire;
But if upon my flight your honour frowns,
The muse folds up her wings, and dying—justice owns.

ON MRS. MENDEZ' BIRTHDAY.

WHO WAS BORN ON VALENTINE'S DAY.

Thine is the gentle day of love,
When youths and virgins try their fate;
When, deep retiring to the grove,
Each feather'd songster weds his mate.

* This was written at a very early period of Thomson's life, probably before he was sixteen; and the reason for inserting it is, that the first productions of genius are objects of rational curiosity.

With temper'd beams the skies are bright,
  Earth decks in smiles her pleasing face;
Such is the day that gave thee light,
  And speaks as such thy every grace.

AN ELEGY UPON JAMES THERBURN.

IN CHATTO.

Now, Chatto, you 're a dreary place,
Pale sorrow broods on ilka face;
Therburn has run his race,
And now, and now, ah me, alas!
            The carl lies dead.

Having his paternoster said,
He took a dram and went to bed;
He fell asleep, and death was glad
            That he had catch'd him;
For Therburn was e'en ill bested,
            That none did watch him.

For had the carl but been aware,
That meagre death, who none does spare,
T' attempt sic things should ever dare,
            As stop his pipe;
He might have come to flee or skare:
            The greedy gipe.

How he 'd had but a gill or twae,
Death wou'd nae got the victory sae,
Nor put poor Therburn o'er the brae,
Into the grave;
. . . .
. . . . *

The fumbling fellow, some folks say,
Should be jobb'd on baith night and day;
She had without'en better play,
Remained still,
Barren for ever and for aye,
Do what he will.

Therefore they say he got some help
In getting of the little whelp;
But passing that, it makes me yelp,
But what remead?
Death lent him sic a cursed skelp,
That now he 's dead.

Therburn, for evermore farewell,
And be thy grave both dry and deep;
And rest thy carcass soft and well,
Free from . . . .
. . . . no night . . . . . .
Disturb . . . .

* The MS. is imperfect in this place.

TO THE MEMORY OF THE RIGHT HON. LORD TALBOT,

LATE CHANCELLOR OF GREAT BRITAIN.

ADDRESSED TO HIS SON.

[First printed 1737.]

While with the public, you, my Lord, lament
A friend and father lost; permit the Muse,
The Muse assign'd of old a double theme,
To praise dead worth and humble living pride,
Whose generous task begins where interest ends;
Permit her on a Talbot's tomb to lay
This cordial verse sincere, by truth inspired,
Which means not to bestow but borrow fame.
Yes, she may sing his matchless virtues now —
Unhappy that she may. — But where begin?
How from the diamond single out each ray,
Where all, tho' trembling with ten thousand hues,
Effuse one dazzling undivided light?
  Let the low-minded of these narrow days
No more presume to deem the lofty tale
Of ancient times, in pity to their own,
Romance. In Talbot we united saw
The piercing eye, the quick enlighten'd soul,
The graceful ease, the flowing tongue of Greece,
Join'd to the virtues and the force of Rome.
  Eternal Wisdom, that all-quickening sun,

Whence every life, in just proportion, draws
Directing life and actuating flame,
Ne'er with a larger portion of its beams
Awaken'd mortal clay. Hence steady, calm,
Diffusive, deep, and clear, his reason saw,
With instantaneous view, the truth of things;
Chief what to human life and human bliss
Pertains, that noblest science, fit for man:
And hence, responsive to his knowledge, glow'd
His ardent virtue. Ignorance and vice,
In consort foul, agree; each heightening each;
While virtue draws from knowledge brighter fire.
  What grand, what comely, or what tender sense,
What talent, or what virtue was not his;
What that can render man or great, or good,
Give useful worth, or amiable grace?
Nor could he brook in studious shade to lie,
In soft retirement, indolently pleased
With selfish peace. The Syren of the wise,
(Who steals the Aonian song, and, in the shape
Of Virtue, woos them from a worthless world,)
Though deep he felt her charms, could never melt
His strenuous spirit, recollected, calm,
As silent night, yet active as the day.
The more the bold, the bustling, and the bad,
Press to usurp the reigns of power, the more
Behoves it virtue, with indignant zeal,
To check their combination. Shall low views
Of sneaking interest or luxurious vice,
The villain's passions quicken more to toil,

And dart a livelier vigour through the soul,
Than those that mingled with our truest good,
With present honour and immortal fame,
Involve the good of all? An empty form
Is the weak Virtue, that amid the shade
Lamenting lies, with future schemes amused,
While Wickedness and Folly, kindred powers,
Confound the world. A Talbot's, different far,
Sprung ardent into action: action, that disdain'd
To lose in death-like sloth one pulse of life,
That might be saved; disdain'd for coward ease,
And her insipid pleasures, to resign
The prize of glory, the keen sweets of toil,
And those high joys that teach the truly great
To live for others, and for others die.
  Early, behold! he breaks benign on life.
Not breathing more beneficence, the Spring
Leads in her swelling train the gentle airs:
While gay, behind her, smiles the kindling waste
Of ruffian storms and Winter's lawless rage.
In him Astrea, to this dim abode
Of ever wandering men, return'd again:
To bless them his delight, to bring them back
From thorny error, from unjoyous wrong,
Into the paths of kind primeval faith,
Of happiness and justice. All his parts,
His virtues all, collected, sought the good
Of humankind. For that he, fervent, felt
The throb of patriots, when they model states:
Anxious for that, nor needful sleep could hold

His still-awakened soul; nor friends had charms
To steal, with pleasing guile, one useful hour;
Toil knew no languor, no attraction joy.
Thus with unwearied steps, by Virtue led,
He gain'd the summit of that sacred hill,
Where, raised above black Envy's darkening clouds,
Her spotless temple lifts its radiant front.
Be named, victorious ravagers, no more!
Vanish, ye human comets! shrink your blaze!
Ye that your glory to your terrors owe,
As, o'er the gazing desolated earth,
You scatter famine, pestilence, and war;
Vanish! before this vernal sun of fame;
Effulgent sweetness! beaming life and joy.
  How the heart listen'd while he, pleading, spoke!
While on the enlighten'd mind, with winning art,
His gentle reason so persuasive stole,
That the charm'd hearer thought it was his own.
Ah! when, ye studious of the laws, again
Shall such enchanting lessons bless your ear?
When shall again the darkest truths, perplex'd,
Be set in ample day? when shall the harsh
And arduous open into smiling ease?
The solid mix with elegant delight?
His was the talent with the purest light
At once to pour conviction on the soul,
And warm with lawful flame the impassion'd heart.
That dangerous gift with him was safely lodged
By Heaven — He, sacred to his country's cause,
To trampled want and worth, to suffering right,

To the lone widow's and her orphan's woes,
Reserved the mighty charm. With equal brow,
Despising then the smiles or frowns of power,
He all that noblest eloquence effused,
Which generous passion, taught by reason, breathes
Then spoke the man; and over barren art,
Prevail'd abundant nature. Freedom then
His client was, humanity and truth.
Placed on the seat of justice, there he reign'd,
In a superior sphere of cloudless day,
A pure intelligence. No tumult there,
No dark emotion, no intemperate heat,
No passion e'er disturb'd the clear serene
That round him spread. A zeal for right alone,
The love of justice, like the steady sun,
Its equal ardour lent; and sometimes raised
Against the sons of violence, of pride,
And bold deceit, his indignation gleam'd,
Yet still by sober dignity restrain'd.
As intuition quick, he snatch'd the truth,
Yet with progressive patience, step by step,
Self-diffident, or to the slower kind,
He through the maze of falsehood traced it on,
Till, at the last, evolved, it full appear'd,
And e'en the loser own'd the just decree.
But when, in senates, he, to freedom firm,
Enlighten'd Freedom, plann'd salubrious laws,
His various learning, his wide knowledge, then,
His insight deep into Britannia's weal,
Spontaneous seem'd from simple sense to flow,

And the plain patriot smooth'd the brow of law.
To specious swell, no frothy pomp of words
Fell on the cheated ear; no studied maze
Of declamation, to perplex the right,
He darkening threw around: safe in itself,
In its own force, all-powerful Reason spoke;
While on the great the ruling point, at once,
He stream'd decisive day, and show'd it vain
To lengthen further out the clear debate.
Conviction breathes conviction; to the heart,
Pour'd ardent forth in eloquence unbid,
The heart attends: for let the venal try
Their every hardening stupifying art,
Truth must prevail, zeal will enkindle zeal,
And Nature, skilful touch'd, is honest still.
  Behold him in the councils of his prince.
What faithful light he lends! How rare, in courts,
Such wisdom! such abilities! and join'd
To virtue so determined, public zeal,
And honour of such adamantine proof,
As e'en corruption, hopeless, and o'erawed,
Durst not have tempted! yet of manners mild,
And winning every heart, he knew to please,
Nobly to please; while equally he scorn'd
Or adulation to receive, or give.
Happy the state, where wakes a ruling eye
Of such inspection keen, and general care!
Beneath a guard so vigilant, so pure,
Toil may resign his careless head to rest,
And ever jealous freedom sleep in peace.

Ah! lost untimely! lost in downward days!
And many a patriot-counsel with him lost!
Counsels, that might have humbled Britain's foe,
Her native foe, from eldest time by fate
Appointed, as did once a Talbot's arms.
Let learning, arts, let universal worth,
Lament a patron lost, a friend and judge,
Unlike the sons of vanity, that veil'd
Beneath the patron's prostituted name,
Dare sacrifice a worthy man to pride,
And flush confusion o'er an honest cheek.
When he conferr'd a grace, it seem'd a debt
Which he to merit, to the public, paid,
And to the great all-bounteous Source of good!
His sympathizing heart itself received
The generous obligation he bestow'd.
This, this indeed, is patronizing worth.
Their kind protector him the Muses own,
But scorn with noble pride the boasted aid
Of tasteless vanity's insulting hand.
The gracious stream, that cheers the letter'd world,
Is not the noisy gift of summer's noon,
Whose sudden current, from the naked root,
Washes the little soil which yet remain'd,
And only more dejects the blushing flowers:
No, 'tis the soft-descending dews at eve,
The silent treasures of the vernal year,
Indulging deep their stores, the still night long;
Till, with returning morn, the freshen'd world,
Is fragrance all, all beauty, joy, and song.

Still let me view him in the pleasing light
Of private life, where pomp forgets to glare,
And where the plain unguarded soul is seen.
There, with that truest greatness he appear'd,
Which thinks not of appearing; kindly veil'd
In the soft graces of the friendly scene,
Inspiring social confidence and ease.
As free the converse of the wise and good,
As joyous, disentangling every power,
And breathing mix'd improvement with delight,
As when amid the various-blossom'd spring,
Or gentle beaming autumn's pensive shade,
The philosophic mind with nature talks.
Say ye, his sons, his dear remains, with whom
The father laid superfluous state aside,
Yet raised your filial duty thence the more,
With friendship raised it, with esteem, with love,
Beyond the ties of love, oh! speak the joy,
The pure serene, the cheerful wisdom mild,
The virtuous spirit, which his vacant hours,
In semblance of amusement, through the breast
Infused. And thou, O Rundle!* lend thy strain,
Thou darling friend! thou brother of his soul!
In whom the head and heart their stores unite:
Whatever fancy paints, invention pours,
Judgment digests, the well tuned bosom feels,
Truth natural, moral, or divine, has taught,
The virtues dictate, or the Muses sing.

* Dr. Rundle, Bishop of Derry in Ireland. See the Memoir.

Lend me the plaint, which, to the lonely main,
With memory conversing, you will pour,
As on the pebbled shore you, pensive, stray,
Where Derry's mountains a bleak crescent form,
And 'mid their ample round receive the waves,
That from the frozen pole, resounding, rush,
Impetuous. Though from native sunshine driven,
Driven from your friends, the sunshine of the soul,
By slanderous zeal, and politics infirm,
Jealous of worth; yet will you bless your lot,
Yet will you triumph in your glorious fate,
Whence Talbot's friendship glows to future times,
Intrepid, warm; of kindred tempers born;
Nursed, by experience, into slow esteem,
Calm confidence unbounded, love not blind,
And the sweet light from mingled minds disclosed,
From mingled chymic oils as bursts the fire.

I too remember well that cheerful bowl,
Which round his table flow'd. The serious there
Mix'd with the sportive, with the learn'd the plain;
Mirth soften'd wisdom, candour temper'd mirth;
And wit its honey lent, without the sting.
Not simple nature's unaffected sons,
The blameless Indians, round their forest-cheer,
In sunny lawn or shady covert set,
Hold more unspotted converse; nor, of old,
Rome's awful consuls, her dictator swains,
As on the product of their Sabine farms
They fared, with stricter virtue fed the soul:
Nor yet in Athens, at an Attic meal,

Where Socrates presided, fairer truth,
More elegant humanity, more grace,
Wit more refined, or deeper science reign'd.
  But far beyond the little vulgar bounds
Of family, or friends, or native land,
By just degrees, and with proportion'd flame,
Extended his benevolence: a friend
To humankind, to parent nature's works.
Of free access, and of engaging grace,
Such as a brother to a brother owes,
He kept an open judging ear for all,
And spread an open countenance, where smiled
The fair effulgence of an open heart;
While on the rich, the poor, the high, the low,
With equal ray, his ready goodness shone:
For nothing human foreign was to him.
  Thus to a dread inheritance, my Lord,
And hard to be supported, you succeed:
But, kept by virtue, as by virtue gain'd,
It will, through latest time, enrich your race,
When grosser wealth shall moulder into dust,
And with their authors in oblivion sunk
Vain titles lie, the servile badges oft
Of mean submission, not the meed of worth.
True genuine honor its large patent holds
Of all mankind, through every land and age,
Of universal reason's various sons,
And e'en of God himself, sole perfect Judge!
Yet know these noblest honors of the mind
On rigid terms descend: the high-placed heir,

Scann'd by the public eye, that, with keen gaze,
Malignant seeks out faults, cannot through life,
Amid the nameless insects of a court,
Unheeded steal: but, with his sire compared,
He must be glorious, or he must be scorn'd.
This truth to you, who merit well to bear
A name to Britons dear, the officious Muse
May safely sing, and sing without reserve.

Vain were the plaint, and ignorant the tear
That should a Talbot mourn. Ourselves, indeed,
Our country robb'd of her delight and strength,
We may lament. Yet let us, grateful, joy
That we such virtues knew, such virtues felt,
And feel them still, teaching our views to rise
Through ever brightening scenes of future worlds.
Be dumb, ye worst of zealots! ye that, prone
To thoughtless dust, renounce that generous hope,
Whence every joy below its spirit draws,
And every pain its balm: a Talbot's light,
A Talbot's virtues claim another source
Than the blind maze of undesigning blood;
Nor when that vital fountain plays no more,
Can they be quench'd amid the gelid stream.

Methinks I see his mounting spirit, freed
From tangling earth, regain the realms of day,
Its native country: whence to bless mankind,
Eternal goodness on this darksome spot
Had ray'd it down awhile. Behold! approved
By the tremendous Judge of heaven and earth
And to the Almighty Father's presence join'd,

He takes his rank, in glory, and in bliss,
Amid the human worthies. Glad around
Crowd his compatriot shades, and point him out,
With joyful pride, Britannia's blameless boast.
Ah! who is he, that with a fonder eye
Meets thine enraptured?—'Tis the best of sons!
The best of friends!——Too soon is realized
That hope, which once forbad thy tears to flow!
Meanwhile the kindred souls of every land,
(Howe'er divided in the fretful days
Of prejudice and error,) mingled now,
In one selected never jarring state,
Where God himself their only monarch reigns,
Partake the joy; yet, such the sense that still
Remains of earthly woes, for us below,
And for our loss, they drop a pitying tear.
But cease, presumptuous Muse, nor vainly strive
To quit this cloudy sphere, that binds thee down:
'Tis not for mortal hand to trace these scenes—
Scenes, that our gross ideas groveling cast
Behind, and strike our boldest language dumb.
    Forgive, immortal shade! if aught from earth,
From dust low warbled, to those groves can rise,
Where flows celestial harmony, forgive
This fond superfluous verse. With deep-felt voice,
On every heart impress'd, thy deeds themselves
Attest thy praise. Thy praise the widow's sighs,
And orphan's tears embalm. The good, the bad,
The sons of justice and the sons of strife,
All who or freedom or who interest prize,

A deep-divided nation's parties all,
Conspire to swell thy spotless praise to Heaven.
Glad Heaven receives it, and seraphic lyres
With songs of triumph thy arrival hail.
How vain this tribute then! this lowly lay!
Yet nought is vain that gratitude inspires.
The Muse, besides, her duty thus approves
To virtue, to her country, to mankind,
To ruling nature, that, in glorious charge,
As to her priestess, gives it her to hymn
Whatever good and excellent she forms.

TO THE MEMORY OF SIR ISAAC NEWTON.

INSCRIBED TO THE RIGHT HON. SIR ROBERT WALPOLE.

[First printed 1727.]

SHALL the great soul of Newton quit this earth,
To mingle with his stars; and every Muse,
Astonish'd into silence, shun the weight
Of honours due to his illustrious name?
But what can man?—E'en now the sons of light,
In strains high warbled to seraphic lyre,
Hail his arrival on the coast of bliss.
Yet am not I deterr'd, though high the theme,
And sung to harps of angels, for with you,
Ethereal flames! ambitious, I aspire
In Nature's general symphony to join.

And what new wonders can ye show your guest!
Who, while on this dim spot, where mortals toil
Clouded in dust, from Motion's simple laws,
Could trace the secret hand of Providence,
Wide-working through this universal frame.
Have ye not listen'd while he bound the suns
And Planets, to their spheres! the unequal task
Of humankind till then. Oft had they roll'd
O'er erring man the year, and oft disgraced
The pride of schools, before their course was known
Full in its causes and effects to him,
All-piercing sage! Who sat not down and dream'd
Romantic schemes, defended by the din
Of specious words, and tyranny of names;
But, bidding his amazing mind attend,
And with heroic patience years on years
Deep-searching, saw at last the system dawn,
And shine, of all his race, on him alone.
What were his raptures then! how pure! how strong!
And what the triumphs of old Greece and Rome,
By his diminish'd, but the pride of boys
In some small fray victorious! when instead
Of shatter'd parcels of this earth usurp'd
By violence unmanly, and sore deeds
Of cruelty and blood, Nature herself
Stood all subdued by him, and open laid
Her every latent glory to his view.
All intellectual eye, our solar round
First gazing through, he by the blended power

Of gravitation and projection saw
The whole in silent harmony revolve.
From unassisted vision hid, the moons
To cheer remoter planets numerous form'd,
By him in all their mingled tracts were seen.
He also fix'd our wandering Queen of Night,
Whether she wanes into a scanty orb,
Or, waxing broad, with her pale shadowy light,
In a soft deluge overflows the sky.
Her every motion clear-discerning, He
Adjusted to the mutual Main, and taught
Why now the mighty mass of waters swells
Resistless, heaving on the broken rocks,
And the full river turning : till again
The tide revertive, unattracted, leaves
A yellow waste of idle sands behind.
  Then breaking hence, he took his ardent flight
Through the blue infinite ; and every star,
Which the clear concave of a winter's night
Pours on the eye, or astronomic tube,
Far stretching, snatches from the dark abyss ;
Or such as further in successive skies
To fancy shine alone, at his approach
Blazed into suns, the living centre each
Of an harmonious system : all combined,
And ruled unerring by that single power,
Which draws the stone projected to the ground.
  O unprofuse magnificence divine !
O wisdom truly perfect ! thus to call
From a few causes such a scheme of things,

Effects so various, beautiful, and great,
A universe complete! And O, beloved
Of Heaven! whose well purged penetrating eye,
The mystic veil transpiercing, inly scann'd
The rising, moving, wide-establish'd frame.
He, first of men, with awful wing pursued
The Comet through the long elliptic curve,
As round innumerous worlds he wound his way;
Till, to the forehead of our evening sky
Return'd, the blazing wonder glares anew,
And o'er the trembling nations shakes dismay.
The heavens are all his own; from the wide rule
Of whirling Vortices, and circling Spheres,
To their first great simplicity restored.
The schools astonish'd stood; but found it vain
To combat still with demonstration strong,
And unawaken'd dream beneath the blaze
Of truth. At once their pleasing visions fled,
With the gay shadows of the morning mix'd,
When Newton rose, our philosophic sun!
The aërial flow of Sound was known to him,
From whence it first in wavy circles breaks,
Till the touch'd organ takes the message in.
Nor could the darting beam of speed immense
Escape his swift pursuit, and measuring eye.
E'en Light itself, which every thing displays,
Shone undiscover'd, till his brighter mind
Untwisted all the shining robe of day;
And, from the whitening undistinguish'd blaze,
Collecting every ray into his kind,

To the charm'd eye educed the gorgeous train
Of parent colours. First the flaming Red
Sprung vivid forth; the tawny Orange next;
And next delicious Yellow; by whose side
Fell the kind beams of all-refreshing Green.
Then the pure Blue, that swells autumnal skies,
Ethereal play'd: and then, of sadder hue,
Emerged the deepen'd Indico, as when
The heavy-skirted evening droops with frost.
While the last gleamings of refracted light
Died in the fainting Violet away.
These, when the clouds distil the rosy shower,
Shine out distinct adown the watery bow;
While o'er our heads the dewy vision bends
Delightful, melting on the fields beneath.
Myriads of mingling dyes from these result,
And myriads still remain; infinite source
Of beauty, ever blushing, ever new.
Did ever poet image aught so fair,
Dreaming in whispering groves, by the hoarse brook!
Or prophet, to whose rapture heaven descends?
E'en now the setting sun and shifting clouds,
Seen, Greenwich, from thy lovely heights, declare
How just, how beauteous the refractive law.
The noiseless tide of Time, all bearing down
To vast eternity's unbounded sea,
Where the green islands of the happy shine,
He stemm'd alone; and to the source (involved
Deep in primeval gloom) ascending, raised

His lights at equal distances, to guide
Historian, wilder'd on his darksome way.
But who can number up his labours? who
His high discoveries sing? but when a few
Of the deep-studying race can stretch their minds
To what he knew: in fancy's lighter thought,
How shall the muse then grasp the mighty theme?
What wonder thence that his devotion swell'd
Responsive to his knowledge? For could he,
Whose piercing mental eye diffusive saw
The finish'd university of things,
In all its order, magnitude, and parts,
Forbear incessant to adore that power
Who fills, sustains, and actuates the whole?
Say, ye who best can tell, ye happy few,
Who saw him in the softest lights of life,
All unwithheld, indulging to his friends
The vast unborrow'd treasures of his mind,
Oh, speak the wondrous man! how mild, how calm,
How greatly humble, how divinely good;
How firmly stablish'd on eternal truth;
Fervent in doing well, with every nerve
Still pressing on, forgetful of the past,
And panting for perfection: far above
Those little cares, and visionary joys,
That so perplex the fond impassion'd heart
Of ever cheated, ever trusting man.
And you, ye hopeless gloomy-minded tribe,
You who, unconscious of those nobler flights
That reach impatient at immortal life,

Against the prime endearing privilege
Of Being dare contend, — say, can a soul
Of such extensive, deep, tremendous powers,
Enlarging still, be but a finer breath
Of spirits dancing through their tubes awhile,
And then for ever lost in vacant air?
But hark! methinks I hear a warning voice,
Solemn as when some awful change is come,
Sound through the world — ''Tis done! — The measure 's full;
And I resign my charge.' — Ye mouldering stones,
That build the towering pyramid, the proud
Triumphal arch, the monument effaced
By ruthless ruin, and whate'er supports
The worshipp'd name of hoar antiquity,
Down to the dust! what grandeur can ye boast
While Newton lifts his column to the skies,
Beyond the waste of time. Let no weak drop
Be shed for him. The virgin in her bloom
Cut off, the joyous youth, and darling child,
These are the tombs that claim the tender tear,
And elegiac song. But Newton calls
For other notes of gratulation high,
That now he wanders through those endless worlds
He here so well descried, and wondering talks,
And hymns their author with his glad compeers.
O Britain's boast! whether with angels thou
Sittest in dread discourse, or fellow-bless'd,
Who joy to see the honour of their kind;
Or whether, mounted on cherubic wing,

Thy swift career is with the whirling orbs,
Comparing things with things, in rapture lost,
And grateful adoration, for that light
So plenteous ray'd into thy mind below,
From light himself; oh, look with pity down
On humankind, a frail erroneous race!
Exalt the spirit of a downward world!
O'er thy dejected Country chief preside,
And be her Genius call'd! her studies raise,
Correct her manners, and inspire her youth.
For, though depraved and sunk, she brought thee
forth,
And glories in thy name: she points thee out
To all her sons, and bids them eye thy star:
While in expectance of the second life,
When time shall be no more, thy sacred dust
Sleeps with her kings, and dignifies the scene.

BRITANNIA.

[First printed 1727.]

——Et tantas audetis tollere moles?
Quos ego — sed motos præstat componere fluctus.
Post mihi non simili pœna commissa luetis.
Maturate fugam, regique hæc dicite vestro:
Non illi imperium pelagi, sævumque tridentem,
Sed mihi sorte datum. VIRGIL.

As on the sea-beat shore Britannia sat,
Of her degenerate sons the faded fame,
Deep in her anxious heart, revolving sad:
Bare was her throbbing bosom to the gale,
That, hoarse and hollow, from the bleak surge blew;
Loose flow'd her tresses; rent her azure robe.
Hung o'er the deep from her majestic brow
She tore the laurel, and she tore the bay.
Nor ceased the copious grief to bathe her cheek;
Nor ceased her sobs to murmur to the main.
Peace discontented, nigh departing, stretch'd
Her dove-like wings: and War, tho' greatly roused,
Yet mourns his fetter'd hands. While thus the queen
Of nations spoke; and what she said the muse
Recorded, faithful, in unbidden verse.

'E'en not yon sail, that from the sky-mixt wave
Dawns on the sight, and wafts the Royal Youth,*
A freight of future glory to my shore;
E'en not the flattering view of golden days,
And rising periods yet of bright renown,
Beneath the Parents, and their endless line
Through late revolving time, can soothe my rage;
While, unchastised, the insulting Spaniard dares
Infest the trading flood, full of vain war
Despise my navies, and my merchants seize;
As, trusting to false peace, they fearless roam
The world of waters wild; made, by the toil,
And liberal blood of glorious ages, mine:
Nor bursts my sleeping thunder on their head.
Whence this unwonted patience? this weak doubt?
This tame beseeching of rejected peace?
This meek forbearance? this unnative fear,
To generous Britons never known before?
And sail'd my fleets for this; on Indian tides
To float, inactive, with the veering winds?
The mockery of war! while hot disease,
And sloth distemper'd, swept off burning crowds,
For action ardent; and amid the deep,
Inglorious, sunk them in a watery grave.
There now they lie beneath the rolling flood,
Far from their friends, and country, unavenged;
And back the drooping war ship comes again,
Dispirited and thin; her sons ashamed

* Frederick Prince of Wales, then lately arrived.

Thus idly to review their native shore;
With not one glory sparkling in their eye,
One triumph on their tongue. A passenger,
The violated merchant comes along;
That far sought wealth, for which the noxious gale
He drew, and sweat beneath equator suns,
By lawless force detain'd; a force that soon
Would melt away, and every spoil resign,
Were once the British lion heard to roar.
Whence is it that the proud Iberian thus,
In their own well asserted element,
Dares rouse to wrath the masters of the main?
Who told him, that the big incumbent war
Would not, ere this, have roll'd his trembling ports
In smoky ruin? and his guilty stores,
Won by the ravage of a butcher'd world,
Yet unatoned, sunk in the swallowing deep,
Or led the glittering prize into the Thames?
'There was a time, (oh let my languid sons
Resume their spirit at the rousing thought!)
When all the pride of Spain, in one dread fleet,
Swell'd o'er the labouring surge; like a whole heaven
Of clouds, wide roll'd before the boundless breeze.
Gaily the splendid armament along
Exultant plough'd, reflecting a red gleam,
As sunk the sun, o'er all the flaming Vast;
Tall, gorgeous, and elate; drunk with the dream
Of easy conquest; while their bloated war,
Stretch'd out from sky to sky, the gather'd force
Of ages held in its capacious womb.

But soon, regardless of the cumbrous pomp,
My dauntless Britons came, a gloomy few,
With tempests black, the goodly scene deform'd,
And laid their glory waste. The bolts of fate
Resistless thunder'd through their yielding sides;
Fierce o'er their beauty blazed the lurid flame;
And seized in horrid grasp, or shatter'd wide,
Amid the mighty waters, deep they sunk.
Then too from every promontory chill,
Rank fen, and cavern where the wild wave works,
I swept confederate winds, and swell'd a storm.
Round the glad isle, snatch'd by the vengeful blast,
The scatter'd remnants drove; on the blind shelve,
And pointed rock, that marks the indented shore,
Relentless dash'd, where loud the northern main
Howls through the fractured Caledonian isles.
'Such were the dawnings of my watery reign;
But since how vast it grew, how absolute,
E'en in those troubled times, when dreadful Blake
Awed angry nations with the British name,
Let every humbled state, let Europe say,
Sustain'd, and balanced, by my naval arm.
Ah, what must those immortal spirits think
Of your poor shifts? Those, for their country's good,
Who faced the blackest danger, knew no fear,
No mean submission, but commanded peace.
Ah, how with indignation must they burn?
(If aught, but joy, can touch ethereal breasts)
With shame? with grief? to see their feeble sons
Shrink from that empire o'er the conquer'd seas,

For which their wisdom plann'd, their councils
glow'd,
And their veins bled through many a toiling age.
'Oh, first of human blessings! and supreme!
Fair Peace! how lovely, how delightful thou!
By whose wide tie the kindred sons of men
Like brothers live, in amity combined
And unsuspicious faith; while honest toil
Gives every joy, and to those joys a right,
Which idle, barbarous rapine but usurps.
Pure is thy reign; when, unaccursed by blood,
Nought, save the sweetness of indulgent showers,
Trickling distils into the vernant glebe;
Instead of mangled carcasses, sad-seen,
When the blithe sheaves lie scatter'd o'er the field;
When only shining shares, the crooked knife,
And hooks imprint the vegetable wound;
When the land blushes with the rose alone,
The falling fruitage and the bleeding vine.
Oh, Peace! thou source and soul of social life;
Beneath whose calm inspiring influence,
Science his views enlarges, Art refines,
And swelling Commerce opens all her ports;
Bless'd be the man divine who gives us thee!
Who bids the trumpet hush his horrid clang,
Nor blow the giddy nations into rage;
Who sheaths the murderous blade; the deadly gun
Into the well piled armoury returns;
And every vigour, from the work of death,
To grateful industry converting, makes

The country flourish, and the city smile.
Unviolated, him the virgin sings;
And him the smiling mother to her train.
Of him the shepherd, in the peaceful dale,
Chants; and, the treasures of his labour sure,
The husbandman of him, as at the plough,
Or team, he toils. With him the sailor soothes,
Beneath the trembling moon, the midnight wave;
And the full city, warm, from street to street,
And shop to shop, responsive, rings of him.
'Nor joys one land alone: his praise extends
Far as the sun rolls the diffusive day;
Far as the breeze can bear the gifts of peace;
Till all the happy nations catch the song.
'What would not, Peace! the patriot bear for thee?
What painful patience? What incessant care?
What mix'd anxiety? What sleepless toil?
E'en from the rash protected what reproach?
For he thy value knows; thy friendship he
To human nature: but the better thou,
The richer of delight, sometimes the more
Inevitable war; when ruffian force
Awakes the fury of an injured state.
E'en the good patient man, whom reason rules,
Roused by bold insult, and injurious rage,
With sharp and sudden check the astonish'd sons
Of violence confounds; firm as his cause,
His bolder heart; in awful justice clad;
His eyes effulging a peculiar fire:

And, as he charges through the prostrate war,
His keen arm teaches faithless men no more
To dare the sacred vengeance of the just.
'And what, my thoughtless sons, should fire you more
Than when your well earn'd empire of the deep
The least beginning injury receives?
What better cause can call your lightning forth?
Your thunder wake? your dearest life demand?
What better cause, than when your country sees
The sly destruction at her vitals aim'd?
For oh! it much imports you, 'tis your all,
To keep your trade entire, entire the force
And honour of your fleets; o'er that to watch,
E'en with a hand severe, and jealous eye.
In intercourse be gentle, generous, just,
By wisdom polish'd, and of manners fair;
But on the sea be terrible, untamed,
Unconquerable still: let none escape,
Who shall but aim to touch your glory there.
Is there the man into the lion's den
Who dares intrude, to snatch his young away?
And is a Briton seized? and seized beneath
The slumbering terrors of a British fleet?
Then ardent rise! Oh, great in vengeance rise!
O'erturn the proud, teach rapine to restore:
And as you ride sublimely round the world,
Make every vessel stoop, make every state
At once their welfare and their duty know.
This is your glory: this your wisdom; this

The native power for which you were design'd
By fate, when fate design'd the firmest state,
That e'er was seated on the subject sea;
A state, alone, where Liberty should live,
In these late times, this evening of mankind,
When Athens, Rome, and Carthage are no more,
The world almost in slavish sloth dissolved.
For this, these rocks around your coast were thrown;
For this, your oaks, peculiar harden'd, shoot
Strong into sturdy growth: for this, your hearts
Swell with a sullen courage, growing still
As danger grows; and strength and toil for this
Are liberal pour'd o'er all the fervent land.
Then cherish this, this unexpensive power,
Undangerous to the public, ever prompt,
By lavish nature thrust into your hand:
And, unencumber'd with the bulk immense
Of conquest, whence huge empires rose, and fell
Self-crush'd, extend your reign from shore to shore,
Where'er the wind your high behests can blow;
And fix it deep on this eternal base.
For should the sliding fabric once give way,
Soon slacken'd quite, and past recovery broke,
It gathers ruin as it rolls along,
Steep rushing down to that devouring gulf,
Where many a mighty empire buried lies.
And should the big redundant flood of trade,
In which ten thousand thousand labours join
Their several currents, till the boundless tide
Rolls in a radiant deluge o'er the land;

Should this bright stream, the least inflected, point
Its course another way, o'er other lands
The various treasure would resistless pour,
Ne'er to be won again; its ancient tract
Left a vile channel, desolate, and dead,
With all around a miserable waste.
Not Egypt, were her better heaven, the Nile,
Turn'd in the pride of flow; when o'er his rocks,
And roaring cataracts, beyond the reach
Of dizzy vision piled, in one wide flash
An Ethiopian deluge foams amain;
(Whence wondering fable traced him from the sky)
E'en not that prime of earth, where harvests crowd
On untill'd harvests, all the teeming year,
If of the fat o'erflowing culture robb'd,
Were then a more uncomfortable wild,
Steril, and void; than of her trade deprived,
Britons, your boasted isle: her princes sunk;
Her high built honour moulder'd to the dust;
Unnerved her force; her spirit vanish'd quite;
With rapid wing her riches fled away;
Her unfrequented ports alone the sign
Of what she was; her merchants scatter'd wide;
Her hollow shops shut up; and in her streets,
Her fields, woods, markets, villages, and roads,
The cheerful voice of labour heard no more.
  'Oh, let not then waste luxury impair
That manly soul of toil which strings your nerves,
And your own proper happiness creates!
Oh, let not the soft, penetrating plague

Creep on the freeborn mind! and working there,
With the sharp tooth of many a new-form'd want,
Endless, and idle all, eat out the heart
Of liberty; the high conception blast;
The noble sentiment, the impatient scorn
Of base subjection, and the swelling wish
For general good, erasing from the mind:
While nought save narrow selfishness succeeds,
And low design, the sneaking passions all
Let loose, and reigning in the rankled breast.
Induced at last, by scarce perceived degrees,
Sapping the very frame of government,
And life, a total dissolution comes;
Sloth, ignorance, dejection, flattery, fear.
Oppression raging o'er the waste he makes;
The human being almost quite extinct;
And the whole state in broad corruption sinks.
Oh, shun that gulf: that gaping ruin shun!
And countless ages roll it far away
From you, ye heaven-beloved! May liberty,
The light of life! the sun of humankind!
Whence heroes, bards, and patriots borrow flame,
E'en where the keen depressive north descends,
Still spread, exalt, and actuate your powers!
While slavish southern climates beam in vain.
And may a public spirit from the throne,
Where every virtue sits, go copious forth,
Live o'er the land! the finer arts inspire;
Make thoughtful Science raise his pensive head,
Blow the fresh bay, bid Industry rejoice,

And the rough sons of lowest labour smile.
As when, profuse of Spring, the loosen'd West
Lifts up the pining year, and balmy breathes
Youth, life, and love, and beauty, o'er the world.
'But haste we from these melancholy shores,
Nor to deaf winds, and waves, our fruitless plaint
Pour weak; the country claims our active aid;
That let us roam; and where we find a spark
Of public virtue, blow it into flame.
Lo! now, my sons, the sons of freedom! meet
In awful senate; thither let us fly;
Burn in the patriot's thought, flow from his tongue
In fearless truth; myself, transform'd, preside,
And shed the spirit of Britannia round.'
This said; her fleeting form and airy train
Sunk in the gale; and nought but ragged rocks
Rush'd on the broken eye; and nought was heard
But the rough cadence of the dashing wave.

LIBERTY.

[First printed 1735.]

TO HIS ROYAL HIGHNESS FREDERICK PRINCE OF WALES.

SIR,

WHEN I reflect upon that ready condescension, that preventing generosity, with which your Royal Highness received the following poem under your protection; I can alone ascribe it to the recommendation and influence of the subject. In you the cause and concerns of Liberty have so zealous a patron, as entitles whatever may have the least tendency to promote them, to the distinction of your favour. And who can entertain this delightful reflection, without feeling a pleasure far superior to that of the fondest author; and of which all true lovers of their country must participate? To behold the noblest dispositions of the prince, and of the patriot, united: an overflowing benevolence, generosity, and candour of heart, joined to an enlightened zeal for Liberty, an intimate persuasion that on it depends the happiness and glory both of kings and people: to see these shining out in public virtues, as they have hitherto smiled in all the social lights and private accomplishments of life, is a prospect that cannot but inspire a general sentiment of satisfaction and gladness, more easy to be felt than expressed.

If the following attempt to trace Liberty, from the first ages down to her excellent establishment in Great Britain, can at all merit your approbation, and prove an entertainment to your Royal Highness; if it can in any degree answer the dignity of the subject, and of the name under which I presume to shelter it; I have my best reward: particularly as it affords me an opportunity of declaring that I am, with the greatest zeal and respect,

Sir,

Your Royal Highness's

most obedient

and most devoted servant,

James Thomson.

CONTENTS.

Part I.

Ancient and Modern Italy compared.

The following Poem is thrown into the form of a Poetical Vision. Its scene, the ruins of ancient Rome. The Goddess of Liberty, who is supposed to speak through the whole, appears, characterized as British Liberty. Gives a view of ancient Italy, and particularly of Republican Rome, in all her magnificence and glory. This contrasted by modern Italy; its valleys, mountains, culture, cities, people: the difference appearing strongest in the capital city Rome. The ruins of the great works of Liberty more magnificent than the borrowed pomp of Oppression; and from them revived Sculpture, Painting, and Architecture. The old Romans apostrophized, with regard to the several melancholy changes in Italy: Horace, Tully, and Virgil, with regard to their Tibur, Tusculum, and Naples. That once finest and most ornamented part of Italy, all along the coast of Baiæ, how changed. This desolation of Italy applied to Britain. Address to the Goddess of Liberty, that she would deduce from the first ages, her chief establishments, the description of which constitute the subject of the following parts of this Poem. She assents, and commands what she says to be sung in Britain; whose happiness, arising from freedom, and a limited monarchy, she marks. An immediate Vision attends, and paints her words. Invocation.

Part II. — Greece.

Liberty traced from the pastoral ages, and the first uniting of neighbouring families into civil government. The several establishments of Liberty, in Egypt, Persia, Phœnicia, Palestine, slightly touched upon, down to her great establishment in Greece. Geographical description of Greece. Sparta and Athens, the two principal states of Greece, described. Influence of Liberty over all the Grecian states; with regard to their Government, their Politeness, their Virtues, their Arts, and Sciences. The vast superiority it gave them, in point of force and bravery, over the Persians, exemplified by the action of Thermopylæ, the battle of Marathon, and the retreat of the Ten Thousand. Its full exertion, and most beautiful effects in Athens. Liberty the source of free Philosophy. The various schools which took their rise from Socrates. Enumeration of Fine Arts: Eloquence, Poetry, Music, Sculpture, Painting, and Architecture; the effects of Liberty in Greece, and brought to their utmost perfection there. Transition to the modern state of Greece. Why Liberty declined, and was at last entirely lost among the Greeks. Concluding Reflection.

Part III. — Rome.

As this part contains a description of the establishment of Liberty in Rome, it begins with a view of the Grecian Colonies settled in the southern parts of Italy, which with Sicily constituted the Great Greece of the Ancients. With these colonies, the Spirit of Liberty, and of Republics, spreads over Italy. Transition to Pythagoras and his philosophy, which he taught through those free states and cities. Amidst the many small Republics in Italy, Rome the destined seat of Liberty. Her establishment there dated from the expulsion of the Tarquins. How differing from that in

Greece. Reference to a view of the Roman Republic given in the First Part of this Poem: to mark its Rise and Fall the peculiar purport of this. During its first ages, the greatest force of Liberty and Virtue exerted. The source whence derived. The Heroic Virtues of the Romans. Enumeration of these virtues. Thence their security at home; their glory, success, and empire abroad. Bounds of the Roman Empire geographically described. The states of Greece restored to Liberty, by Titus Quintus Flaminius, the highest instance of public generosity and beneficence. The loss of Liberty in Rome. Its causes, progress, and completion in the death of Brutus. Rome under the Emperors. From Rome the Goddess of Liberty goes among the Northern Nations; where, by infusing into them her Spirit and general principles, she lays the groundwork of her future establishments; sends them in vengeance on the Roman Empire, now totally enslaved; and then, with Arts and Sciences in her train, quits earth during the Dark Ages. The celestial regions, to which Liberty retired, not proper to be opened to the view of mortals.

Part IV. — Britain.

Difference betwixt the Ancients and Moderns slightly touched upon. Description of the Dark Ages. The Goddess of Liberty, who during these is supposed to have left earth, returns, attended with Arts and Science. She first descends on Italy. Sculpture, Painting, and Architecture fix at Rome, to revive their several arts by the great models of antiquity there, which many barbarous invasions had not been able to destroy. The revival of these arts marked out. That sometimes arts may flourish for a while under despotic governments, though never the natural and genuine production of them. Learning begins to dawn. The Muse and Science attend Liberty, who in her progress towards Great Britain raises several free states and cities. These enumerated. Author's exclamation of joy, upon seeing the British seas and coasts rise in the vision, which painted whatever the Goddess of Liberty said. She resumes her narration. The Genius of the Deep appears, and addressing Liberty, associates Great Britain into his dominion. Liberty received and congratulated by Britannia, and the Native Genii or Virtues of the Island. These described. Animated by the presence of Liberty, they begin their operations. Their beneficent influence contrasted with the works and delusions of opposing Demons. Concludes with an abstract of the English history, marking the several Advances of Liberty, down to her complete establishment at the Revolution.

Part V.—The Prospect.

The author addresses the Goddess of Liberty, marking the happiness and grandeur of Great Britain, as arising from her influence. She resumes her discourse, and points out the chief Virtues which are necessary to maintain her establishment there. Recommends, as its last ornament and finishing, Sciences, Fine Arts, and Public Works. The encouragement of these urged from the example of France, though under a despotic government. The whole concludes with a prospect of future times, given by the Goddess of Liberty: this described by the author, as it passes in vision before him.

LIBERTY.

PART I.

ANCIENT AND MODERN ITALY COMPARED.

O MY lamented Talbot! while with thee
The Muse gay roved the glad Hesperian round,
And drew the inspiring breath of ancient arts;
Ah! little thought she her returning verse
Should sing our darling subject to thy Shade.
And does the mystic veil, from mortal beam,
Involve those eyes where every virtue smiled,
And all thy Father's candid spirit shone?
The light of reason, pure, without a cloud;
Full of the generous heart, the mild regard;
Honour disdaining blemish, cordial faith,
And limpid truth, that looks the very soul.
But to the death of mighty nations turn
My strain; be there absorpt the private tear.
Musing, I lay; warm from the sacred walks,
Where at each step imagination burns:
While scatter'd wide around, awful, and hoar,
Lies, a vast monument, once glorious Rome,
The tomb of empire! Ruins! that efface
Whate'er, of finish'd, modern pomp can boast.

Snatch'd by these wonders to that world where thought
Unfetter'd ranges, Fancy's magic hand
Led me anew o'er all the solemn scene,
Still in the mind's pure eye more solemn dress'd:
When straight, methought, the fair majestic Power
Of Liberty appear'd. Not, as of old,
Extended in her hand the cap, and rod,
Whose slave-enlarging touch gave double life:
But her bright temples bound with British oak,
And naval honours nodded on her brow.
Sublime of port: loose o'er her shoulder flow'd
Her sea-green robe, with constellations gay.
An island-goddess now; and her high care
The Queen of Isles, the mistress of the main.
My heart beat filial transport at the sight;
And, as she moved to speak, the awaken'd Muse
Listen'd intense. Awhile she look'd around,
With mournful eye the well known ruins mark'd,
And then, her sighs repressing, thus began:
'Mine are these wonders, all thou seest is mine;
But ah, how changed! the falling poor remains
Of what exalted once the Ausonian shore.
Look back through time: and, rising from the gloom,
Mark the dread scene, that paints whate'er I say.
'The great Republic see! that glow'd, sublime,
With the mix'd freedom of a thousand states;
Raised on the thrones of kings her curule chair,
And by her fasces awed the subject world.

See busy millions quickening all the land,
With cities throng'd, and teeming culture high:
For Nature then smiled on her free-born sons,
And pour'd the plenty that belongs to men.
Behold, the country cheering, villas rise,
In lively prospect; by the secret lapse
Of brooks now lost, and streams renown'd in song;
In Umbria's closing vales, or on the brow
Of her brown hills that breathe the scented gale:
On Baiæ's viny coast; where peaceful seas,
Fann'd by kind zephyrs, ever kiss the shore;
And suns unclouded shine, through purest air:
Or in the spacious neighbourhood of Rome;
Far shining upward to the Sabine hills,
To Anio's roar, and Tibur's olive shade;
To where Prenestè lifts her airy brow;
Or downward spreading to the sunny shore,
Where Alba breathes the freshness of the main.
'See distant mountains leave their valleys dry,
And o'er the proud Arcade their tribute pour,
To lave imperial Rome. For ages laid,
Deep, massy, firm, diverging every way,
With tombs of heroes sacred, see her roads;
By various nations trod, and suppliant kings;
With legions flaming, or with triumph gay.
'Full in the centre of these wondrous works,
The pride of earth! Rome in her glory see!
Behold her demigods, in senate met;
All head to counsel, and all heart to act:
The commonweal inspiring every tongue

With fervent eloquence, unbribed, and bold;
Ere tame Corruption taught the servile herd
To rank obedient to a master's voice.
'Her Forum see, warm, popular, and loud,
In trembling wonder hush'd, when the two Sires,*
As they the private father greatly quell'd,
Stood up the public fathers of the state.
See Justice judging there, in human shape.
Hark! how with freedom's voice it thunders high,
Or in soft murmurs sinks to Tully's tongue.
'Her tribes, her census, see; her generous troops,
Whose pay was glory, and their best reward
Free for their country and for me to die;
Ere mercenary murder grew a trade.
'Mark, as the purple triumph waves along,
The highest pomp and lowest fall of life.
'Her festive games, the school of heroes, see;
Her Circus, ardent with contending youth:
Her streets, her temples, palaces, and baths,
Full of fair forms, of Beauty's eldest born,
And of a people cast in virtue's mould:
While sculpture lives around, and Asian hills
Lend their best stores to heave the pillar'd dome:
All that to Roman strength the softer touch
Of Grecian art can join. But language fails
To paint this sun, this centre of mankind;
Where every virtue, glory, treasure, art,
Attracted strong, in heighten'd lustre met.

* Lucius Junius Brutus, and Virginius.

'Need I the contrast mark? unjoyous view!
A land in all, in government and arts,
In virtue, genius, earth, and heaven, reversed,
Who but these far famed ruins to behold,
Proofs of a people, whose heroic aims
Soar'd far above the little selfish sphere
Of doubting modern life; who but inflamed
With classic zeal, these consecrated scenes
Of men and deeds to trace; unhappy land,
Would trust thy wilds, and cities loose of sway?
'Are these the vales, that, once, exulting states
In their warm bosom fed? The mountains these,
On whose high-blooming sides my sons, of old,
I bred to glory? These dejected towns,
Where, mean and sordid, life can scarce subsist,
The scenes of ancient opulence and pomp?
'Come! by whatever sacred name disguised,
Oppression, come! and in thy works rejoice!
See nature's richest plains to putrid fens
Turn'd by thy fury. From their cheerful bounds,
See razed the enlivening village, farm, and seat.
First, rural toil, by thy rapacious hand
Robb'd of his poor reward, resign'd the plough;
And now he dares not turn the noxious glebe.
'Tis thine entire. The lonely swain himself,
Who loves at large along the grassy downs
His flocks to pasture, thy drear champaign flies.
Far as the sickening eye can sweep around,
'Tis all one desert, desolate, and grey,
Grazed by the sullen buffalo alone;

And where the rank uncultivated growth
Of rotting ages taints the passing gale.
Beneath the baleful blast the city pines,
Or sinks enfeebled, or infected burns.
Beneath it mourns the solitary road,
Roll'd in rude mazes o'er the abandon'd waste;
While ancient ways, ingulf'd, are seen no more.
'Such thy dire plains, thou self-destroyer! foe
To humankind! thy mountains too, profuse,
Where savage nature blooms, seem their sad plaint
To raise against thy desolating rod.
There on the breezy brow, where thriving states
And famous cities, once, to the pleased sun,
Far other scenes of rising culture spread,
Pale shine thy ragged towns. Neglected round,
Each harvest pines; the livid, lean produce
Of heartless labour: while thy hated joys,
Not proper pleasure, lift the lazy hand.
Better to sink in sloth the woes of life,
Than wake their rage with unavailing toil.
Hence, drooping art almost to nature leaves
The rude unguided year. Thin wave the gifts
Of yellow Ceres, thin the radiant blush
Of orchard reddens in the warmest ray.
To weedy wildness run, no rural wealth
(Such as dictators fed) the garden pours.
Crude the wild olive flows, and foul the vine;
Nor juice Cæcubian, nor Falernian, more,
Streams life and joy, save in the Muse's bowl.
Unseconded by art, the spinning race

Draw the bright thread in vain, and idly toil.
In vain, forlorn in wilds, the citron blows;
And flowering plants perfume the desert gale.
Through the vile thorn the tender myrtle twines:
Inglorious droops the laurel, dead to song,
And long a stranger to the hero's brow.
'Nor half thy triumph this: cast, from brute fields,
Into the haunts of men thy ruthless eye.
There buxom Plenty never turns her horn;
The grace and virtue of exterior life,
No clean convenience reigns; e'en sleep itself,
Least delicate of powers, reluctant, there,
Lays on the bed impure his heavy head.
Thy horrid walk! dead, empty, unadorn'd,
See streets whose echoes never know the voice
Of cheerful hurry, commerce many-tongued,
And art mechanic at his various task,
Fervent, employ'd. Mark the desponding race,
Of occupation void, as void of hope;
Hope, the glad ray, glanced from Eternal Good,
That life enlivens, and exalts its powers,
With views of fortune — madness all to them!
By thee relentless seized their better joys,
To the soft aid of cordial airs they fly,
Breathing a kind oblivion o'er their woes.
And love and music melt their souls away.
From feeble Justice, see how rash Revenge,
Trembling, the balance snatches; and the sword,
Fearful himself, to venal ruffians gives.

See where God's altar, nursing murder, stands,
With the red touch of dark assassins stain'd.
'But chief let Rome, the mighty city! speak
The full-exerted genius of thy reign.
Behold her rise amid the lifeless waste,
Expiring nature all corrupted round;
While the lone Tiber, through the desert plain,
Winds his waste stores, and sullen sweeps along.
Patch'd from my fragments, in unsolid pomp,
Mark how the temple glares; and artful dress'd,
Amusive, draws the superstitious train.
Mark how the palace lifts a lying front,
Concealing often, in magnific jail,
Proud want; a deep unanimated gloom!
And oft adjoining to the drear abode
Of misery, whose melancholy walls
Seem its voracious grandeur to reproach.
Within the city bounds the desert see.
See the rank vine o'er subterranean roofs,
Indecent, spread; beneath whose fretted gold
It once, exulting, flow'd. The people mark,
Matchless, while fired by me; to public good
Inexorably firm, just, generous, brave,
Afraid of nothing but unworthy life,
Elate with glory, an heroic soul
Known to the vulgar breast: behold them now
A thin despairing number, all-subdued,
The slaves of slaves, by superstition fool'd,
By vice unmann'd and a licentious rule;
In guile ingenious, and in murder brave.

Such in one land, beneath the same fair clime,
Thy sons, Oppression, are; and such were mine.
'E'en with thy labour'd Pomp, for whose vain show
Deluded thousands starve; all age-begrimed,
Torn, robb'd, and scatter'd in unnumbered sacks,
And by the tempest of two thousand years
Continual shaken, let my ruins vie.
These roads that yet the Roman hand assert,
Beyond the weak repair of modern toil;
These fractured arches, that the chiding stream
No more delighted hear; these rich remains
Of marbles now unknown, where shines imbibed
Each parent ray; these massy columns, hew'd
From Afric's farthest shore; one granite all.
These obelisks high-towering to the sky,
Mysterious mark'd with dark Egyptian lore;
These endless wonders that this sacred * way
Illumine still, and consecrate to fame;
These fountains, vases, urns, and statues, charged
With the fine stores of art-completing Greece.
Mine is, besides, thy every later boast:
Thy Buonarotis, thy Palladios mine;
And mine the fair designs, which Raphael's † soul
O'er the live canvass, emanating, breathed.
'What would you say, ye conquerors of earth!

* Via Sacra.

† Michael Angelo Buonaroti, Palladio, and Raphael d'Urbino; the three great modern masters in sculpture, architecture, and painting.

Ye Romans! could you raise the laurel'd head;
Could you the country see, by seas of blood,
And the dread toil of ages, won so dear;
Your pride, your triumph, your supreme delight!
For whose defence oft, in the doubtful hour,
You rush'd with rapture down the gulf of fate,
Of death ambitious! till by awful deeds,
Virtues, and courage, that amaze mankind,
The queen of nations rose; possess'd of all
Which nature, art, and glory could bestow:
What would you say, deep in the last abyss
Of slavery, vice, and unambitious want,
Thus to behold her sunk? your crowded plains,
Void of their cities; unadorn'd your hills;
Ungraced your lakes; your ports to ships unknown;
Your lawless floods, and your abandon'd streams;
These could you know; these could you love again?
Thy Tiber, Horace, could it now inspire,
Content, poetic ease, and rural joy,
Soon bursting into song: while through the groves
Of headlong Anio, dashing to the vale,
In many a tortured stream, you mused along?
Yon wild retreat,* where superstition dreams,
Could, Tully, you your Tusculum believe?
And could you deem yon naked hills, that form,
Famed in old song, the ship-forsaken bay,†

* Tusculum is reckoned to have stood at a place now called Grotta Ferrata, a convent of monks.

† The bay of Mola (anciently Formiæ) into which Homer brings Ulysses and his companions. Near Formiæ Cicero had a villa.

Your Formian shore? Once the delight of earth,
Where art and nature, ever smiling, join'd
On the gay land to lavish all their stores.
How changed, how vacant, Virgil, wide around,
Would now your Naples seem? disaster'd less
By Black Vesuvius thundering o'er the coast
His midnight earthquakes, and his mining fires,
Than by despotic rage:* that inward gnaws
A native foe; a foreign, tears without.
First from your flatter'd Cæsars this began:
Till, doom'd to tyrants an eternal prey,
Thin peopled spreads, at last, the syren plain,†
That the dire soul of Hannibal disarm'd;
And wrapt in weeds the shore ‡ of Venus lies.
There Baiæ sees no more the joyous throng;
Her bank all beaming with the pride of Rome:
No generous vines now bask along the hills,
Where sport the breezes of the Tyrrhene main:
With baths and temples mix'd, no villas rise;
Nor, art-sustain'd amid reluctant waves,
Draw the cool murmurs of the breathing deep:
No spreading ports their sacred arms extend:
No mighty moles the big intrusive storm,
From the calm station, roll resounding back.

* Naples, then under the Austrian government.

† Campagna Felice, adjoining to Capua.

‡ The coast of Baiæ, which was formerly adorned with the works mentioned in the following lines; and where, amidst many magnificent ruins, those of a temple erected to Venus are still to be seen.

An almost total desolation sits,
A dreary stillness, saddening o'er the coast;
Where,* when soft suns and tepid winters rose,
Rejoicing crowds inhaled the balm of peace ;
Where citied hill to hill reflected blaze ;
And where with Ceres Bacchus wont to hold
A genial strife. Her youthful form, robust,
E'en Nature yields; by fire, and earthquake rent:
Whole stately cities in the dark abrupt
Swallow'd at once, or vile in rubbish laid,
A nest for serpents ; from the red abyss
New hills, explosive, thrown ; the Lucrine lake
A reedy pool: and all to Cuma's point,
The sea recovering his usurp'd domain,
And pour'd triumphant o'er the buried dome.
'Hence, Britain, learn ; my best establish'd, last,
And more than Greece, or Rome, my steady reign ;
The land where, King and People equal bound
By guardian laws, my fullest blessings flow ;
And where my jealous unsubmitting soul,
The dread of tyrants ! burns in every breast :
Learn hence, if such the miserable fate
Of an heroic race, the masters once
Of humankind ; what, when deprived of ME,
How grievous must be thine ? in spite of climes,
Whose sun-enliven'd ether wakes the soul
To higher powers ; in spite of happy soils,

* All along this coast the ancient Romans had their winter retreats; and several populous cities stood.

That, but by labour's slightest aid impell'd,
With treasures teem to thy cold clime unknown;
If there desponding fail the common arts,
And sustenance of life: could life itself,
Far less a thoughtless tyrant's hollow pomp,
Subsist with thee? against depressing skies,
Join'd to full spread oppression's cloudy brow,
How could thy spirits hold? where vigour find,
Forced fruits to tear from their unnative soil?
Or, storing every harvest in thy ports,
To plough the dreadful all producing wave?'
Here paused the Goddess. By the cause assured,
In trembling accents thus I moved my prayer:
'Oh first, and most benevolent of powers!
Come from eternal splendours, here on earth,
Against despotic pride, and rage, and lust,
To shield mankind; to raise them to assert
The native rights and honour of their race:
Teach me, thy lowest subject, but in zeal
Yielding to none, the progress of thy reign,
And with a strain from THEE enrich the Muse.
As thee alone she serves, her patron, THOU,
And great inspirer be! then will she joy,
Though narrow life her lot, and private shade:
And when her venal voice she barters vile,
Or to thy open or thy secret foes;
May ne'er those sacred raptures touch her more,
By slavish hearts unfelt! and may her song
Sink in oblivion with the nameless crew!

Vermin of state! to thy o'erflowing light
That owe their being, yet betray thy cause.'
  Then, condescending kind, the heavenly Power
Return'd:—'What here, suggested by the scene,
I slight unfold, record and sing at home,
In that bless'd isle, where (so we spirits move)
With one quick effort of my will I am.
There Truth, unlicensed, walks; and dares accost
E'en kings themselves, the monarchs of the free!
Fix'd on my rock, there, an indulgent race
O'er Britons wield the sceptre of their choice:
And there, to finish what his sires began,
A Prince behold! for me who burns sincere,
E'en with a subject's zeal. He my great work
Will parent-like sustain; and added give
The touch the Graces and the Muses owe.
For Britain's glory swells his panting breast;
And ancient arts he emulous revolves:
His pride to let the smiling heart abroad,
Through clouds of pomp, that but conceal the man;
To please his pleasure; bounty his delight;
And all the soul of Titus dwells in him.'
  Hail, glorious theme! but how, alas! shall verse,
From the crude stores of mortal language drawn,
How faint and tedious, sing, what, piercing deep,
The Goddess flash'd at once upon my soul.
For, clear precision all, the tongue of gods
Is harmony itself; to every ear
Familiar known, like light to every eye.
Meantime disclosing ages, as she spoke,

In long succession pour'd their empires forth;
Scene after scene, the human drama spread;
And still the embodied picture rose to sight.
  Oh THOU! to whom the Muses owe their flame;
Who bidd'st, beneath the pole, Parnassus rise,
And Hippocrenè flow; with thy bold ease,
The striking force, the lightning of thy thought,
And thy strong phrase, that rolls profound and clear;
Oh, gracious Goddess! reinspire my song;
While I, to nobler than poetic fame
Aspiring, thy commands to Britons bear.

LIBERTY.

PART II.—GREECE.

Thus spoke the Goddess of the fearless eye;
And at her voice, renew'd, the Vision rose:
'First, in the dawn of time, with eastern swains,
In woods, and tents, and cottages, I lived;
While on from plain to plain they led their flocks,
In search of clearer spring, and fresher field.
These, as increasing families disclosed
The tender state, I taught an equal sway.
Few were offences, properties, and laws.
Beneath the rural portal, palm-o'erspread,
The father senate met. There Justice dealt,
With reason then and equity the same,
Free as the common air, her prompt decree;
Nor yet had stain'd her sword with subjects' blood.
The simpler arts were all their simple wants
Had urged to light. But instant, these supplied,
Another set of fonder wants arose,
And other arts with them of finer aim;
Till, from refining want to want impell'd,
The mind by thinking push'd her latent powers,
And life began to glow, and arts to shine.

'At first, on brutes alone the rustic war
Launch'd the rude spear; swift, as he glared along,
On the grim lion, or the robber wolf.
For then young sportive life was void of toil,
Demanding little, and with little pleased:
But when to manhood grown, and endless joys,
Led on by equal toils, the bosom fired;
Lewd lazy rapine broke primeval peace,
And, hid in caves and idle forests drear,
From the lone pilgrim, and the wandering swain,
Seized what he durst not earn. Then brother's blood
First, horrid, smoked on the polluted skies.
Awful in justice, then the burning youth,
Led by their temper'd sires, on lawless men,
The last worst monsters of the shaggy wood,
Turn'd the keen arrow, and the sharpen'd spear.
Then war grew glorious. Heroes then arose;
Who, scorning coward self, for others lived,
Toil'd for their ease, and for their safety bled.
West, with the living day, to Greece I came:
Earth smiled beneath my beam: the Muse before
Sonorous flew, that low till then in woods
Had tuned the reed, and sigh'd the shepherd's pain;
But now, to sing heroic deeds, she swell'd
A nobler note, and bade the banquet burn.
'For Greece my sons of Egypt I forsook;
A boastful race, that in the vain abyss
Of fabling ages loved to lose their source,
And with their river traced it from the skies.

While there my laws alone despotic reign'd,
And king, as well as people, proud obey'd;
I taught them science, virtue, wisdom, arts;
By poets, sages, legislators sought;
The school of polish'd life, and humankind.
But when mysterious Superstition came,
And, with her Civil Sister * leagued, involved
In studied darkness the desponding mind;
Then Tyrant Power the righteous scourge unloosed:
For yielded reason speaks the soul a slave.
Instead of useful works, like nature's, great,
Enormous, cruel wonders crush'd the land;
And round a tyrant's tomb,† who none deserved,
For one vile carcass perish'd countless lives.
Then the great Dragon ‡ couch'd amid his floods,
Swell'd his fierce heart, and cried, "This flood is mine,
'Tis I that bid it flow." But, undeceived,
His frenzy soon the proud blasphemer felt;
Felt that, without my fertilizing power,
Suns lost their force, and Niles o'erflow'd in vain.
Nought could retard me: nor the frugal state
Of rising Persia, sober in extreme,
Beyond the pitch of man, and thence reversed
Into luxurious waste: nor yet the ports
Of old Phœnicia; first for letters famed,
That paint the voice, and silent speak to sight;

* Civil Tyranny. † The Pyramids.
‡ The Tyrants of Egypt.

Of arts prime source, and guardian! by fair stars,
First tempted out into the lonely deep;
To whom I first disclosed mechanic arts,
The winds to conquer, to subdue the waves,
With all the peaceful power of ruling trade;
Earnest of Britain. Nor by these retain'd;
Nor by the neighbouring land, whose palmy shore
The silver Jordan laves. Before me lay
The promised Land of Arts, and urged my flight.
'Hail, Nature's utmost boast! unrival'd Greece!
My fairest reign! where every power benign
Conspired to blow the flower of humankind,
And lavish'd all that genius can inspire.
Clear sunny climates, by the breezy main,
Ionian or Ægean, temper'd kind:
Light, airy soils: a country rich, and gay;
Broke into hills with balmy odours crown'd,
And, bright with purple harvest, joyous vales;
Mountains, and streams, where verse spontaneous flow'd;
Whence deem'd by wondering men the seat of gods,
And still the mountains and the streams of song.
All that boon Nature could luxuriant pour
Of high materials, and my restless Arts
Frame into finish'd life. How many states,
And clustering towns, and monuments of fame,
And scenes of glorious deeds, in little bounds?
From the rough tract of bending mountains, beat
By Adria's here, there by Ægean waves;
To where the deep adorning Cyclade Isles

In shining prospect rise, and on the shore
Of farthest Crete resounds the Libyan main.
'O'er all two rival cities rear'd the brow,
And balanced all. Spread on Eurotas' bank,
Amid a circle of soft rising hills,
The patient Sparta one: the sober, hard,
And man-subduing city; which no shape
Of pain could conquer, nor of pleasure charm.
Lycurgus there built, on the solid base
Of equal life, so well a temper'd state;
Where mix'd each government, in such just poise;
Each power so checking, and supporting each;
That firm for ages, and unmoved, it stood,
The fort of Greece! without one giddy hour,
One shock of faction, or of party rage.
For, drain'd the springs of wealth, Corruption there
Lay wither'd at the root. Thrice happy land!
Had not neglected art, with weedy vice
Confounded, sunk. But if Athenian arts
Loved not the soil; yet there the calm abode
Of wisdom, virtue, philosophic ease,
Of manly sense and wit, in frugal phrase
Confined, and press'd into Laconic force.
There too, by rooting thence still treacherous self,
The Public and the Private grew the same.
The children of the nursing Public all,
And at its table fed; for that they toil'd,
For that they lived entire, and even for that
The tender mother urged her son to die.
'Of softer genius, but not less intent

To seize the palm of empire, Athens rose.
Where, with bright marbles big and future pomp,
Hymettus * spread, amid the scented sky,
His thymy treasures to the labouring bee,
And to botanic hand the stores of health;
Wrapt in a soul-attenuating clime,
Between Ilissus and Cephissus † glow'd
This hive of science, shedding sweets divine,
Of active arts, and animated arms.
There, passionate for me, an easy moved,
A quick, refined, a delicate, humane,
Enlighten'd people reign'd. Oft on the brink
Of ruin, hurried by the charm of speech,
Inforcing hasty counsel immature,
Totter'd the rash Democracy; unpoised,
And by the rage devour'd, that ever tears
A populace unequal; part too rich,
And part or fierce with want or abject grown.
Solon at last, their mild restorer, rose:
Allay'd the tempest; to the calm of laws
Reduced the settling whole; and, with the weight
Which the two senates ‡ to the public lent,
As with an anchor fix'd the driving state.
'Nor was my forming care to these confined.

* A mountain near Athens.

† Two rivers, betwixt which Athens was situated.

‡ The Areopagus, or Supreme Court of Judicature, which Solon reformed and improved: and the council of Four Hundred, by him instituted. In this Council all affairs of state were deliberated, before they came to be voted in the assembly of the people.

For emulation through the whole I pour'd,
Noble contention! who should most excel
In government well poised, adjusted best
To public weal: in countries cultured high:
In ornamented towns, where order reigns,
Free social life, and polish'd manners fair:
In exercise, and arms; arms only drawn
For common Greece, to quell the Persian pride:
In moral science, and in graceful arts.
Hence, as for glory peacefully they strove,
The prize grew greater, and the prize of all.
By contest brighten'd, hence the radiant youth,
Pour'd every beam; by generous pride inflamed,
Felt every ardour burn: their great reward
The verdant wreath, which sounding Pisa* gave.
'Hence flourish'd Greece; and hence a race of men,
As gods by conscious future times adored:
In whom each virtue wore a smiling air,
Each science shed o'er life a friendly light,
Each art was nature. Spartan valour hence,
At the famed pass,† firm as an isthmus stood;
And the whole eastern ocean, waving far
As eye could dart its vision, nobly check'd.
While in extended battle, at the field
Of Marathon, my keen Athenians drove
Before their ardent band a host of slaves.

* Or Olympia, the city where the Olympic games were celebrated.

† The Straits of Thermopylæ.

'Hence thro' the continent ten thousand Greeks
Urged a retreat, whose glory not the prime
Of victories can reach. Deserts, in vain,
Opposeu their course; and hostile lands, unknown;
And deep rapacious floods, dire bank'd with death;
And mountains, in whose jaws destruction grinn'd;
Hunger, and toil; Armenian snows, and storms;
And circling myriads still of barbarous foes.
Greece in their view, and glory yet untouch'd,
Their steady column pierced the scattering herds,
Which a whole empire pour'd; and held its way
Triumphant, by the sage-exalted Chief*
Fired and sustain'd. Oh light and force of mind,
Almost almighty in severe extremes!
The sea at last from Colchian mountains seen,
Kind-hearted transport round their captains threw
The soldiers' fond embrace; o'erflow'd their eyes
With tender floods, and loosed the general voice
To cries resounding loud — "The sea! The sea!"
'In Attic bounds hence heroes, sages, wits,
Shone thick as stars, the milky way of Greece!
And though gay wit, and pleasing grace was theirs,
All the soft modes of elegance, and ease;
Yet was not courage less, the patient touch
Of toiling art, and disquisition deep.
'My spirit pours a vigour through the soul,
The unfetter'd thought with energy inspires,
Invincible in arts, in the bright field

* Xenophon.

Of nobler Science, as in that of Arms.
Athenians thus not less intrepid burst
The bonds of tyrant darkness, than they spurn'd
The Persian chains: while through the city full
Of mirthful quarrel and of witty war,
Incessant struggled taste, refining taste,
And friendly free discussion, calling forth
From the fair jewel Truth its latent ray.
O'er all shone out the great Athenian Sage,*
And Father of Philosophy: the sun,
From whose white blaze emerged, each various sect
Took various tints, but with diminish'd beam.
Tutor of Athens! he, in every street,
Dealt priceless treasure: goodness his delight,
Wisdom his wealth, and glory his reward.
Deep through the human heart, with playful art,
His simple question stole; as into truth,
And serious deeds, he smiled the laughing race;
Taught moral happy life, whate'er can bless,
Or grace mankind; and what he taught he was.
Compounding high, though plain, his doctrine broke
In different Schools: the bold poetic phrase
Of figured Plato; Xenophon's pure strain,
Like the clear brook that steals along the vale;
Dissecting truth, the Stagyrite's keen eye;
The exalted Stoic pride; the Cynic sneer;
The slow-consenting Academic doubt;
And, joining bliss to virtue, the glad ease

* Socrates.

Of Epicurus, seldom understood.
They, ever candid, reason still opposed
To reason; and, since virtue was their aim,
Each by sure practice tried to prove his way
The best. Then stood untouch'd the solid base
Of Liberty, the liberty of mind:
For systems yet, and soul-enslaving creeds,
Slept with the monsters of succeeding times.
From priestly darkness sprung the enlightening arts
Of fire, and sword, and rage, and horrid names.
'O Greece! thou sapient nurse of finer arts!
Which to bright science blooming fancy bore;
Be this thy praise, that thou, and thou alone,
In these hast led the way, in these excell'd,
Crown'd with the laurel of assenting Time.
'In thy full language, speaking mighty things;
Like a clear torrent close, or else diffused
A broad majestic stream, and rolling on
Through all the winding harmony of sound:
In it the power of Eloquence, at large,
Breathed the persuasive or pathetic soul;
Still'd by degrees the democratic storm,
Or bade it threatening rise, and tyrants shook,
Flush'd at the head of their victorious troops.
In it the Muse, her fury never quench'd,
By mean unyielding phrase, or jarring sound,
Her unconfined divinity display'd;
And, still harmonious, form'd it to her will:
Or soft depress'd it to the shepherd's moan,
Or raised it swelling to the tongue of gods.

'Heroic song was thine; the Fountain Bard,*
Whence each poetic stream derives its course.
Thine the dread moral scene, thy chief delight!
Where idle Fancy durst not mix her voice,
When Reason spoke august; the fervent heart
Or plain'd, or storm'd; and in the impassioned man,
Concealing art with art, the poet sunk.
This potent school of manners, but when left
To loose neglect, a land-corrupting plague,
Was not unworthy deem'd of public care,
And boundless cost, by thee; whose every son,
E'en last mechanic, the true taste possess'd
Of what had flavour to the nourish'd soul.
'The sweet enforcer of the poet's strain,
Thine was the meaning music of the heart.
Not the vain trill, that, void of passion, runs
In giddy mazes, tickling idle ears;
But that deep-searching voice, and artful hand,
To which respondent shakes the varied soul.
'Thy fair ideas, thy delightful forms,
By Love imagined, by the Graces touch'd,
The boast of well pleased Nature! Sculpture seized,
And bade them ever smile in Parian stone.
Selecting Beauty's choice, and that again
Exalting, blending in a perfect whole,
Thy workmen left e'en Nature's self behind.
From those far different, whose prolific hand

* Homer.

Peoples a nation; they for years on years,
By the cool touches of judicious toil,
Their rapid genius curbing, pour'd it all
Through the live features of one breathing stone.
There, beaming full, it shone; expressing gods:
Jove's awful brow, Apollo's air divine,
The fierce atrocious frown of sinewed Mars,
Or the sly graces of the Cyprian Queen.
Minutely perfect all! Each dimple sunk,
And every muscle swell'd, as nature taught.
In tresses, braided gay, the marble waved;
Flow'd in loose robes, or thin transparent veils;
Sprung into motion; softened into flesh;
Was fired to passion, or refined to soul.
'Nor less thy pencil, with creative touch,
Shed mimic life, when all thy brightest dames,
Assembled, Zeuxis in his Helen mix'd.
And when Apelles, who peculiar knew
To give a grace that more than mortal smiled,
The soul of beauty! call'd the Queen of Love,
Fresh from the billows, blushing orient charms.
E'en such enchantment then thy pencil pour'd,
That cruel-thoughted War the impatient torch
Dash'd to the ground; and, rather than destroy
The patriot picture,* let the city scape.

* When Demetrius besieged Rhodes, and could have reduced the city, by setting fire to that quarter of it where stood the house of the celebrated Protogenes; he chose rather to raise the siege, than hazard the burning of a famous picture called Jasylus, the masterpiece of that painter.

'First, elder Sculpture taught her sister art
Correct design; where great ideas shone,
And in the secret trace expression spoke:
Taught her the graceful attitude; the turn,
And beauteous airs of head; the native act,
Or bold, or easy; and, cast free behind,
The swelling mantle's well adjusted flow.
Then the bright Muse, their eldest sister, came;
And bade her follow where she led the way:
Bade earth, and sea, and air, in colours rise;
And copious action on the canvass glow:
Gave her gay Fable; spread Invention's store;
Enlarged her View; taught Composition high,
And just Arrangement, circling round one point,
That starts to sight, binds and commands the whole.
Caught from the heavenly Muse a nobler aim,
And scorning the soft trade of mere delight,
O'er all thy temples, porticos, and schools,
Heroic deeds she traced, and warm display'd
Each moral beauty to the ravish'd eye.
There, as the imagined presence of the god
Aroused the mind, or vacant hours induced
Calm contemplation, or assembled youth
Burn'd in ambitious circle round the sage,
The living lesson stole into the heart,
With more prevailing force than dwells in words.
These rouse to glory; while, to rural life,
The softer canvass oft reposed the soul.
There gaily broke the sun-illumined cloud;
The lessening prospect, and the mountain blue,

Vanish'd in air; the precipice frown'd, dire;
White, down the rock, the rushing torrent dash'd;
The sun shone, trembling, o'er the distant main;
The tempest foam'd, immense; the driving storm
Sadden'd the skies, and, from the doubling gloom,
On the scath'd oak the ragged lightning fell;
In closing shades, and where the current strays,
With Peace, and Love, and innocence around,
Piped the lone shepherd to his feeding flock:
Round happy parents smiled their younger selves;
And friends conversed, by death divided long.
 'To public virtue thus the smiling arts,
Unblemish'd handmaids, served; the Graces they
To dress this fairest Venus. Thus revered,
And placed beyond the reach of sordid care,
The high awarders of immortal fame,
Alone for glory thy great masters strove;
Courted by kings, and by contending states
Assumed the boasted honour of their birth.
 'In Architecture too thy rank supreme!
That art where most magnificent appears
The little builder man; by thee refined,
And, smiling high, to full perfection brought.
Such thy sure rules, that Goths of every age,
Who scorn'd their aid, have only loaded earth
With labour'd heavy monuments of shame.
Not those gay domes that o'er thy splendid shore
Shot, all proportion, up. First unadorn'd,
And nobly plain, the manly Doric rose;
The Ionic then, with decent matron grace,

Her airy pillar heaved; luxuriant last,
The rich Corinthian spread her wanton wreath.
The whole so measured true, so lessen'd off
By fine proportion, that the marble pile,
Form'd to repel the still or stormy waste
Of rolling ages, light as fabrics look'd
That from the magic wand aërial rise.
'These were the wonders that illumined Greece,
From end to end' —— Here interrupting warm,
'Where are they now? (I cried) say, goddess, where?
And what the land, thy darling thus of old?'
'Sunk! (she resumed) deep in the kindred gloom
Of Superstition, and of Slavery, sunk!
No glory now can touch their hearts, benumb'd
By loose dejected sloth and servile fear:
No science pierce the darkness of their minds;
No nobler art the quick ambitious soul
Of imitation in their breast awake.
E'en to supply the needful arts of life,
Mechanic toil denies the hopeless hand.
Scarce any trace remaining, vestige gray,
Or nodding column on the desert shore,
To point where Corinth, or where Athens stood.
A faithless land of violence, and death!
Where commerce parleys, dubious, on the shore;
And his wild impulse curious search restrains,
Afraid to trust the inhospitable clime.
Neglected nature fails; in sordid want
Sunk, and debased, their beauty beams no more.

The sun himself seems, angry, to regard,
Of light unworthy, the degenerate race;
And fires them oft with pestilential rays:
While earth, blue poison steaming on the skies,
Indignant, shakes them from her troubled sides.
But as from man to man, Fate's first decree,
Impartial Death the tide of riches rolls,
So states must die and Liberty go round.
'Fierce was the stand, ere Virtue, Valour, Arts,
And the soul fired by me (that often, stung
With thoughts of better times and old renown,
From hydra-tyrants tried to clear the land)
Lay quite extinct in Greece, their works effaced
And gross o'er all unfeeling bondage spread.
Sooner I moved my much reluctant flight,
Poised on the doubtful wing: when Greece with Greece
Embroil'd in foul contention fought no more
For common glory, and for common weal:
But false to Freedom, sought to quell the free;
Broke the firm band of Peace, and sacred Love,
That lent the whole irrefragable force;
And, as around the partial trophy blush'd,
Prepared the way for total overthrow.
Then to the Persian power, whose pride they scorn'd,
When Xerxes pour'd his millions o'er the land,
Sparta, by turns, and Athens, vilely sued;
Sued to be venal parricides, to spill
Their country's bravest blood, and on themselves
To turn their matchless mercenary arms.

Peaceful in Susa, then, sat the Great King;*
And by the trick of treaties, the still waste
Of sly corruption, and barbaric gold,
Effected what his steel could ne'er perform.
Profuse he gave them the luxurious draught,
Inflaming all the land: unbalanced wide
Their tottering states; their wild assemblies ruled,
As the winds turn at every blast the seas:
And by their listed orators, whose breath
Still with a factious storm infested Greece,
Roused them to civil war, or dash'd them down
To sordid peace — Peace!† that, when Sparta shook
Astonish'd Artaxerxes on his throne,
Gave up, fair-spread o'er Asia's sunny shore,
Their kindred cities to perpetual chains.
What could so base, so infamous a thought
In Spartan hearts inspire? Jealous, they saw
Respiring Athens ‡ rear again her walls:
And the pale fury fired them, once again
To crush this rival city to the dust.
For now no more the noble social soul
Of Liberty my families combined;

* So the kings of Persia were called by the Greeks.

† The peace made by Antalcidas, the Lacedemonian admiral, with the Persians; by which the Lacedemonians abandoned all the Greeks established in the lesser Asia, to the dominion of the King of Persia.

‡ Athens had been dismantled by the Lacedemonians, at the end of the first Peloponnesian war, and was at this time restored by Conon to its former splendour.

But by short views, and selfish passions, broke,
Dire as when friends are rankled into foes,
They mix'd severe, and waged eternal war:
Nor felt they, furious, their exhausted force;
Nor, with false glory, discord, madness blind,
Saw how the blackening storm from Thracia came.
Long years roll'd on, by many a battle stain'd,*
The blush and boast of Fame! where courage, art,
And military glory shone supreme:
But let detesting ages, from the scene
Of Greece self-mangled, turn the sickening eye.
At last, when bleeding from a thousand wounds,
She felt her spirits fail; and in the dust
Her latest heroes, Nicias, Conon, lay,
Agesilaus, and the Theban friends: †
The Macedonian vulture mark'd his time,
By the dire scent of Cheronæa ‡ lured,
And, fierce descending, seized his hapless prey.
'Thus tame submitted to the victor's yoke
Greece, once the gay, the turbulent, the bold;
For every grace, and muse, and science born;
With arts of War, of Government elate;
To tyrants dreadful, dreadful to the best;
Whom I myself could scarcely rule: and thus
The Persian fetters, that inthrall'd the mind,
Were turn'd to formal and apparent chains.

* The Peloponnesian war

† Pelopidas and Epaminondas.

‡ The battle of Cheronæa, in which Philip of Macedon utterly defeated the Greeks.

'Unless Corruption first deject the pride,
And guardian vigour of the free-born soul,
All crude attempts of Violence are vain;
For firm within, and while at heart untouch'd,
Ne'er yet by force was freedom overcome.
But soon as Independence stoops the head,
To Vice enslaved, and vice-created Wants;
Then to some foul corrupting hand, whose waste
These heighten'd wants with fatal bounty feeds:
From man to man the slackening ruin runs,
Till the whole state unnerved in Slavery sinks.'

LIBERTY.

PART III.—ROME.

Here melting mixed with air the ideal forms
That painted still whate'er the goddess sung.
Then I, impatient.—'From extinguish'd Greece,
To what new region stream'd the Human Day?'
She softly sighing, as when Zephyr leaves,
Resign'd to Boreas, the declining year,
Resumed.—'Indignant, these last scenes I fled; *
And long ere then, Leucadia's cloudy cliff,
And the Ceraunian hills behind me thrown,
All Latium stood aroused. Ages before,
Great mother of republics! Greece had pour'd,
Swarm after swarm, her ardent youth around.
On Asia, Afric, Sicily, they stoop'd,
But chief on fair Hesperia's winding shore;
Where, from Lacinium † to Etrurian vales,
They roll'd increasing colonies along,
And lent materials for my Roman reign.
With them my spirit spread; and numerous states,

* The last struggles of Liberty in Greece.
† A promontory in Calabria.

And cities rose, on Grecian models formed;
As its parental policy and arts
Each had imbibed. Besides, to each assign'd
A guardian Genius, o'er the public weal,
Kept an unclosing eye; tried to sustain,
Or more sublime, the soul infused by me:
And strong the battle rose, with various wave,
Against the tyrant demons of the land.
Thus they their little wars and triumphs knew;
Their flows of fortune, and receding times,
But almost all below the proud regard
Of story vow'd to Rome, on deeds intent
That Truth beyond the flight of Fable bore.
'Not so the Samian sage;* to him belongs
The brightest witness of recording Fame.
For these free states his native isle † forsook,
And a vain tyrant's transitory smile,
He sought Crotona's pure salubrious air;
And thro' Great Greece ‡ his gentle wisdom taught;
Wisdom that calm'd for listening years § the mind,
Nor ever heard amid the storm of zeal.
His mental eye first launch'd into the deeps
Of boundless ether; where unnumber'd orbs,
Myriads on myriads, through the pathless sky
Unerring roll, and wind their steady way.

* Pythagoras.

† Samos, over which then reigned the tyrant Polycrates.

‡ The southern parts of Italy and Sicily, so called because of the Grecian colonies there settled.

§ His scholars were enjoined silence for five years.

There he the full consenting choir beheld;
There first discern'd the secret band of love,
The kind attraction, that to central suns
Binds circling earths, and world with world unites.
Instructed thence, he great ideas form'd
Of the whole-moving, all-informing God,
The Sun of beings! beaming unconfined
Light, life, and love, and ever active power:
Whom nought can image, and who best approves
The silent worship of the moral heart,
That joys in bounteous Heaven, and spreads the joy.
Nor scorn'd the soaring sage to stoop to life,
And bound his reason to the sphere of man.
He gave the four yet reigning virtues * name;
Inspired the study of the finer arts,
That civilize mankind, and laws devised
Where with enlighten'd justice mercy mix'd.
He e'en, into his tender system, took
Whatever shares the brotherhood of life:
He taught that life's indissoluble flame,
From brute to man and man to brute again,
For ever shifting, runs the eternal round;
Thence tried against the blood-polluted meal,
And limbs yet quivering with some kindred soul,
To turn the human heart. Delightful truth!
Had he beheld the living chain ascend,
And not a circling form but rising whole.
'Amid these small republics one arose

* The four cardinal virtues.

On yellow Tiber's bank, almighty Rome,
Fated for me. A nobler spirit warm'd
Her sons; and, roused by tyrants, nobler still
It burn'd in Brutus; the proud Tarquins chased,
With all their crimes; bade radiant eras rise,
And the long honours of the Consul-line.
'Here from the fairer, not the greater, plan
Of Greece I varied; whose unmixing states,
By the keen soul of emulation pierced,
Long waged alone the bloodless war of arts,
And their best empire gain'd. But to diffuse
O'er men an empire was my purpose now:
To let my martial majesty abroad;
Into the vortex of one state to draw
The whole mix'd force, and liberty, on earth;
To conquer tyrants, and set nations free.
'Already have I given, with flying touch,
A broken view of this my amplest reign.
Now, while its first, last, periods you survey,
Mark how it labouring rose, and rapid fell.
'When Rome in noon-tide empire grasp'd the world,
And, soon as her resistless legions shone,
The nations stoop'd around; though then appear'd
Her grandeur most; yet in her dawn of power,
By many a jealous equal people press'd,
Then was the toil, the mighty struggle then;
Then for each Roman I a hero told;
And every passing sun, and Latian scene,
Saw patriot virtues then, and awful deeds,

That or surpass the faith of modern times,
Or, if believed, with sacred horror strike.
'For then, to prove my most exalted power,
I to the point of full perfection push'd,
To fondness and enthusiastic zeal,
The great, the reigning passion of the free.
That godlike passion! which, the bounds of self
Divinely bursting, the whole public takes
Into the heart, enlarged, and burning high
With the mix'd ardour of unnumber'd selves;
Of all who safe beneath the voted laws
Of the same parent state, fraternal, live.
From this kind sun of moral nature flow'd
Virtues, that shine the light of humankind,
And, ray'd through story, warm remotest time.
These virtues too, reflected to their source,
Increased its flame. The social charm went round,
The fair idea, more attractive still,
As more by virtue mark'd; till Romans, all
One band of friends, unconquerable grew.
'Hence, when their country raised her plaintive voice,
The voice of pleading Nature was not heard;
And in their hearts the fathers throbb'd no more;
Stern to themselves, but gentle to the whole.
Hence sweeten'd Pain, the luxury of toil;
Patience, that baffled fortune's utmost rage;
High-minded Hope, which at the lowest ebb,
When Brennus conquer'd, and when Cannæ bled,
The bravest impulse felt, and scorn'd despair.

Hence Moderation a new conquest gain'd:
As on the vanquish'd, like descending heaven,
Their dewy mercy dropp'd, the bounty beam'd,
And by the labouring hand were crowns bestow'd.
Fruitful of men, hence hard laborious life,
Which no fatigue can quell, no season pierce.
Hence, Independence, with his little pleased
Serene, and self-sufficient, like a god;
In whom Corruption could not lodge one charm,
While he his honest roots to gold preferr'd;
While truly rich, and by his Sabine field,
The man maintain'd, the Roman's splendour all
Was in the public wealth and glory placed:
Or ready, a rough swain, to guide the plough;
Or else, the purple o'er his shoulder thrown,
In long majestic flow, to rule the state,
With Wisdom's purest eye; or, clad in steel,
To drive the steady battle on the foe.
Hence every passion, e'en the proudest, stoop'd
To common good: Camillus, thy revenge;
Thy glory, Fabius. All submissive hence,
Consuls, Dictators, still resign'd their rule,
The very moment that the laws ordain'd.
Though Conquest o'er them clapp'd her eagle-wings,
Her laurels wreath'd, and yoked her snowy steeds
To the triumphal car; soon as expired
The latest hour of sway, taught to submit,
(A harder lesson that than to command,)
Into the private Roman sunk the chief.

If Rome was served, and glorious, careless they
By whom. Their country's fame they deem'd their own;
And above envy, in a rival's train,
Sung the loud Iös by themselves deserved.
Hence matchless courage. On Cremera's bank,
Hence fell the Fabii; hence the Decii died;
And Curtius plunged into the flaming gulf.
Hence Regulus the wavering fathers firm'd,
By dreadful counsel never given before;
For Roman honour sued, and his own doom.
Hence he sustain'd to dare a death prepar'd
By Punic rage. On earth his manly look
Relentless fix'd, he from a last embrace,
By chains polluted, put his wife aside,
His little children climbing for a kiss;
Then dumb through rows of weeping, wondering friends,
A new illustrious exile! press'd along.
Nor less impatient did he pierce the crowds
Opposing his return, than if, escaped
From long litigious suits, he glad forsook
The noisy town awhile and city cloud,
To breathe Venafrian, or Tarentine air.
Need I these high particulars recount?
The meanest bosom felt a thirst for fame;
Flight their worst death, and shame their only fear.
Life had no charms, nor any terrors fate,
When Rome and glory call'd. But, in one view,
Mark the rare boast of these unequal'd times.

Ages revolved unsullied by a crime:
Astrea reign'd, and scarcely needed laws
To bind a race elated with the pride
Of virtue, and disdaining to descend
To meanness, mutual violence, and wrongs.
While war around them raged, in happy Rome
All peaceful smiled, all save the passing clouds
That often hang on Freedom's jealous brow;
And fair unblemish'd centuries elapsed,
When not a Roman bled but in the field.
Their virtue such, that an unbalanced state,
Still between Noble and Plebeian tost,
As flow'd the wave of fluctuating power,
Was then kept firm, and with triumphant prow
Rode out the storms. Oft though the native feuds,
That from the first their constitution shook,
(A latent ruin, growing as it grew,)
Stood on the threatening point of civil war
Ready to rush: yet could the lenient voice
Of wisdom, soothing the tumultuous soul,
Those sons of virtue calm. Their generous hearts
Unpetrified by self, so naked lay
And sensible to Truth, that o'er the rage
Of giddy faction, by oppression swell'd,
Prevail'd a simple fable, and at once
To peace recover'd the divided state.
But if their often cheated hopes refused
The soothing touch; still, in the love of Rome,
The dread Dictator found a sure resource.
Was she assaulted? was her glory stain'd?

One common quarrel wide inflamed the whole.
Foes in the forum in the field were friends,
By social danger bound; each fond for each,
And for their dearest country all, to die.
'Thus up the hill of empire slow they toil'd:
Till, the bold summit gain'd, the thousand states
Of proud Italia blended into one;
Then o'er the nations they resistless rush'd,
And touch'd the limits of the failing world.
'Let Fancy's eye the distant lines unite.
See that which borders wild the western main,
Where storms at large resound, and tides immense;
From Caledonia's dim cerulean coast,
And moist Hibernia, to where Atlas, lodged
Amid the restless clouds and leaning heaven,
Hangs o'er the deep that borrows thence its name.
Mark that opposed, where first the springing morn
Her roses sheds, and shakes around her dews:
From the dire deserts by the Caspian laved,
To where the Tigris and Euphrates, join'd,
Impetuous tear the Babylonian plain;
And bless'd Arabia aromatic breathes.
See that dividing far the watery north,
Parent of floods! from the majestic Rhine,
Drunk by Batavian meads, to where, seven-mouth'd,
In Euxine waves the flashing Danube roars;
To where the frozen Tanais scarcely stirs
The dead Meotic pool, or the long Rha,*

* The ancient name of the Volga.

In the black Scythian sea,* his torrent throws.
Last, that beneath the burning zone behold:
See where it runs, from the deep-loaded plains
Of Mauritania to the Libyan sands,
Where Ammon lifts amid the torrid waste
A verdant isle, with shade and fountain fresh;
And farther to the full Egyptian shore,
To where the Nile from Ethiopian clouds,
His never drain'd ethereal urn, descends.
In this vast space what various tongues, and states!
What bounding rocks, and mountains, floods, and seas!
What purple tyrants quell'd, and nations freed!
'O'er Greece, descended chief, with stealth divine,
The Roman bounty in a flood of day:
As at her Isthmian games, a fading pomp!
Her full-assembled youth innumerous swarm'd.
On a tribunal raised, Flaminius sat:
A victor he, from the deep phalanx pierced
Of iron-coated Macedon, and back
The Grecian tyrant † to his bounds repell'd.
In the high thoughtless gaiety of game,
While sport alone their unambitious hearts
Possess'd; the sudden trumpet, sounding hoarse,
Bade silence o'er the bright assembly reign.
Then thus a herald: — "To the states of Greece
The Roman people, unconfined, restore

* The Caspian Sea. † The King of Macedonia.

Their countries, cities, liberties, and laws:
Taxes remit, and garrisons withdraw."
The crowd astonish'd half, and half inform'd,
Stared dubious round; some question'd, some exclaim'd.
(Like one who dreaming, between hope and fear,
Is lost in anxious joy,) 'Be that again,
Be that again proclaim'd, distinct, and loud.'
Loud, and distinct, it was again proclaim'd;
And still as midnight in the rural shade,
When the gale slumbers, they the words devour'd.
Awhile severe amazement held them mute,
Then bursting broad, the boundless shout to Heaven
From many a thousand hearts ecstatic sprung.
On every hand rebellow'd to their joy
The swelling sea, the rocks, and vocal hills:
Through all her turrets stately Corinth * shook,
And, from the void above of shatter'd air,
The flitting bird fell breathless to the ground.
What piercing bliss, how keen a sense of fame,
Did then, Flaminius, reach thy inmost soul!
And with what deep-felt glory didst thou then
Escape the fondness of transported Greece?
Mix'd in a tempest of superior joy,
They left the sports; like Bacchanals they flew,
Each other straining in a strict embrace,
Nor strain'd a slave; and loud acclaims till night
Round the Proconsul's tent repeated rung.

* The Isthmian games were celebrated at Corinth.

Then, crown'd with garlands, came the festive hours;
And music, sparkling wine, and converse warm,
Their raptures waked anew. "Ye gods! (they cried)
Ye guardian gods of Greece! and are we free?
Was it not madness deem'd the very thought?
And is it true? How did we purchase chains?
At what a dire expense of kindred blood?
And are they now dissolved? And scarce one drop
For the fair first of blessings have we paid?
Courage, and conduct, in the doubtful field,
When rages wide the storm of mingling war,
Are rare indeed; but how to generous ends
To turn success, and conquest, rarer still:
That the great gods and Romans only know.
Lives there on earth, almost to Greece unknown,
A people so magnanimous, to quit
Their native soil, traverse the stormy deep,
And by their blood and treasure, spent for us,
Redeem our states, our liberties, and laws!
There does! there does! Oh saviour, Titus! Rome!"
Thus thro' the happy night they pour'd their souls,
And in my last reflected beams rejoiced.
As when the shepherd, on the mountain-brow,
Sits piping to his flocks and gamesome kids;
Meantime the sun, beneath the green earth sunk,
Slants upward o'er the scene a parting gleam:
Short is the glory that the mountain gilds,

Plays on the glittering flocks, and glads the swain;
To western worlds irrevocable roll'd,
Rapid, the source of light recalls his ray.'
Here interposing I — 'Oh, Queen of men!
Beneath whose sceptre in essential rights
Equal they live; though placed for common good,
Various, or in subjection or command;
And that by common choice: alas! the scene,
With virtue, freedom, and with glory bright,
Streams into blood, and darkens into woe.'
Thus she pursued: — 'Near this great era, Rome
Began to feel the swift approach of fate,
That now her vitals gain'd: still more and more
Her deep divisions kindling into rage,
And war with chains and desolation charged.
From an unequal balance of her sons
These fierce contentions sprung: and, as increased
This hated inequality, more fierce
They flamed to tumult. Independence fail'd;
Here by luxurious wants, by real there;
And with this virtue every virtue sunk,
As, with the sliding rock, the pile sustain'd.
A last attempt, too late, the Gracchi made,
To fix the flying scale, and poise the state.
On one side swell'd aristocratic Pride;
With Usury, the villain! whose fell gripe
Bends by degrees to baseness the free soul;
And Luxury rapacious, cruel, mean,
Mother of vice! While on the other crept
A populace in want, with pleasure fired;

Fit for proscriptions, for the darkest deeds,
As the proud feeder bade; inconstant, blind,
Deserting friends at need, and duped by foes;
Loud and seditious, when a chief inspired
Their headlong fury, but of him deprived,
Already slaves that lick'd the scourging hand.
'This firm republic, that against the blast
Of opposition rose; that (like an oak,
Nursed on ferocious Algidum,* whose boughs
Still stronger shoot beneath the rigid axe,)
By loss, by slaughter, from the steel itself,
E'en force and spirit drew; smit with the calm,
The dead serene of prosperous fortune, pined.
Nought now her weighty legions could oppose;
Her † terror once, on Afric's tawny shore,
Now smoked in dust, a stabling now for wolves;
And every dreaded power received the yoke.
Besides, destructive, from the conquer'd East,
In the soft plunder came that worst of plagues,
That pestilence of mind, a fever'd thirst
For the false joys which Luxury prepares.
Unworthy joys! that wasteful leave behind
No mark of honour, in reflecting hour,
No secret ray to glad the conscious soul;
At once involving in one ruin wealth,
And wealth-acquiring powers: while stupid self,
Of narrow gust, and hebetating sense,
Devour the noble faculties of bliss.

* A town of Latium, near Tusculum. † Carthage.

Hence Roman virtue slacken'd into sloth;
Security relax'd the softening state;
And the broad eye of government lay closed.
No more the laws inviolable reign'd,
And public weal no more: but party raged;
And partial power, and license unrestrain'd,
Let Discord through the deathful city loose.
First, mild Tiberius,* on thy sacred head
The fury's vengeance fell; the first, whose blood
Had since the consuls stain'd contending Rome.
Of precedent pernicious! with thee bled
Three hundred Romans; with thy brother, next,
Three thousand more: till, into battles turn'd
Debates of peace, and forced the trembling laws,
The Forum and Comitia horrid grew,
A scene of barter'd power, or reeking gore.
When, half-ashamed, Corruption's thievish arts,
And ruffian force begin to sap the mounds
And majesty of laws; if not in time
Repress'd severe, for human aid too strong
The torrent turns, and overbears the whole.
'Thus Luxury, Dissension, a mix'd rage
Of boundless pleasure and of boundless wealth,
Want-wishing change, and waste-repairing war,
Rapine for ever lost to peaceful toil,
Guilt unatoned, profuse of blood Revenge,
Corruption all avow'd, and lawless Force,
Each heightening each, alternate shook the state.

* Tiberius Gracchus.

Meantime Ambition, at the dazzling head
Of hardy legions, with the laurels heap'd
And spoil of nations, in one circling blast
Combined in various storm, and from its base
The broad republic tore. By Virtue built,
It touch'd the skies, and spread o'er shelter'd earth
An ample roof: by Virtue too sustain'd,
And balanced steady, every tempest sung
Innoxious by, or bade it firmer stand.
But when, with sudden and enormous change,
The first of mankind sunk into the last,
As once in Virtue, so in Vice extreme,
This universal fabric yielded loose,
Before Ambition still; and thundering down,
At last, beneath its ruins crush'd a world.
A conquering people, to themselves a prey,
Must ever fall; when their victorious troops,
In blood and rapine savage grown, can find
No land to sack and pillage but their own.
'By brutal Marius, and keen Sylla, first
Effused the deluge dire of civil blood,
Unceasing woes began, and this, or that,
Deep-drenching their revenge, nor virtue spared,
Nor sex, nor age, nor quality, nor name;
Till Rome, into a human shambles turn'd,
Made deserts lovely. — Oh, to well earn'd chains,
Devoted race! — If no true Roman then,
No Scævola there was, to raise for me
A vengeful hand: was there no father, robb'd
Of blooming youth to prop his wither'd age?

No son, a witness to his hoary sire
In dust and gore defiled? no friend, forlorn?
No wretch that doubtful trembled for himself?
None brave, or wild, to pierce a monster's heart,
Who, heaping horror round, no more deserved
The sacred shelter of the laws he spurn'd?
No:—Sad o'er all profound dejection sat;
And nerveless fear. The slave's asylum theirs:
Or flight, ill-judging, that the timid back
Turns weak to slaughter; or partaken guilt.
In vain from Sylla's vanity I drew
An unexampled deed. The power resign'd,
And all unhoped the commonwealth restored,
Amazed the public, and effaced his crimes.
Through streets yet streaming from his murderous hand
Unarm'd he stray'd, unguarded, unassail'd,
And on the bed of peace his ashes laid;
A grace, which I to his demission gave.
But with him died not the despotic soul.
Ambition saw that stooping Rome could bear
A master, nor had virtue to be free.
Hence, for succeeding years, my troubled reign
No certain peace, no spreading prospect knew.
Destruction gather'd round. Still the black soul,
Or of a Catiline, or Rullus,* swell'd

* Publius Servilius Rullus, tribune of the people, proposed an Agrarian Law, in appearance very advantageous for the people, but destructive of their liberty: and which was defeated by the eloquence of Cicero, in his speech against Rullus.

With fell designs; and all the watchful art
Of Cicero demanded, all the force,
All the state-wielding magic of his tongue;
And all the thunder of my Cato's zeal.
With these I linger'd; till the flame anew
Burst out, in blaze immense, and wrapt the world.
The shameful contest sprung; to whom mankind
Should yield the neck: to Pompey, who conceal'd
A rage impatient of an equal name;
Or to the nobler Cæsar, on whose brow
O'er daring vice deluding virtue smiled,
And who no less a vain superior scorn'd.
Both bled, but bled in vain. New traitors rose.
The venal will be bought, the base have lords.
To these vile wars I left ambitious slaves;
And from Philippi's field, from where in dust
The last of Romans, matchless Brutus! lay,
Spread to the north untamed a rapid wing.
'What tho' the first smooth Cæsars arts caress'd,
Merit, and virtue, simulating me?
Severely tender! cruelly humane!
The chain to clinch, and make it softer sit
On the new-broken still ferocious state.
From the dark Third,* succeeding, I beheld
The imperial monsters all. — A race on earth
Vindictive, sent the scourge of humankind!
Whose blind profusion drain'd a bankrupt world;
Whose lust to forming nature seems disgrace;
And whose infernal rage bade every drop

* Tiberius.

Of ancient blood, that yet retain'd my flame,
To that of Pætus,* in the peaceful bath,
Or Rome's affrighted streets, inglorious flow.
But almost just the meanly patient death,
That waits a tyrant's unprevented stroke.
Titus indeed gave one short evening gleam;
More cordial felt, as in the midst it spread
Of storm, and horror. The delight of men!
He who the day, when his o'erflowing hand
Had made no happy heart, concluded lost;
Trajan and he, with the mild sire † and son,
His son of virtue! eased awhile mankind;
And arts revived beneath their gentle beam.
Then was their last effort; what sculpture raised
To Trajan's glory, following triumphs stole;
And mix'd with Gothic forms, (the chisel's shame,)
On that triumphal arch,‡ the forms of Greece.
'Meantime o'er rocky Thrace, and the deep vales
Of gelid Hæmus, I pursued my flight;
And, piercing farthest Scythia, westward swept
Sarmatia,§ traversed by a thousand streams,

* Thrasea Pætus, put to death by Nero. Tacitus introduces the account he gives of his death, thus:—'After having inhumanly slaughtered so many illustrious men, he (Nero) burned at last with a desire of cutting off virtue itself in the person of Thrasea,' &c.

† Antoninus Pius, and his adopted son Marcus Aurelius, afterwards called Antoninus Philosophus.

‡ Constantine's arch, to build which, that of Trajan was destroyed, sculpture having been then almost entirely lost.

§ The ancient Sarmatia contained a vast tract of country running all along the north of Europe and Asia.

A sullen land of lakes, and fens immense,
Of rocks, resounding torrents, gloomy heaths,
And cruel deserts black with sounding pine;
Where nature frowns: tho' sometimes into smiles
She softens; and immediate, at the touch
Of southern gales, throws from the sudden glebe
Luxuriant pasture, and a waste of flowers.
But, cold-compress'd, when the whole loaded heaven
Descends in snow, lost in one white abrupt,
Lies undistinguish'd earth; and, seized by frost,
Lakes, headlong streams, and floods, and oceans sleep.
Yet there life glows; the furry millions there
Deep dig their dens beneath the sheltering snows:
And there a race of men prolific swarms,
To various pain, to little pleasure used;
On whom, keen-parching, beat Riphæan winds;
Hard like their soil, and like their climate fierce,
The nursery of nations!—These I roused,
Drove land on land, on people people pour'd;
Till from almost perpetual night they broke,
As if in search of day; and o'er the banks
Of yielding empire, only slave-sustain'd,
Resistless raged; in vengeance urged by me.
'Long in the barbarous heart the buried seeds
Of Freedom lay, for many a wintry age;
And though my spirit work'd, by slow degrees,
Nought but its pride and fierceness yet appear'd.
Then was the night of time, that parted worlds.

I quitted earth the while. As when the tribes
Aërial, warn'd of rising winter, ride
Autumnal winds, to warmer climates borne;
So, arts and each good genius in my train,
I cut the closing gloom, and soar'd to Heaven.
'In the bright regions there of purest day,
Far other scenes, and palaces, arise,
Adorn'd profuse with other arts divine.
All beauty here below, to them compared,
Would, like a rose before the midday sun,
Shrink up its blossom; like a bubble break
The passing poor magnificence of kings.
For there the King of Nature, in full blaze,
Calls every splendour forth; and there his court,
Amid ethereal powers, and virtues, holds:
Angel, archangel, tutelary gods,
Of cities, nations, empires, and of worlds.
But sacred be the veil, that kindly clouds
A light too keen for mortals; wraps a view
Too softening fair, for those that here in dust
Must cheerful toil out their appointed years.
A sense of higher life would only damp
The schoolboy's task, and spoil his playful hours.
Nor could the child of Reason, feeble man,
With vigour through this infant-being drudge;
Did brighter worlds, their unimagined bliss
Disclosing, dazzle and dissolve his mind.'

LIBERTY.

PART IV.—BRITAIN.

STRUCK with the rising scene, thus I amazed:
'Ah, Goddess, what a change! is earth the same?
Of the same kind the ruthless race she feeds?
And does the same fair sun and ether spread
Round this vile spot their all-enlivening soul?
Lo! beauty fails; lost in unlovely forms
Of little pomp, magnificence no more
Exalts the mind, and bids the public smile:
While to rapacious interest Glory leaves
Mankind, and every grace of life is gone.'
To this the Power, whose vital radiance calls
From the brute mass of man an order'd world:
'Wait till the morning shines, and from the depth
Of Gothic darkness springs another day.
True, Genius droops; the tender ancient taste
Of Beauty, then fresh blooming in her prime,
But faintly trembles through the callous soul;
And Grandeur, or of morals, or of life,
Sinks into safe pursuits, and creeping cares.
E'en cautious Virtue seems to stoop her flight,
And aged life to deem the generous deeds

Of youth romantic. Yet in cooler thought
Well reason'd, in researches piercing deep
Through nature's works, in profitable arts,
And all that calm experience can disclose,
(Slow guide, but sure,) behold the world anew
Exalted rise; with other honours crown'd;
And, where my Spirit wakes the finer powers,
Athenian laurels still afresh shall bloom.
'Oblivious ages pass'd; while earth, forsook
By her best Genii, lay to Demons foul,
And unchain'd Furies, an abandon'd prey.
Contention led the van; first small of size,
But soon dilating to the skies she towers:
Then, wide as air, the livid Fury spread,
And high her head above the stormy clouds,
She blazed in omens, swell'd the groaning winds
With wild surmises, battlings, sounds of war:
From land to land the maddening trumpet blew,
And pour'd her venom through the heart of man.
Shook to the pole, the North obey'd her call.
Forth rush'd the bloody power of Gothic war,
War against humankind: Rapine, that led
Millions of raging robbers in his train:
Unlistening, barbarous Force, to whom the sword
Is reason, honour, law: the foe of arts
By monsters follow'd, hideous to behold,
That claim'd their place. Outrages mix'd with these
Another species of tyrannic * rule;

* Church power, or ecclesiastical tyranny.

Unknown before, whose cankerous shackles seized
The envenom'd soul; a wilder Fury, she
Even o'er her Elder Sister* tyrannized;
Or, if perchance agreed, inflamed her rage.
Dire was her train, and loud: the sable band,
Thundering;—"Submit, ye Laity! ye profane!
Earth is the Lord's, and therefore ours; let kings
Allow the common claim, and half be theirs;
If not, behold! the sacred lightning flies!"
Scholastic Discord, with a hundred tongues,
For science uttering jangling words obscure,
Where frighted reason never yet could dwell:
Of peremptory feature, cleric Pride,
Whose reddening cheek no contradiction bears;
And holy Slander, his associate firm,
On whom the lying Spirit still descends:
Mother of tortures! persecuting Zeal,
High flashing in her hand the ready torch,
Or poniard bathed in unbelieving blood;
Hell's fiercest fiend! of saintly brow demure,
Assuming a celestial seraph's name,
While she beneath the blasphemous pretence
Of pleasing Parent Heaven, the Source of Love!
Has wrought more horrors, more detested deeds,
Than all the rest combined. Led on by her,
And wild of head to work her fell designs,
Came idiot superstition; round with ears
Innumerous strow'd, ten thousand monkish forms
With legends ply'd them, and with tenets, meant

* Civil tyranny.

To charm or scare the simple into slaves,
And poison reason; gross, she swallows all,
The most absurd believing ever most.
Broad o'er the whole her universal night,
The gloom still doubling, Ignorance diffused.
'Nought to be seen, but visionary monks
To councils strolling, and embroiling creeds;
Banditti Saints,* disturbing distant lands;
And unknown nations, wandering for a home.
All lay reversed: the sacred arts of rule
Turn'd to flagitious leagues against mankind,
And arts of plunder more and more avow'd;
Pure plain Devotion † to a solemn farce;
To holy dotage Virtue, even to guile,
To murder, and a mockery of oaths;
Brave ancient Freedom to the rage of slaves,‡
Proud of their state, and fighting for their chains;
Dishonour'd Courage to the bravo's trade,§
To civil broil; and Glory to romance.
Thus human life, unhinged, to ruin reel'd,
And giddy Reason totter'd on her throne.
'At last Heaven's best inexplicable scheme,
Disclosing, bade new brightening eras smile.
The high command gone forth, Arts in my train,
And azure-mantled Science, swift we spread
A sounding pinion. Eager pity, mix'd

* Crusades.

† The corruptions of the church of Rome.

‡ Vassalage, whence the attachment of clans to their chief.

§ Duelling.

With indignation, urged her downward flight.
On Latium first we stoop'd, for doubtful life
That panted, sunk beneath unnumber'd woes.
Ah, poor Italia! what a bitter cup
Of vengeance hast thou drain'd? Goth, Vandals, Huns,
Lombards, barbarians broke from every land,
How many a ruffian form hast thou beheld?
What horrid jargons heard, where rage alone
Was all thy frighted ear could comprehend?
How frequent by the red inhuman hand,
Yet warm with brother's, husband's, father's blood,
Hast thou thy matrons and thy virgins seen
To violation dragg'd, and mingled death?
What conflagrations, earthquakes, ravage, floods,
Have turn'd thy cities into stony wilds;
And succourless, and bare, the poor remains
Of wretches forth to Nature's common cast?
Added to these the still continued waste
Of imbred foes that on thy vitals prey,*
And double tyrants, seize the very soul.
Where hadst thou treasures for this rapine all?
These hungry myriads, that thy bowels tore,
Heap'd sack on sack, and buried in their rage
Wonders of art; whence this grey scene, a mine
Of more than gold becomes and orient gems,
Where Egypt, Greece, and Rome united glow.
'Here Sculpture, Painting, Architecture, bent

* The Hierarchy.

From ancient models to restore their arts,
Remain'd. A little trace we how they rose.
'Amid the hoary ruins, Sculpture first,
Deep digging, from the cavern dark and damp,
Their grave for ages, bid her marble race
Spring to new light. Joy sparkled in her eyes,
And old remembrance thrill'd in every thought,
As she the pleasing resurrection saw.
In leaning site, respiring from his toils,
The well known Hero,* who deliver'd Greece,
His ample chest, all tempested with force,
Unconquerable rear'd. She saw the head,
Breathing the hero, small, of Grecian size,
Scarce more extensive than the sinewy neck:
The spreading shoulders, muscular, and broad;
The whole a mass of swelling sinews, touch'd
Into harmonious shape; she saw, and joy'd.
The yellow hunter, Meleager, raised
His beauteous front, and through the finish'd whole
Shows what ideas smiled of old in Greece.
Of raging aspect, rush'd impetuous forth
The Gladiator: † pitiless his look,
And each keen sinew braced, the storm of war,
Ruffling, o'er all his nervous body frowns.
The dying other ‡ from the gloom she drew:
Supported on his shorten'd arm he leans,
Prone, agonizing; with incumbent fate,

* The Hercules of Farnese.
† Fighting Gladiator.
‡ Dying Gladiator.

Heavy declines his head; yet dark beneath
The suffering feature sullen vengeance lours,
Shame, indignation, unaccomplish'd rage,
And still the cheated eye expects his fall.
All conquest-flush'd, from prostrate Python, came
The quiver'd God.* In graceful act he stands,
His arm extended with the slacken'd bow:
Light flows his easy robe, and fair displays
A manly soften'd form. The bloom of gods
Seems youthful o'er the beardless cheek to wave:
His features yet heroic ardour warms;
And sweet subsiding to a native smile,
Mix'd with the joy elating conquest gives,
A scatter'd frown exalts his matchless air.
On Flora moved; her full proportion'd limbs
Rise through the mantle fluttering in the breeze.
The Queen of Love † arose, as from the deep
She sprung in all the melting pomp of charms.
Bashful she bends, her well taught look aside
Turns in enchanting guise, where dubious mix
Vain conscious beauty, a dissembled sense
Of modest shame, and slippery looks of love.
The gazer grows enamour'd, and the stone,
As if exulting in its conquest, smiles.
So turn'd each limb, so swell'd with softening art,
That the deluded eye the marble doubts.
At last her utmost masterpiece ‡ she found,

* Apollo of Belvidere. † Venus of Medici.

‡ The group of Laocoon and his two sons, destroyed by two serpents.

That Maro fired; * the miserable sire,
Wrapt with his sons in fate's severest grasp:
The serpents, twisting round, their stringent folds
Inextricable tie. Such passion here,
Such agonies, such bitterness of pain,
Seem so to tremble through the tortured stone,
That the touch'd heart engrosses all the view.
Almost unmark'd the best proportions pass,
That ever Greece beheld; and, seen alone,
On the rapt eye the imperious passions seize:
The father's double pangs, both for himself
And sons convulsed; to Heaven his rueful look,
Imploring aid, and half accusing, cast;
His fell despair with indignation mix'd,
As the strong curling monsters from his side
His full extended fury cannot tear.
More tender touch'd, with varied art, his sons
All the soft rage of younger passions show.
In a boy's helpless fate one sinks oppress'd;
While, yet unpierced, the frighted other tries
His foot to steal out of the horrid twine.
  'She bore no more, but straight from Gothic rust
Her chisel clear'd, and dust † and fragments drove
Impetuous round. Successive as it went
From son to son, with more enlivening touch,

* See Æneid II. ver. 199-227.

† It is reported of Michael Angelo Buonaroti, the most celebrated master of modern sculpture, that he wrought with a kind of inspiration, or enthusiastical fury, which produced the effect here mentioned.

From the brute rock it call'd the breathing form;
Till, in a legislator's awful grace
Dress'd, Buonaroti bid a Moses * rise,
And, looking love immense, a Saviour God.*
'Of these observant, Painting felt the fire
Burn inward. Then ecstatic she diffused
The canvass, seized the pallet, with quick hand
The colours brew'd; and on the void expanse
Her gay creation pour'd, her mimic world.
Poor was the manner of her eldest race,
Barren, and dry; just struggling from the taste,
That had for ages scared in cloisters dim
The superstitious herd: yet glorious then
Were deem'd their works; where undeveloped lay
The future wonders that enrich'd mankind,
And a new light and grace o'er Europe cast.
Arts gradual gather streams. Enlarging This,
To each his portion of her various gifts
The Goddess dealt, to none indulging all;
No, not to Raphael. At kind distance still
Perfection stands, like Happiness, to tempt
The eternal chase. In elegant design,
Improving nature: in ideas fair,
Or great, extracted from the fine antique;
In attitude, expression, airs divine;
Her sons of Rome and Florence bore the prize.
To those of Venice she the magic art
Of colours melting into colours gave.

* Esteemed the two finest pieces of modern sculpture.

Theirs too it was by one embracing mass
Of light and shade, that settles round the whole,
Or varies tremulous from part to part,
O'er all a binding harmony to throw,
To raise the picture, and repose the sight.
The Lombard school,* succeeding, mingled both.
'Meantime dread fanes, and palaces, around,
Rear'd the magnific front. Music again
Her universal language of the heart
Renew'd; and, rising from the plaintive vale,
To the full concert spread, and solemn quire.
'E'en bigots smiled; to their protection took
Arts not their own, and from them borrow'd pomp:
For in a tyrant's garden these awhile
May bloom, though Freedom be their parent soil.
'And now confess'd, with gently growing gleam
The morning shone, and westward stream'd its light.
The Muse awoke. Not sooner on the wing
Is the gay bird of dawn. Artless her voice,
Untaught and wild, yet warbling through the woods
Romantic lays. But as her northern course
She, with her tutor Science, in my train,
Ardent pursued, her strains more noble grew:
While Reason drew the plan, the Heart inform'd
The moral page, and Fancy lent it grace.
'Rome and her circling deserts cast behind,
I pass'd not idle to my great sojourn.

* The school of the Caracci.

'On Arno's* fertile plain, where the rich vine
Luxuriant o'er Etrurian mountains roves,
Safe in the lap reposed of private bliss,
I small republics † raised. Thrice happy they!
Had social Freedom bound their peace, and arts,
Instead of ruling Power, ne'er meant for them,
Employ'd their little cares, and saved their fate.
'Beyond the rugged Apennines, that roll
Far through Italian bounds their wavy tops,
My path, too, I with public blessings strow'd:
Free states and cities, where the Lombard plain,
In spite of culture negligent and gross,
From her deep bosom pours unbidden joys,
And green o'er all the land a garden spreads.
'The barren rocks themselves beneath my foot,
Relenting bloom'd on the Ligurian shore.
Thick swarming people ‡ there, like emmets, seized,
Amid surrounding cliffs, the scatter'd spots,
Which Nature left in her destroying rage.§
Made their own fields, nor sigh'd for other lands.
There, in white prospect from the rocky hill
Gradual descending to the shelter'd shore,
By me proud Genoa's marble turrets rose.
And while my genuine spirit warm'd her sons,

* The river Arno runs through Florence.

† The republics of Florence, Pisa, Lucca, and Sienna.

‡ The Genoese territory is reckoned very populous; but the towns and villages for the most part lie hid among the Apennine rocks and mountains.

§ According to Dr. Burnet's system of the Deluge.

Beneath her Dorias, not unworthy, she
Vied for the trident of the narrow seas,
Ere Britain yet had open'd all the main.
'Nor be the then triumphant state forgot;*
Where,† push'd from plunder'd earth, a remnant still
Inspired by me, through the dark ages kept
Of my old Roman flame some sparks alive:
The seeming god-built city! which my hand
Deep in the bosom fix'd of wondering seas.
Astonish'd mortals sail'd, with pleasing awe,
Around the sea-girt walls, by Neptune fenced,
And down the briny street; where on each hand,
Amazing seen amid unstable waves,
The splendid palace shines; and rising tides,
The green steps marking, murmur at the door.
To this fair Queen of Adria's stormy gulf,
The mart of nations! long, obedient seas
Roll'd all the treasure of the radiant East.
But now no more. Than one great tyrant worse,
(Whose shared oppression lightens, as diffused,)
Each subject tearing, many tyrants rose.
The least the proudest. Join'd in dark cabal,
They jealous, watchful, silent, and severe,

* Venice was the most flourishing city in Europe, with regard to trade, before the passage to the East Indies by the Cape of Good Hope and America was discovered.

† Those who fled to some marshes in the Adriatic gulf, from the desolation spread over Italy by an irruption of the Huns, first founded there this famous city, about the beginning of the fifth century.

Cast o'er the whole indissoluble chains:
The softer shackles of luxurious ease
They likewise added, to secure their sway.
Thus Venice fainter shines; and Commerce thus,
Of toil impatient, flags the drooping sail.
Bursting, besides, his ancient bounds, he took
A larger circle:* found another seat,†
Opening a thousand ports, and, charm'd with toil,
Whom nothing can dismay, far other sons.
'The mountains then, clad with eternal snow,
Confess'd my power. Deep as the rampant rocks,
By Nature thrown insuperable round,
I planted there a league of friendly states,‡
And bade plain Freedom there ambition be.
There in the vale, where rural plenty fills,
From lakes, and meads, and furrow'd fields, her horn,
Chief,§ where the Leman pure emits the Rhone,
Rare to be seen! unguilty cities rise,
Cities of brothers form'd: while equal life,
Accorded gracious with revolving power,
Maintains them free; and, in their happy streets,
Nor cruel deed, nor misery, is known.
For valour, faith, and innocence of life,
Renown'd, a rough laborious people, there,
Not only give the dreadful Alps to smile,

* The Main Ocean. † Great Britain.

‡ Swiss Cantons.

§ Geneva, situated on Lacus Lemanus, a small state, but noble example of the blessings of civil and religious liberty.

And press their culture on retiring snows;
But, to firm order train'd and patient war,
They likewise know, beyond the nerve remiss
Of mercenary force, how to defend
The tasteful little their hard toil has earn'd,
And the proud arm of Bourbon to defy.
'E'en, cheer'd by me, their shaggy mountains charm,
More than or Gallic or Italian plains;
And sickening Fancy oft, when absent long,
Pines * to behold their Alpine views again:
The hollow-winding stream: the vale, fair spread
Amid an amphitheatre of hills;
Whence, vapour-wing'd, the sudden tempest springs:
From steep to steep ascending, the gay train
Of fogs, thick-roll'd into romantic shapes:
The flitting cloud, against the summit dash'd;
And, by the sun illumined, pouring bright
A gemmy shower; hung o'er amazing rocks,
The mountain ash, and solemn sounding pine:
The snow-fed torrent, in white mazes tost,
Down to the clear ethereal lake below:
And, high o'ertopping all the broken scene,
The mountain fading into sky; where shines
On winter, winter shivering, and whose top
Licks from their cloudy magazine the snows.

* The Swiss, after having been long absent from their native country, are seized with such a violent desire of seeing it again, as affects them with a kind of languishing indispo sition, called the Swiss-sickness.

'From these descending, as I waved my course
O'er vast Germania, the ferocious nurse
Of hardy men, and hearts affronting death,
I gave some favour'd cities * there to lift
A nobler brow, and through their swarming streets,
More busy, wealthy, cheerful, and alive,
In each contented face to look my soul.
'Thence the loud Baltic passing, black with storm,
To wintry Scandinavia's utmost bound;
There I the manly race,† the parent hive
Of the mix'd kingdoms, form'd into a state
More regularly free. By keener air
Their genius purged, and temper'd hard by frost,
Tempest and toil their nerves, the sons of those
Whose ‡ only terror was a bloodless death,
They, wise and dauntless, still sustain my cause.
Yet there I fix'd not. Turning to the south,
The whispering zephyrs sigh'd at my delay.'
Here, with the shifted vision, burst my joy:—
'O the dear prospect! O majestic view!
See Britain's empire! lo! the watery vast
Wide waves, diffusing the cerulean plain.
And now, methinks, like clouds at distance seen,
Emerging white from deeps of ether, dawn
My kindred cliffs; whence, wafted in the gale,
Ineffable, a secret sweetness breathes.
Goddess, forgive!—My heart, surprised, o'erflows
With filial fondness for the land you bless.'

* The Hans Towns.
† The Swedes.
‡ See note †, p. 203.

As parents to a child complacent deign
Approvance, the celestial brightness smiled;
Then thus—'As o'er the wave resounding deep,
To my near reign, the happy isle, I steer'd
With easy wing; behold! from surge to surge,
Stalk'd the tremendous Genius of the Deep.
Around him clouds, in mingled tempest, hung;
Thick flashing meteors crown'd his starry head;
And ready thunder reddened in his hand,
Or from it stream'd compress'd the gloomy cloud.
Where'er he look'd, the trembling waves recoil'd.
He needs but strike the conscious flood, and shook
From shore to shore, in agitation dire,
It works his dreadful will. To me his voice,
(Like that hoarse blast that round the cavern howls,
Mix'd with the murmurs of the falling main,)
Address'd began—"By Fate commission'd, go,
My Sister-Goddess now, to yon bless'd isle,
Henceforth the partner of my rough domain.
All my dread walks to Britons open lie.
Those that refulgent, or with rosy morn,
Or yellow evening, flame; those that, profuse,
Drunk by equator suns, severely shine;
Or those that, to the poles approaching, rise
In billows rolling into Alps of ice.
E'en, yet untouch'd by daring keel, be theirs
The vast Pacific; that on other worlds,
Their future conquest, rolls resounding tides.
Long I maintain'd inviolate my reign;
Nor Alexanders me, nor Cæsars braved.

Still, in the crook of shore, the coward sail
Till now low crept; and peddling commerce ply'd
Between near joining lands. For Britons, chief,
It was reserved, with star-directed prow,
To dare the middle deep, and drive assured
To distant nations through the pathless main.
Chief, for their fearless hearts the glory waits,
Long months from land, while the black stormy night
Around them rages, on the groaning mast
With unshook knee to know their giddy way;
To sing, unquell'd, amid the lashing wave;
To laugh at danger. Theirs the triumph be,
By deep Invention's keen pervading eye,
The heart of Courage, and the hand of Toil,
Each conquer'd ocean staining with their blood,
Instead of treasure robb'd by ruffian war,
Round social earth to circle fair exchange,
And bind the nations in a golden chain.
To these I honour'd stoop. Rushing to light
A race of men behold! whose daring deeds
Will in renown exalt my nameless plains
O'er those of fabling earth, as hers to mine
In terror yield. Nay, could my savage heart
Such glories check, their unsubmitting soul
Would all my fury brave, my tempest climb,
And might in spite of me my kingdom force."
Here, waiting no reply, the shadowy power
Eased the dark sky, and to the deeps return'd:
While the loud thunder rattling from his hand,
Auspicious, shook opponent Gallia's shore.

'Of this encounter glad, my way to land
I quick pursued, that from the smiling sea
Received me joyous. Loud acclaims were heard;
And music, more than mortal, warbling, fill'd
With pleased astonishment the labouring hind,
Who for a while the unfinish'd furrow left,
And let the listening steer forget his toil.
Unseen by grosser eye, Britannia breathed,
And her aërial train, these sounds of joy.
For of old time, since first the rushing flood,
Urged by almighty power, this favour'd isle
Turn'd flashing from the continent aside,
Indented shore to shore responsive still,
Its guardian she — the Goddess, whose staid eye
Beams the dark azure of the doubtful dawn.
Her tresses, like a flood of soften'd light
Through clouds imbrown'd, in waving circles play.
Warm on her cheek sits Beauty's brightest rose,
Of high demeanour, stately, shedding grace
With every motion. Full her rising chest;
And new ideas, from her finish'd shape,
Charm'd Sculpture taking might improve her art.
Such the fair Guardian of an isle that boasts,
Profuse as vernal blooms, the fairest dames.
High shining on the promontory's brow,
Awaiting me, she stood; with hope inflamed,
By my mixed spirit burning in her sons,
To firm, to polish, and exalt the state.
'The native Genii, round her, radiant smiled.
Courage, of soft deportment, aspect calm,

Unboastful, suffering long, and, till provoked,
As mild and harmless as the sporting child;
But, on just reason, once his fury roused,
No lion springs more eager to his prey:
Blood is a pastime; and his heart, elate,
Knows no depressing fear. That Virtue known
By the relenting look, whose equal heart
For others feels, as for another self:
Of various name, as various objects wake,
Warm into action, the kind sense within:
Whether the blameless poor, the nobly maim'd,
The lost to reason, the declined in life,
The helpless young that kiss no mother's hand,
And the grey second infancy of age,
She gives in public families to live,
A sight to gladden Heaven! whether she stands
Fair beckoning at the hospitable gate,
And bids the stranger take repose and joy:
Whether, to solace honest labour, she
Rejoices those that make the land rejoice:
Or whether to Philosophy, and Arts,
(At once the basis and the finish'd pride
Of government and life,) she spreads her hand;
Nor knows the gift profuse, nor seems to know,
Doubling her bounty, that she gives at all.
Justice to these her awful presence join'd,
The mother of the state! no low revenge,
No turbid passions in her breast ferment:
Tender, serene, compassionate of vice,
As the last woe that can afflict mankind,

She punishment awards; yet of the good
More piteous still, and of the suffering whole,
Awards it firm. So fair her just decree,
That, in his judging peers, each on himself
Pronounces his own doom. O happy land!
Where reigns alone this justice of the free!
Mid the bright group Sincerity his front,
Diffusive, rear'd; his pure untroubled eye
The fount of truth. The thoughtful Power, apart,
Now, pensive, cast on earth his fix'd regard,
Now, touch'd celestial, launch'd it on the sky.
The Genius he whence Britain shines supreme,
The land of light, and rectitude of mind.
He, too, the fire of fancy feeds intense,
With all the train of passions thence derived:
Not kindling quick, a noisy transient blaze,
But gradual, silent, lasting, and profound.
Near him Retirement, pointing to the shade,
And Independence stood: the generous pair,
That simple life, the quiet-whispering grove,
And the still raptures of the free-born soul,
To cates prefer by Virtue bought, not earn'd,
Proudly prefer them to the servile pomp,
And to the heart-embitter'd joys of slaves.
Or should the latter, to the public scene
Demanded, quit his silvan friend awhile;
Nought can his firmness shake, nothing seduce
His zeal, still active for the commonweal;
Nor stormy tyrants, nor corruption's tools,
Foul ministers, dark-working by the force

Of secret-sapping gold. All their vile arts,
Their shameful honours, their perfidious gifts,
He greatly scorns; and, if he must betray
His plunder'd country, or his power resign,
A moment's parley were eternal shame:
Illustrious into private life again,
From dirty levees he unstain'd ascends,
And firm in senates stands the patriot's ground,
Or draws new vigour in the peaceful shade.
Aloof the bashful virtue hover'd coy,
Proving by sweet distrust distrusted worth.
Rough Labour closed the train: and in his hand
Rude, callous, sinew-swell'd, and black with toil,
Came manly Indignation. Sour he seems,
And more than seems, by lawless pride assail'd;
Yet kind at heart, and just, and generous, there
No vengeance lurks, no pale insidious gall:
Even in the very luxury of rage,
He softening can forgive a gallant foe;
The nerve, support, and glory of the land!
Nor be Religion, rational and free,
Here pass'd in silence; whose enraptured eye
Sees Heaven with earth connected, human things
Link'd to divine: who not from servile fear,
By rights for some weak tyrant incense fit,
The God of Love adores, but from a heart
Effusing gladness, into pleasing awe
That now astonish'd swells, now in a calm
Of fearless confidence that smiles serene;
That lives devotion, one continual hymn,

And then most grateful, when Heaven's bounty most
Is right enjoy'd. This ever cheerful Power
O'er the raised circle ray'd superior day.
'I joy'd to join the Virtues, whence my reign
O'er Albion was to rise. Each cheering each,
And, like the circling planets from the sun,
All borrowing beams from me, a heighten'd zeal
Impatient fired us to commence our toils,
Or pleasures rather. Long the pungent time
Pass'd not in mutual hails; but, through the land
Darting our light, we shone the fogs away.
'The Virtues conquer with a single look.
Such grace, such beauty, such victorious light,
Live in their presence, stream in every glance,
That the soul won, enamour'd, and refined,
Grows their own image, pure ethereal flame.
Hence the foul Demons, that oppose our reign,
Would still from us deluded mortals wrap;
Or in gross shades they drown the visual ray,
Or by the fogs of prejudice, where mix
Falsehood and truth confounded, foil the sense
With vain refracted images of bliss.
But chief around the court of flatter'd kings
They roll the dusky rampart, wall o'er wall
Of darkest pile, and with their thickest shade
Secure the throne. No savage Alp, the den
Of wolves, and bears, and monstrous things obscene,
That vex the swain and waste the country round,
Protected lies beneath a deeper cloud.

Yet there we sometimes send a searching ray,
As, at the sacred opening of the morn,
The prowling race retire; so, pierced severe,
Before our potent blaze these Demons fly,
And all their works dissolve—— the whisper'd tale,
That, like the fabling Nile, no fountain knows.
Fair-faced Deceit, whose wily conscious eye
Ne'er looks direct. The tongue that licks the dust,
But, when it safely dares, as prompt to sting:
Smooth crocodile Destruction, whose fell tears
Ensnare. The Janus-face of courtly Pride;
One to superiors heaves submissive eyes,
On hapless worth the other scowls disdain:
Cheeks that for some weak tenderness, alone,
Some virtuous slip, can wear a blush. The laugh
Profane, when midnight bowls disclose the heart,
At starving Virtue, and at Virtue's fools.
Determined to be broke, the plighted faith;
Nay more, the godless oath, that knows no ties.
Soft-buzzing Slander; silky moths, that eat
An honest name. The harpy hand, and maw,
Of avaricious Luxury; who makes
The throne his shelter, venal laws his fort,
And, his service, who betrays his king.
'Now turn your view, and mark from Celtic* night
To present grandeur, how my Britain rose.
'Bold were those Britons, who, the careless sons

* Great Britain was peopled by the Celtæ or Gauls.

Of Nature, roam'd the forest-bounds, at once
Their verdant city, high-embowering fane,
And the gay circle of their woodland wars:
For by the Druid * taught, that death but shifts
The vital scene, they that prime fear despised;
And, prone to rush on steel, disdain'd to spare
An ill saved life, that must again return.
Erect from Nature's hand, by tyrant force,
And still more tyrant custom, unsubdued,
Man knows no master save creating Heaven,
Or such as choice and common good ordain.
This general sense, with which the nations I
Promiscuous fire, in Britons burn'd intense,
Of future times prophetic. Witness, Rome,
Who saw'st thy Cæsar, from the naked land,
Whose only fort was British hearts, repell'd,
To seek Pharsalian wreaths. Witness, the toil,
The blood of ages, bootless to secure,
Beneath an empire's † yoke, a stubborn isle,
Disputed hard, and never quite subdued.
The North ‡ remain'd untouch'd, where those who scorn'd
To stoop retired; and, to their keen effort
Yielding at last, recoil'd the Roman power.

* The Druids, among the ancient Gauls and Britons, had the care and direction of all religious matters.

† The Roman empire.

‡ Caledonia, inhabited by the Scots and Picts; whither a great many Britons, who would not submit to the Romans, retired.

In vain, unable to sustain the shock,
From sea to sea desponding legions raised
The wall immense,* and yet, on summer's eve,
While sport his lambkins round, the shepherd's
gaze.
Continual o'er it burst the northern storm,†
As often, check'd, receded; threatening hoarse
A swift return. But the devouring flood
No more endured control, when, to support
The last remains of empire,‡ was recall'd
The weary Roman, and the Briton lay
Unnerved, exhausted, spiritless, and sunk.
Great proof! how men enfeeble into slaves.
The sword § behind him flash'd; before him roar'd,
Deaf to his woes, the deep. Forlorn, around
He roll'd his eye, not sparkling ardent flame,
As when Caractacus ‖ to battle led

* The wall of Severus, built upon Adrian's rampart, which ran for eighty miles quite across the country, from the mouth of the Tyne to Solway Frith.

† Irruptions of the Scots and Picts.

‡ The Roman empire being miserably torn by the northern nations, Britain was for ever abandoned by the Romans in the year 426 or 427.

§ The Britons applying to Ætius, the Roman general, for assistance, thus expressed their miserable condition:—'We know not which way to turn us. The Barbarians drive us to sea, and the sea forces us back to the Barbarians; between which we have only the choice of two deaths, either to be swallowed up by the waves, or butchered by the sword.'

‖ King of the Silures, famous for his great exploits, and accounted the best general Great Britain had ever produced.

Silurian swains, and Boadicea * taught
Her raging troops the miseries of slaves.
'Then (sad relief!) from the bleak coast, that hears
The German ocean roar, deep-blooming, strong,
And yellow-hair'd, the blue-eyed Saxon came.
He came implored, but came with other aim
Than to protect: for conquest and defence
Suffices the same arm. With the fierce race
Pour'd in a fresh invigorating stream,
Blood, where unquell'd a mighty spirit glow'd.
Rash war, and perilous battle, their delight;
And immature, and red with glorious wounds,
Unpeaceful death their choice: deriving thence
A right to feast, and drain immortal bowls,
In Odin's hall; † whose blazing roof resounds

The Silures were esteemed the bravest and most powerful of all the Britons: they inhabited Herefordshire, Radnorshire, Brecknockshire, Monmouthshire, and Glamorganshire.

* Queen of the Iceni.

† It is certain, that an opinion was fixed and general among them (the Goths) that death was but the entrance into another life; that all men who lived lazy and unactive lives, and died natural deaths, by sickness or by age, went into vast caves under ground, all dark and miry, full of noisome creatures usual to such places, and there for ever groveled in endless stench and misery. On the contrary, all who gave themselves to warlike actions and enterprises, to the conquest of their neighbours and the slaughter of their enemies, and died in battle, or of violent deaths upon bold adventures or resolutions, went immediately to the vast hall or palace of Odin, their god of war, who eternally kept open house for all such guests, where they were entertained at infinite tables, in per-

The genial uproar of those shades, who fall
In desperate fight, or by some brave attempt;
And though more polish'd times the martial creed
Disown, yet still the fearless habit lives.
Nor were the surly gifts of war their all.
Wisdom was likewise theirs, indulgent laws,
The calm gradations of art-nursing peace,
And matchless orders, the deep basis still
On which ascends my British reign. Untamed
To the refining subtleties of slaves,
They brought a happy government along;
Form'd by that freedom, which, with secret voice,
Impartial Nature teaches all her sons,
And which of old through the whole Scythian mass
I strong inspired. Monarchical their state,
But prudently confined, and mingled wise
Of each harmonious power: only, too much,
Imperious war into their rule infused,
Prevail'd their General-King, and Chieftain-Thanes.

'In many a field, by civil fury stain'd,
Bled the discordant Heptarchy;* and long

petual feasts and mirth, carousing in bowls made of the skulls of their enemies they had slain; according to the number of whom, every one in these mansions of pleasure was the most honoured and best entertained.—*Sir William Temple's Essay on Heroic Virtue.*

* The seven kingdoms of the Anglo-Saxons, considered as being united into one common government, under a general in chief or monarch, and by the means of an assembly general, or wittenagemot.

(Educing good from ill) the battle groan'd;
Ere, blood-cemented, Anglo-Saxon saw
Egbert* and peace on one united throne.
'No sooner dawn'd the fair disclosing calm
Of brighter days, when lo! the North anew,
With stormy nations black, on England pour'd
Woes the severest e'er a people felt.
The Danish Raven,† lured by annual prey,
Hung o'er the land incessant. Fleet on fleet
Of barbarous pirates unremitting tore
The miserable coast. Before them stalk'd,
Far seen, the Demon of devouring Flame;
Rapine, and Murder, all with blood besmear'd,
Without or ear, or eye, or feeling heart;
While close behind them march'd the sallow Power
Of desolating famine, who delights
In grass-grown cities, and in desert fields;
And purple-spotted Pestilence, by whom
E'en Friendship scared, in sickening horror sinks
Each social sense and tenderness of life.
Fixing at last, the sanguinary race
Spread, from the Humber's loud resounding shore
To where the Thames devolves his gentle maze,
And with superior arm the Saxon awed.
But Superstition first, and monkish dreams,

* Egbert, King of Wessex, who, after having reduced all the other kingdoms of the Heptarchy under his dominion, was the first king of England.

† A famous Danish standard was called Reafan, or Raven. The Danes imagined that, before a battle, the Raven wrought upon this standard clapt its wings or hung down its head, in token of victory or defeat.

And monk-directed cloister-seeking kings,
Had eat away his vigour, eat away
His edge of Courage, and depress'd the soul
Of conquering Freedom, which he once respired.
Thus cruel ages pass'd; and rare appear'd
White-mantled Peace, exulting o'er the vale,
As when, with Alfred,* from the wilds she came
To policed cities and protected plains.
Thus by degrees the Saxon empire sunk,
Then set entire in Hastings' † bloody field.
  'Compendious war! (on Britain's glory bent,
So fate ordain'd) in that decisive day,
The haughty Norman seized at once an isle,
For which, through many a century, in vain,
The Roman, Saxon, Dane, had toil'd and bled.
Of Gothic nations this the final burst;
And, mix'd the genius of these people all,
Their virtues mix'd in one exalted stream,
Here the rich tide of English blood grew full.
  'Awhile my Spirit slept; the land awhile,
Affrighted, droop'd beneath despotic rage.
Instead of Edward's ‡ equal gentle laws,

* Alfred the Great, renowned in war, and no less famous in peace for his many excellent institutions, particularly that of juries.

† The battle of Hastings, in which Harold II. the last of the Saxon kings, was slain, and William the Conqueror made himself master of England.

‡ Edward III. the Confessor, who reduced the West Saxon, Mercian, and Danish laws into one body; which from that time became common to all England, under the name of 'The Laws of Edward.'

The furious victor's partial will prevail'd.
All prostrate lay; and, in the secret shade,
Deep stung but fearful Indignation gnash'd
His teeth. Of freedom, property, despoil'd,
And of their bulwark, arms; with castles crush'd,
With ruffians quarter'd o'er the bridled land;
The shivering wretches, at the curfew * sound,
Dejected shrunk into their sordid beds,
And, through the mournful gloom, of ancient times
Mused sad, or dreamt of better. E'en to feed
A tyrant's idle sport the peasant starved:
To the wild herd, the pasture of the tame,
The cheerful hamlet, spiry town, was given,
And the brown forest † roughen'd wide around.
'But this so dead, so vile submission, long
Endured not. Gathering force, my gradual flame
Shook off the mountain of tyrannic sway.
Unused to bend, impatient of control,
Tyrants themselves the common tyrant check'd.
The Church, by kings intractable and fierce,
Denied her portion of the plunder'd state,
Or tempted, by the timorous and weak,
To gain new ground, first taught their rapine law.
The Barons next a nobler league began,

* The Curfew-Bell (from the French Couvrefeu) which was rung every night at eight of the clock, to warn the English to put out their fires and candles, under the penalty of a severe fine.

† The New Forest in Hampshire; to make which, the country for above thirty miles in compass was laid waste.

Both those of English and of Norman race,
In one fraternal nation blended now,
The nation of the Free! press'd by a band *
Of Patriots, ardent as the summer's noon
That looks delighted on, the tyrant see!
Mark! how with feign'd alacrity he bears
His strong reluctance down, his dark revenge,
And gives the Charter, by which life indeed
Becomes of price, a glory to be man.
'Thro' this, and thro' succeeding reigns affirm'd
These long-contested rights, the wholesome winds
Of Opposition † hence began to blow,
And often since have lent the country life.
Before their breath Corruption's insect-blights,
The darkening clouds of evil counsel fly;
Or should they sounding swell, a putrid court,
A pestilential ministry, they purge,
And ventilated states renew their bloom.
'Though with the temper'd Monarchy here mix'd
Aristocratic sway, the People still,
Flatter'd by this or that, as interest lean'd,
No full protection knew. For me reserved,
And for my Commons, was that glorious turn.
They crown'd my first attempt, in senates ‡ rose

* On the 5th of June, 1215, King John, met by the Barons on Runnemede, signed the Great Charter of Liberties, or Magna Charta.

† The league formed by the Barons, during the reign of John, in the year 1213, was the first confederacy made in England in defence of the nation's interest against the King.

‡ The commons are generally thought to have been first

The fort of Freedom! Slow till then, alone,
Had work'd that general liberty, that soul
Which generous nature breathes, and which, when
left
By me to bondage was corrupted Rome,
I through the northern nations wide diffused.
Hence many a people, fierce with freedom, rush'd
From the rude iron regions of the North,
To Libyan deserts swarm protruding swarm,
And pour'd new spirit through a slavish world.
Yet, o'er these Gothic states, the King and Chiefs
Retain'd the high prerogative of war,
And with enormous property engross'd
The mingled power. But on Britannia's shore
Now present, I to raise my reign began
By raising the Democracy, the third
And broadest bulwark of the guarded state.
Then was the full, the perfect plan disclosed
Of Britain's matchless constitution, mix'd
Of mutual checking and supporting powers,
King, Lords, and Commons; nor the name of free

represented in parliament towards the end of Henry the Third's reign. To a parliament called in the year 1264, each county was ordered to send four knights, as representatives of their respective shires: and to a parliament called in the year following, each county was ordered to send, as their representatives, two knights, and each city and borough as many citizens and burgesses. Till then, history makes no mention of them; whence a very strong argument may be drawn, to fix the original of the House of Commons to that era.

Deserving, while the vassal-many droop'd:
For since the moment of the whole they form,
So, as depress'd or raised, the balance they
Of public welfare and of glory cast.
Mark from this period the continual proof.
'When Kings of narrow genius, minion-rid,
Neglecting faithful worth for fawning slaves;
Proudly regardless of their people's plaints,
And poorly passive of insulting foes;
Double, not prudent, obstinate, not firm,
Their mercy fear, necessity their faith;
Instead of generous fire, presumptuous, hot,
Rash to resolve, and slothful to perform;
Tyrants at once and slaves, imperious, mean,
To want rapacious joining shameful waste;
By counsels weak and wicked, easy roused
To paltry schemes of absolute command,
To seek their splendour in their sure disgrace,
And in a broken ruin'd people wealth:
When such o'ercast the state, no bond of love,
No heart, no soul, no unity, no nerve,
Combined the loose disjointed public, lost
To fame abroad, to happiness at home.
'But when an Edward,* and a Henry † breathed
Through the charm'd whole one all-exerting soul:
Drawn sympathetic from his dark retreat,
When wide-attracted merit round them glow'd:
Then counsels just, extensive, generous, firm,

* Edward III. † Henry V.

Amid the maze of state, determined kept
Some ruling point in view: when, on the stock
Of public good and glory grafted, spread
Their palms, their laurels; or, if thence they stray'd,
Swift to return, and patient of restraint:
When regal state, pre-eminence of place,
They scorn'd to deem pre-eminence of ease,
To be luxurious drones, that only rob
The busy hive: as in distinction, power,
Indulgence, honour, and advantage, first;
When they too claim'd in virtue, danger, toil,
Superior rank; with equal hand, prepared
To guard the subject, and to quell the foe:
When such with me their vital influence shed,
No mutter'd grievance, hopeless sigh, was heard;
No foul distrust through wary senates ran,
Confined their bounty, and their ardour quench'd:
On aid, unquestion'd liberal aid was given:
Safe in their conduct, by their valour fired,
Fond where they led victorious armies rush'd;
And Cressy, Poitiers, Agincourt * proclaim
What Kings supported by almighty Love,
And People fired with Liberty, can do.
'Be veil'd the savage reigns,† when kindred rage
The numerous once Plantagenets devour'd,
A race to vengeance vow'd! and when, oppress'd

* The famous battles, gained by the English over the French.

† During the civil wars, betwixt the families of York and Lancaster.

By private feuds, almost extinguish'd lay
My quivering flame. But, in the next, behold!
A cautious tyrant * lend it oil anew.
'Proud, dark, suspicious, brooding o'er his gold,
As how to fix his throne he jealous cast
His crafty views around; pierced with a ray,
Which on his timid mind I darted full,
He mark'd the Barons of excessive sway,
At pleasure making and unmaking kings; †
And hence, to crush these petty tyrants, plann'd
A law,‡ that let them, by the silent waste
Of luxury, their landed wealth diffuse,
And with that wealth their implicated power.
By soft degrees a mighty change ensued,
E'en working to this day. With streams, deduced
From these diminish'd floods, the country smiled.
As when impetuous from the snow-heap'd Alps,
To vernal suns relenting, pours the Rhine;
While, undivided, oft, with wasteful sweep,
He foams along; but through Batavian meads,
Branch'd into fair canals, indulgent flows;
Waters a thousand fields; and culture, trade,
Towns, meadows, gliding ships, and villas mix'd,
A rich, a wondrous landscape rises round.
His furious son § the soul-enslaving chain,‖

* Henry VII.

† The famous Earl of Warwick, during the reigns of Henry VI. and Edward IV. was called the 'King Maker.'

‡ Permitting the Barons to alienate their lands.

§ Henry VIII.

‖ Of papal dominion.

Which many a doting venerable age
Had link by link strong twisted round the land,
Shook off. No longer could be borne a power,
From Heaven pretended, to deceive, to void
Each solemn tie, to plunder without bounds,
To curb the generous soul, to fool mankind;
And, wild at last, to plunge into a sea
Of blood and horror. The returning light,
That first thro' Wickliff* streak'd the priestly
gloom,
Now burst in open day. Bared to the blaze,
Forth from the haunts of Superstition † crawled
Her motley sons, fantastic figures all;
And, wide dispersed, their useless fetid wealth
In graceful labour bloom'd, and fruits of peace.
'Trade, join'd to these, on every sea display'd
A daring canvass, pour'd with every tide
A golden flood. From other worlds ‡ were roll'd
The guilty glittering stores, whose fatal charms,
By the plain Indian happily despised,
Yet work'd his woe; and to the blissful groves,
Where Nature lived herself among her sons,
And Innocence and Joy for ever dwelt,
Drew rage unknown to pagan climes before,

* John Wickliff, doctor of divinity, who, towards the close of the fourteenth century, published doctrines very contrary to those of the church of Rome, and particularly denying the papal authority. His followers grew very numerous, and were called Lollards.

† Suppression of monasteries.

‡ The Spanish West Indies.

The worst the zeal-inflamed barbarian drew.
Be no such horrid commerce, Britain, thine!
But want for want, with mutual aid, supply.
'The Commons thus enrich'd, and powerful grown,
Against the Barons weigh'd. Eliza then,
Amid these doubtful motions, steady, gave
The beam to fix. She! like the secret Eye,
That never closes on a guarded world,
So sought, so mark'd, so seized the public good,
That self-supported, without one ally,
She awed her inward, quell'd her circling foes.
Inspired by me, beneath her sheltering arm,
In spite of raging universal sway *
And raging seas repress'd, the Belgic states,
My bulwark on the continent, arose.
Matchless in all the spirit of her days!
With confidence, unbounded, fearless love
Elate, her fervent people waited gay,
Cheerful demanded the long threaten'd fleet,†
And dash'd the pride of Spain around their isle.
Nor ceased the British thunder here to rage:
The deep, reclaim'd, obey'd its awful call;
In fire and smoke Iberian ports involved,
The trembling foe even to the centre shook
Of their new conquer'd world, and, skulking, stole
By veering winds their Indian treasure home.

* The dominion of the house of Austria.

† The Spanish Armada. Rapin says, that after proper measures had been taken, the enemy was expected with uncommon alacrity.

Meantime, Peace, Plenty, Justice, Science, Arts,
With softer laurels crown'd her happy reign.
As yet uncircumscribed the regal power,
And wild and vague prerogative remain'd;
A wide voracious gulf, where swallow'd oft
The helpless subject lay. This to reduce
To the just limit was my great effort.
'By means that evil seem to narrow man,
Superior Beings work their mystic will:
From storm and trouble thus a settled calm,
At last, effulgent, o'er Britannia smiled.
'The gathering tempest, Heaven-commission'd came,
Came in the prince,* who, drunk with flattery, dreamt
His vain pacific counsels ruled the world;
Though scorn'd abroad, bewilder'd in a maze
Of fruitless treaties; while, at home enslaved,
And by a worthless crew insatiate drain'd,
He lost his people's confidence and love:
Irreparable loss! whence crowns become
An anxious burden. Years inglorious pass'd:
Triumphant Spain the vengeful draught enjoy'd:
Abandon'd Frederick † pined, and Raleigh bled.

* James I.

† Elector Palatine, and who had been chosen King of Bohemia, but was stripped of all his dominions and dignities by the Emperor Ferdinand, while James the First, his father-in-law, being amused from time to time, endeavoured to mediate a peace.

But nothing that to these internal broils,
That rancour, he began; while lawless sway
He, with his slavish Doctors, tried to rear
On metaphysic,* on enchanted ground,
And all the mazy quibbles of the schools:
As if for one, and sometimes for the worst,
Heaven had mankind in vengeance only made.
Vain the pretence! not so the dire effect,
The fierce, the foolish discord † thence derived,
That tears the country still, by party rage
And ministerial clamour kept alive.
In action weak, and for the wordy war
Best fitted, faint this prince pursued his claim:
Content to teach the subject herd, how great,
How sacred he! how despicable they!
'But his unyielding son ‡ these doctrines drank,
With all a bigot's rage; (who never damps
By reasoning his fire) and what they taught,
Warm, and tenacious, into practice push'd.
Senates, in vain, their kind restraint applied:
The more they struggled to support the laws,
His justice-dreading ministers the more
Drove him beyond their bounds. Tired with the check
Of faithful Love, and with the flattery pleased
Of false designing Guilt, the fountain § he

* The monstrous and till then unheard-of doctrines of divine indefeasible hereditary right, passive obedience, &c.

† The parties of Whig and Tory.

‡ Charles I.

§ Parliaments.

Of Public Wisdom and of Justice shut.
Wide mourn'd the land. Straight to the voted aid
Free, cordial, large, of never failing source,
The illegal imposition follow'd harsh,
With execration given, or ruthless squeezed
From an insulted people, by a band
Of the worst ruffians, those of tyrant power.
Oppression walk'd at large, and pour'd abroad
Her unrelenting train: informers, spies,
Bloodhounds, that sturdy Freedom to the grove
Pursue; projectors of aggrieving schemes,
Commerce to load for unprotected seas,*
To sell the starving many to the few,†
And drain a thousand ways the exhausted land,
E'en from that place, whence healing Peace should flow,
And Gospel truth, inhuman bigots shed
Their poison ‡ round; and on the venal bench,
Instead of justice, party held the scale,
And violence the sword. Afflicted years,
Too patient, felt at last their vengeance full.
'Mid the low murmurs of submissive fear
And mingled rage, my Hampden raised his voice,
And to the laws appeal'd; the laws no more

* Ship-money.

† Monopolies.

‡ The raging High-Church sermons of these times, inspiring a spirit of slavish submission to the court, and of bitter persecution against those whom they call Church and State Puritans.

In judgment sat, behoved some other ear.
When instant from the keen resentive North,
By long oppression, by religion roused,
The guardian army came. Beneath its wing
Was call'd, though meant to furnish hostile aid,
The more than Roman senate. There a flame
Broke out, that clear'd, consumed, renew'd the land.
In deep emotion hurl'd, nor Greece, nor Rome,
Indignant bursting from a tyrant's chain,
While, full of me, each agitated soul
Strung every nerve and flamed in every eye,
Had e'er beheld such light and heat combined!
Such heads and hearts! such dreadful zeal, led on
By calm majestic wisdom, taught its course
What nuisance to devour; such wisdom fired
With unabating zeal, and aim'd sincere
To clear the weedy state, restore the laws,
And for the future to secure their sway.
'This then the purpose of my mildest sons.
But man is blind. A nation once inflamed
(Chief, should the breath of factious fury blow,
With the wild rage of mad enthusiast swell'd)
Not easy cools again. From breast to breast,
From eye to eye, the kindling passions mix
In heighten'd blaze; and, ever wise and just,
High Heaven to gracious ends directs the storm.
Thus in one conflagration Britain wrapt,
And by Confusion's lawless sons despoil'd,
King, Lords, and Commons, thundering to the ground,

Successive, rush'd — Lo! from their ashes rose,
Gay beaming radiant youth, the Phœnix State.*
'The grievous yoke of vassalage, the yoke
Of private life, lay by those flames dissolved;
And, from the wasteful, the luxurious king,†
Was purchased ‡ that which taught the young to
bend.
Stronger restored, the Commons tax'd the whole,
And built on that eternal rock their power.
The Crown, of its hereditary wealth
Despoil'd, on senates more dependent grew,
And they more frequent, more assured. Yet lived,
And in full vigour spread that bitter root,
The passive doctrines, by their patrons first,
Opposed ferocious, when they touch themselves.
'This wild delusive cant; the rash cabal
Of hungry courtiers, ravenous for prey;
The bigot, restless in a double chain
To bind anew the land; the constant need
Of finding faithless means, of shifting forms,
And flattering senates, to supply his waste;
These tore some moments from the careless prince,
And in his breast awaked the kindred plan.
By dangerous softness long he mined his way;
By subtle arts, dissimulation deep;
By sharing what corruption shower'd, profuse;
By breathing wide the gay licentious plague,
And pleasing manners, fitted to deceive.

* At the Restoration. † Charles II.
‡ Court of Wards.

'At last subsided the delirious joy,
On whose high billow, from the saintly reign,
The nation drove too far. A pension'd king,
Against his country bribed by Gallic gold;
The Port * pernicious sold, the Scylla since
And fell Charybdis of the British seas;
Freedom attack'd abroad,† with surer blow
To cut it off at home; the saviour league ‡
Of Europe broke; the progress e'en advanced
Of universal sway,§ which to reduce
Such seas of blood and treasure Britain coast;
The millions, by a generous people given,
Or squander'd vile, or to corrupt, disgrace,
And awe the land with forces ‖ not their own,
Employ'd; the darling church herself betray'd;
All these, broad glaring, oped the general eye,
And waked my spirit, the resisting soul.
'Mild was, at first, and half ashamed, the check
Of senates, shook from the fantastic dream
Of absolute submission, tenets vile!
Which slaves would blush to own, and which reduced
To practice, always honest nature shock.
Not e'en the mask removed, and the fierce front

* Dunkirk.

† The war in conjunction with France, against the Dutch.

‡ The Triple Alliance.

§ Under Lewis XIV.

‖ A standing army, raised without the consent of parliament.

Of tyranny disclosed; nor trampled laws;
Nor seized each badge of freedom * thro' the land;
Nor Sidney bleeding for the unpublish'd page;
Nor on the bench avowed corruption placed,
And murderous rage itself, in Jefferies' form; †
Nor endless acts of arbitrary power,
Cruel, and false, could raise the public arm.
Distrustful, scatter'd, of combining chiefs
Devoid, and dreading blind rapacious war,
The patient public turns not, till impell'd
To the near verge of ruin. Hence I roused
The bigot king,‡ and hurried fated on
His measures immature. But chief his zeal,
Out-flaming Rome herself, portentous scared
The troubled nation: Mary's horrid days
To fancy bleeding rose, and the dire glare
Of Smithfield lighten'd in its eyes anew.
Yet silence reign'd. Each on another scowl'd
Rueful amazement, pressing down his rage:
As, mustering vengeance, the deep thunder frowns,
Awfully still, waiting the high command
To spring. Straight from his country Europe saved,
To save Britannia, lo! my darling son,
Than hero more! the patriot of mankind!
Immortal Nassau came. I hush'd the deep
By demons roused, and bade the listed winds,§

* The charters of corporations.

† Judge Jefferies.

‡ James II.

§ The Prince of Orange, in his passage to England, though

Still shifting as behoved, with various breath,
Waft the deliverer to the longing shore.
See! wide alive, the foaming channel * bright
With swelling sails, and all the pride of war,
Delightful view! when Justice draws the sword:
And mark! diffusing ardent soul around,
And sweet contempt of death, My streaming flag,†
E'en adverse navies ‡ bless'd the binding gale,
Kept down the glad acclaim, and silent joy'd.
Arrived, the pomp, and not the waste of arms
His progress mark'd. The faint opposing host §
For once, in yielding their best victory found,
And by desertion proved exalted faith:
While his the bloodless conquest of the heart,
Shouts without groan, and triumph without war.

his fleet had been at first dispersed by a storm, was afterwards extremely favoured by several changes of wind.

* Rapin, in his History of England.—The third of November the fleet entered the Channel, and lay by between Calais and Dover, to stay for the ships that were behind. Here the Prince called a council of war. It is easy to imagine what a glorious show the fleet made. Five or six hundred ships in so narrow a channel, and both the English and French shores covered with numberless spectators, are no common sight. For my part, who was then on board the fleet, I own it struck me extremely.

† The Prince placed himself in the main body, carrying a flag with English colours, and their highnesses' arms surrounded with this motto, 'The Protestant Religion and the Liberties of England;' and underneath the motto of the house of Nassau, 'Je maintiendrai,' I will maintain.—*Rapin.*

‡ The English fleet.

§ The King's army.

'Then dawn'd the period destined to confine
The surge of wild prerogative, to raise
A mound restraining its imperious rage,
And bid the raving deep no farther flow.
Nor where, without that fence, the swallow'd state
Better than Belgian plains without their dykes,
Sustaining weighty seas. This, often saved
By more than human hand, the public saw,
And seized the white-wing'd moment. Pleased *
to yield
Destructive power, a wise heroic prince †
E'en lent his aid — Thrice happy! did they know
Their happiness, Britannia's bounded kings.
What tho' not theirs the boast, in dungeon glooms,
To plunge bold freedom; or, to cheerless wilds,
To drive him from the cordial face of friend;
Or fierce to strike him at the midnight hour,
By mandate blind, not justice, that delights
To dare the keenest eye of open day.
What though no glory to control the laws,
And make injurious will their only rule,
They deem it. What tho', tools of wanton power,
Pestiferous armies swarm not at their call.
What though they give not a relentless crew
Of civil furies, proud oppression's fangs!
To tear at pleasure the dejected land,
With starving labour pampering idle waste.
To clothe the naked, feed the hungry, wipe

* By the Bill of Rights and the Act of Succession.
† William III.

The guiltless tear from lone affliction's eye;
To raise hid merit, set the alluring light
Of virtue high to view, to nourish arts,
Direct the thunder of an injured state,
Make a whole glorious people sing for joy,
Bless humankind, and thro' the downward depth
Of future times to spread that better sun
Which lights up British soul: for deeds like these,
The dazzling fair career unbounded lies;
While (still superior bliss!) the dark abrupt
Is kindly barr'd, the precipice of ill.
O luxury divine! O poor to this,
Ye giddy glories of despotic thrones!
By this, by this indeed, is imaged Heaven,
By boundless good without the power of ill.
 'And now behold! exalted as the cope
That swells immense o'er many-peopled earth,
And like it free, my fabric stands complete,
The palace of the laws. To the four heavens
Four gates impartial thrown, unceasing crowds,
With kings themselves the hearty peasant mix'd,
Pour urgent in. And though to different ranks
Responsive place belongs, yet equal spreads
The sheltering roof o'er all; while plenty flows,
And glad contentment echoes round the whole.
Ye floods, descend! Ye winds, confirming, blow!
Nor outward tempest, nor corrosive time,
Nought but the felon undermining hand
Of dark Corruption, can its frame dissolve,
And lay the toil of ages in the dust.'

LIBERTY.

PART V.—THE PROSPECT.

HERE interposing, as the Goddess paused;—
'O bless'd Britannia! in thy presence bless'd,
Thou guardian of mankind! whence spring, alone,
All human grandeur, happiness, and fame;
For toil, by thee protected, feels no pain;
The poor man's lot with milk and honey flows;
And, gilded by thy rays, even death looks gay.
Let other lands the potent blessings boast
Of more exalting suns. Let Asia's woods,
Untended, yield the vegetable fleece:
And let the little insect-artist form,
On higher life intent, its silken tomb.
Let wondering rocks, in radiant birth, disclose
The various tinctured children of the sun.
From the prone beam let more delicious fruits,
A flavour drink, that in one piercing taste
Bids each combine. Let Gallic vineyards burst
With floods of joy; with mild balsamic juice
The Tuscan olive. Let Arabia breathe
Her spicy gales, her vital gums distil.
Turbid with gold, let southern rivers flow;
And orient floods draw soft, o'er pearls, their maze.

Let Afric vaunt her treasures; let Peru
Deep in her bowels her own ruin breed,
The yellow traitor that her bliss betray'd, —
Unequal'd bliss —— and to unequal'd rage!
Yet nor the gorgeous East, nor golden South,
Nor, in full prime, that new discover'd world,
Where flames the falling day, in wealth and praise,
Shall with Britannia vie; while, Goddess, she
Derives her praise from thee, her matchless charms.
Her hearty fruits the hand of freedom own;
And warm with culture, her thick clustering fields
Prolific teem. Eternal verdure crowns
Her meads; her gardens smile eternal spring.
She gives the hunter-horse, unquell'd by toil,
Ardent, to rush into the rapid chase;
She, whitening o'er her downs, diffusive, pours
Unnumber'd flocks: she weaves the fleecy robe,
That wraps the nations: she, to lusty droves,
The richest pasture spreads; and, hers, deep-wave
Autumnal seas of pleasing plenty round.
These are delights: and by no baneful herb,
No darting tiger, no grim lion's glare,
No fierce-descending wolf, no serpent roll'd
In spires immense progressive o'er the land,
Disturb'd. Enlivening these, add cities, full
Of wealth, of trade, of cheerful toiling crowds:
Add thriving towns; add villages and farms,
Innumerous sow'd along the lively vale,
Where bold unrival'd peasants happy dwell:
Add ancient seats, with venerable oaks

Embosom'd high, while kindred floods below
Wind through the mead; and those of modern hand,
More pompous, add, that splendid shine afar.
Need I her limpid lakes, her rivers name
Where swarm the finny race? Thee, chief, Thames!
On whose each tide, glad with returning sails,
Flows in the mingled harvest of mankind?
And thee, thou Severn, whose prodigious swell,
And waves, resounding, imitate the main?
Why need I name her deep capacious ports,
That point around the world? and why her seas?
All ocean is her own, and every land
To whom her ruling thunder ocean bears.
She too the mineral feeds: the obedient lead,
The warlike iron, nor the peaceful less,
Forming of life art-civilized the bond;
And that * the Tyrian merchant sought of old,
Not dreaming then of Britain's brighter fame.
She rears to freedom an undaunted race:
Compatriot zealous, hospitable, kind,
Hers the warm Cambrian: hers the lofty Scot,
To hardship tamed, active in arts and arms,
Fired with a restless, an impatient flame,
That leads him raptured where ambition calls:
And English merit hers; where meet, combined,
Whate'er high fancy, sound judicious thought,
An ample generous heart, undrooping soul,

* Tin.

And firm tenacious valor can bestow.
Great nurse of fruits, of flocks, of commerce, she!
Great nurse of men! by thee, O Goddess, taught,
Her old renown I trace, disclose her source
Of wealth, of grandeur, and to Britons sing
A strain the Muses never touch'd before.
'But how shall this thy mighty kingdom stand?
On what unyielding base? how finish'd shine?'
At this her eye, collecting all its fire,
Beam'd more than human; and her awful voice,
Majestic thus she raised: 'To Britons bear
This closing strain, and with intenser note
Loud let it sound in their awaken'd ear:
'On virtue can alone my kingdom stand,
On public virtue, every virtue join'd.
For, lost this social cement of mankind,
The greatest empires, by scarce-felt degrees,
Will moulder soft away; till, tottering loose,
They, prone at last, to total ruin rush.
Unbless'd by virtue, government a league
Becomes, a circling junto of the great,
To rob by law; religion mild, a yoke
To tame the stooping soul, a trick of state
To mask their rapine, and to share the prey.
What are, without it, senates; save a face
Of consultation deep and reason free,
While the determined voice and heart are sold?
What boasted freedom, save a sounding name?
And what election, but a market vile
Of slaves self-barter'd? Virtue! without thee,

There is no ruling eye, no nerve, in states;
War has no vigour, and no safety peace:
E'en justice warps to party, laws oppress,
Wide through the land their weak protection fails,
First broke the balance, and then scorn'd the sword.
Thus nations sink, society dissolves;
Rapine and guile and violence break loose,
Everting life, and turning love to gall;
Man hates the face of man, and Indian woods
And Libya's hissing sands to him are tame.
'By those three virtues be the frame sustain'd
Of British freedom; independent life;
Integrity in office; and, o'er all
Supreme, a passion for the commonweal.
'Hail! Independence, hail! Heaven's next best gift,
To that of life and an immortal soul!
The life of life! that to the banquet high
And sober meal gives taste; to the bow'd roof
Fair-dream'd repose, and to the cottage charms.
Of public freedom, hail, thou secret source!
Whose streams, from every quarter confluent, form
My better Nile, that nurses human life.
By rills from thee deduced, irriguous, fed,
The private field looks gay, with nature's wealth
Abundant flows, and blooms with each delight
That nature craves. Its happy master there,
The only freeman, walks his pleasing round:
Sweet-featured peace attending; fearless truth;
Firm resolution; goodness, blessing all

That can rejoice; contentment, surest friend;
And, still fresh stores from nature's book derived,
Philosophy, companion ever new.
These cheer his rural, and sustain or fire,
When into action call'd, his busy hours.
Meantime true judging moderate desires,
Economy and taste, combined, direct
His clear affairs, and from debauching fiends
Secure his little kingdom. Nor can those
Whom fortune heaps, without these virtues reach
That truce with pain, that animated ease,
That self-enjoyment springing from within;
That independence, active or retired,
Which make the soundest bliss of man below:
But, lost beneath the rubbish of their means,
And drain'd by wants to nature all unknown,
A wandering, tasteless, gaily wretched train,
Though rich, are beggars, and though noble, slaves.
'Lo! damn'd to wealth, at what a gross expense
They purchase disappointment, pain, and shame.
Instead of hearty hospitable cheer,
See! how the hall with brutal riot flows;
While in the foaming flood, fermenting, steep'd,
The country maddens into party rage.
Mark! those disgraceful piles of wood and stone;
Those parks and gardens, where, his haunts be-trimm'd,
And nature by presumptuous art oppress'd,
The woodland genius mourns. See! the full board
That steams disgust, and bowls that give no joy;

No truth invited there, to feed the mind;
Nor wit, the wine-rejoicing reason quaffs.
Hark! how the dome with insolence resounds,
With those retain'd by vanity to scare
Repose and friends. To tyrant fashion, mark!
The costly worship paid, to the broad gaze
Of fools. From still delusive day to day,
Led an eternal round of lying hope,
See! self-abandon'd, how they roam adrift,
Dash'd o'er the town, a miserable wreck!
Then to adore some warbling eunuch turn'd,
With Midas' ears they crowd; or to the buzz
Of masquerade unblushing: or, to show
Their scorn of nature, at the tragic scene
They mirthful sit, or prove the comic true.
But, chief, behold! around the rattling board,
The civil robbers ranged; and e'en the fair,
The tender fair, each sweetness laid aside,
As fierce for plunder as all-licensed troops
In some sack'd city. Thus dissolved their wealth,
Without one generous luxury dissolved,
Or quarter'd on it many a needless want,
At the throng'd levee bends the venal tribe;
With fair but faithless smiles each varnish'd o'er,
Each smooth as those that mutually deceive,
And for their falsehood each despising each;
Till shook their patron by the wintry winds,
Wide flies the wither'd shower, and leaves him bare.
O far superior Afric's sable sons,
By merchant pilfer'd, to these willing slaves!

And rich, as unsqueezed favourite, to them,
Is he who can his virtue boast alone!
'Britons! be firm! — nor let corruption sly
Twine round your heart indissoluble chains!
The steel of Brutus burst the grosser bonds
By Cæsar cast o'er Rome; but still remain'd
The soft enchanting fetters of the mind,
And other Cæsars rose. Determined, hold
Your independence; for, that once destroy'd,
Unfounded, Freedom is a morning dream,
That flits aerial from the spreading eye.
'Forbid it, Heaven! that ever I need urge
Integrity in office on my sons!
Inculcate common honour —— not to rob ——
And whom? — the gracious, the confiding hand,
That lavishly rewards? the toiling poor,
Whose cup with many a bitter drop is mix'd;
The guardian public; every face they see,
And every friend; nay, in effect themselves.
As in familiar life, the villain's fate
Admits no cure; so, when a desperate age
At this arrives, I the devoted race
Indignant spurn, and hopeless soar away.
'But, ah too little known to modern times!
Be not the noblest passion past unsung;
That ray peculiar, from unbounded love
Effused, which kindles the heroic soul;
Devotion to the public. Glorious flame!
Celestial ardour! in what unknown worlds,
Profusely scatter'd through the blue immense,

Hast thou been blessing myriads, since in Rome,
Old virtuous Rome, so many deathless names
From thee their lustre drew? since, taught by thee,
Their poverty put splendour to the blush,
Pain grew luxurious, and e'en death delight?
O wilt thou ne'er, in thy long period, look,
With blaze direct, on this my last retreat?
'Tis not enough, from self right understood
Reflected, that thy rays inflame the heart:
Though virtue not disdains appeals to self,
Dreads not the trial; all her joys are true,
Nor is there any real joy save hers.
Far less the tepid the declaiming race,
Foes to corruption, to its wages friends,
Or those whom private passions, for a while,
Beneath my standard list; can they suffice
To raise and fix the glory of my reign?
'An active flood of universal love
Must swell the breast. First, in effusion wide,
The restless spirit roves creation round,
And seizes every being: stronger then
It tends to life, whate'er the kindred search
Of bliss allies: then, more collected still,
It urges humankind; a passion grown,
At last, the central parent public calls
Its utmost effort forth, awakes each sense,
The comely, grand, and tender. Without this,
This awful pant, shook from sublimer powers
Than those of self, this Heaven-infused delight,
This moral gravitation, rushing prone

To press the public good, my system soon,
Traverse, to several selfish centres drawn,
Will reel to ruin: while for ever shut
Stand the bright portals of desponding fame.
'From sordid self shoot up no shining deeds,
None of those ancient lights, that gladden earth,
Give grace to being, and arouse the brave
To just ambition, virtue's quickening fire!
Life tedious grows, an idly bustling round,
Fill'd up with actions animal and mean,
A dull gazette! The impatient reader scorns
The poor historic page; till kindly comes
Oblivion, and redeems a people's shame.
Not so the times when, emulation-stung,
Greece shone in genius, science, and in arts,
And Rome in virtues dreadful to be told!
To live was glory then! and charm'd mankind,
Through the deep periods of devolving time,
Those, raptured, copy; these, astonish'd, read.
'True, a corrupted state, with every vice
And every meanness foul, this passion damps.
Who can, unshock'd, behold the cruel eye?
The pale inveigling smile? the ruffian front?
The wretch abandon'd to relentless self,
Equally vile if miser or profuse?
Powers not of God, assiduous to corrupt?
The fell deputed tyrant, who devours
The poor and weak,* at distance from redress?

* Lord Molesworth, in his account of Denmark, says, 'It is observed, that in limited monarchies and common-

Delirious faction bellowing loud my name?
The false fair-seeming patriot's hollow boast?
A race resolved on bondage, fierce for chains,
My sacred rights a merchandize alone
Esteeming, and to work their feeder's will
By deeds, a horror to mankind, prepared,
As were the dregs of Romulus of old?
Who these indeed can undetesting see?—
But who unpitying? to the generous eye
Distress is virtue; and, though self-betray'd,
A people struggling with their fate must rouse
The hero's throb. Nor can a land, at once,
Be lost to virtue quite. How glorious then!
Fit luxury for gods! to save the good,
Protect the feeble, dash bold vice aside,
Depress the wicked, and restore the frail.
Posterity, besides! the young are pure,
And sons may tinge their father's cheek with shame.
'Should then the times arrive (which Heaven avert!)
That Britons bend unnerved, not by the force
Of arms, more generous and more manly, quell'd,
But by corruption's soul-dejecting arts,
Arts impudent! and gross! by their own gold,
In part bestow'd, to bribe them to give all,
With party raging, or immersed in sloth,
Should they Britannia's well fought laurels yield

wealths, a neighbourhood to the seat of the government is advantageous to the subjects; whilst the distant provinces are less thriving, and more liable to oppression.'

To slily conquering Gaul; e'en from her brow
Let her own naval oak be basely torn,
By such as tremble at the stiffening gale,
And nerveless sink while others sing rejoiced,
Or (darker prospect! scarce one gleam behind
Disclosing) should the broad corruptive plague
Breathe from the city to the farthest hut,
That sits serene within the forest shade;
The fever'd people fire, inflame their wants,
And their luxurious thirst, so gathering rage,
That, were a buyer found, they stand prepared
To sell their birthright for a cooling draught.
Should shameless pens for plain corruption plead;
The hired assassins of the commonweal!
Deem'd the declaiming rant of Greece and Rome,
Should public virtue grow the public scoff,
Till private, failing, staggers through the land:
Till round the city loose mechanic want,
Dire prowling nightly, makes the cheerful haunts
Of men more hideous than Numidian wilds,
Nor from its fury sleeps the vale in peace;
And murders, horrors, perjuries abound:
Nay, till to lowest deeds the highest stoop;
The rich, like starving wretches, thirst for gold;
And those, on whom the vernal showers of Heaven
All-bounteous fall, and that prime lot bestow,
A power to live to nature and themselves,
In sick attendance wear their anxious days,
With fortune, joyless, and with honours, mean.
Meantime, perhaps, profusion flows around,

The waste of war, without the works of peace;
No mark of millions in the gulf absorpt
Of uncreating vice, none but the rage
Of roused corruption still demanding more.
That very portion, which (by faithful skill
Employ'd) might make the smiling public rear
Her ornamented head, drill'd through the hands
Of mercenary tools, serves but to nurse
A locust band within, and in the bud
Leaves starved each work of dignity and use.
'I paint the worst. But should these times arrive,
If any nobler passion yet remain,
Let all my sons all parties fling aside,
Despise their nonsense, and together join;
Let worth and virtue scorning low despair,
Exerted full, from every quarter shine,
Commix'd in heighten'd blaze. Light flash'd to light,
Moral, or intellectual, more intense
By giving glows. As on pure winter's eve,
Gradual, the stars effulge; fainter, at first,
They, straggling, rise; but when the radiant host,
In thick profusion pour'd, shine out immense,
Each casting vivid influence on each,
From pole to pole a glittering deluge plays,
And worlds above rejoice, and men below.
'But why to Britons this superfluous strain?—
Good nature, honest truth e'en somewhat blunt,
Of crooked baseness an indignant scorn,

A zeal unyielding in their country's cause,
And ready bounty, wont to dwell with them —
Nor only wont — wide o'er the land diffused,
In many a bless'd retirement still they dwell.
'To softer prospect turn we now the view,
To laurel'd science, arts, and public works,
That lend my finish'd fabric comely pride,
Grandeur and grace. Of sullen genius he!
Cursed by the Muses! by the Graces loathed!
Who deems beneath the public's high regard
These last enlivening touches of my reign.
However puff'd with power, and gorged with wealth,
A nation be; let trade enormous rise,
Let East and South their mingled treasure pour,
Till, swell'd impetuous, the corrupting flood
Burst o'er the city and devour the land:
Yet these neglected, these recording arts,
Wealth rots, a nuisance; and, oblivious sunk,
That nation must another Carthage lie.
If not by them, on monumental brass,
On sculptured marble, on the deathless page,
Impress'd, renown had left no trace behind:
In vain, to future times, the sage had thought,
The legislator plann'd, the hero found
A beauteous death, the patriot toil'd in vain.
The awarders they of Fame's immortal wreath,
They rouse ambition, they the mind exalt,
Give great ideas, lovely forms infuse,
Delight the general eye, and, dress'd by them,
The moral Venus glows with double charms.

'Science, my close associate, still attends
Where'er I go. Sometimes, in simple guise,
She walks the furrow with the consul-swain,
Whispering unletter'd wisdom to the heart,
Direct; or, sometimes, in the pompous robe
Of fancy dress'd, she charms Athenian wits,
And a whole sapient city round her burns.
Then o'er her brow Minerva's terrors nod:
With Xenophon, sometimes, in dire extremes,
She breathes deliberate soul, and makes retreat *
Unequal'd glory: with the Theban sage,
Epaminondas, first and best of men!
Sometimes she bids the deep-embattled host,
Above the vulgar reach, resistless form'd,
March to sure conquest — never gain'd before! †
Nor on the treacherous seas of giddy state
Unskilful she: when the triumphant tide
Of high-swoln empire wears one boundless smile,
And the gale tempts to new pursuits of fame,
Sometimes, with Scipio, she collects her sail,
And seeks the blissful shore of rural ease,
Where, but the Aonian maids, no sirens sing;
Or should the deep-brew'd tempest muttering rise,

* The famous Retreat of the Ten Thousand was chiefly conducted by Xenophon.

† Epaminondas, after having beat the Lacedemonians and their allies, in the battle of Leuctra, made an incursion, at the head of a powerful army, into Laconia. It was now six hundred years since the Dorians had possessed this country, and in all that time the face of an enemy had not been seen within their territories. — *Plutarch in Agesilaus.*

While rocks and shoals perfidious lurk around,
With Tully she her wide-reviving light
To senates holds; a Catiline confounds,
And saves awhile from Cæsar sinking Rome.
Such the kind power, whose piercing eye dissolves
Each mental fetter, and sets reason free;
For me inspiring an enlightened zeal,
Tho' more tenacious as the more convinced
How happy freemen, and how wretched slaves.
To Britons not unknown, to Britons full
The Goddess spreads her stores, the secret soul
That quickens trade, the breath unseen that wafts
To them the treasures of a balanced world.
But finer arts (save what the Muse has sung
In daring flight, above all modern wing,)
Neglected droop the head; and public works,
Broke by corruption into private gain,
Not ornament, disgrace; not serve, destroy.
'Shall Britons, by their own joint wisdom ruled
Beneath one Royal Head, whose vital power
Connects, enlivens, and exerts the whole;
In finer arts, and public works, shall they
To Gallia yield? yield to a land that bends
Depress'd, and broke, beneath the will of one?
Of one who, should the unkingly thirst of gold,
Of tyrant passions, or ambition, prompt,
Calls locust-armies o'er the blasted land:
Drains from its thirsty bounds the springs of wealth,
His own insatiate reservoir to fill:
To the lone desert patriot-merit frowns,

Or into dungeons arts, when they, their chains,
Indignant, bursting; for their nobler works
All other license scorn but truth's and mine.
Oh shame to think! shall Britons, in the field
Unconquer'd still, the better laurel lose?
E'en in that monarch's reign,* who vainly dreamt,
By giddy power, betray'd, and flatter'd pride,
To grasp unbounded sway; while, swarming round,
His armies dared all Europe to the field;
To hostile hands while treasure flow'd profuse,
And, that great source of treasure, subjects' blood,
Inhuman squander'd, sicken'd every land;
From Britain, chief, while my superior sons,
In vengeance rushing, dash'd his idle hopes,
And bade his agonizing heart be low:
E'en then, as in the golden calm of peace,
What public works, at home, what arts arose!
What various science shone! what genius glow'd!
'’Tis not for me to paint, diffusive shot
O'er fair extents of land, the shining road;
The flood-compelling arch; the long canal,†
Through mountains piercing and uniting seas;
The dome ‡ resounding sweet with infant joy,
From famine saved, or cruel-handed shame;
And that ‡ where valour counts his noble scars,
The land where social pleasure loves to dwell,
Of the fierce demon, Gothic duel, freed;

* Lewis XIV.
† The Canal of Languedoc.
‡ The hospitals for foundlings and invalids.

The robber from his farthest forest chased;
The turbid city clear'd, and, by degrees,
Into sure peace the best police refined,
Magnificence, and grace, and decent joy.
Let Gallic bards record, how honour'd arts,
And science, by despotic bounty bless'd,
At distance flourish'd from my parent-eye.
Restoring ancient taste, how Boileau rose:
How the big Roman soul shook, in Corneille,
The trembling stage. In elegant Racine;
How the more powerful though more humble voice
Of nature-painting Greece, resistless, breathed
The whole awaken'd heart. How Moliere's scene,
Chastised and regular, with well judged wit,
Not scatter'd wild, and native humour, graced,
Was life itself. To public honours raised,
How learning in warm seminaries * spread;
And, more for glory than the small reward,
How emulation strove. How their pure tongue
Almost obtain'd what was denied their arms.
From Rome, awhile, how Painting, courted long,
With Poussin came; ancient design, that lifts
A fairer front, and looks another soul.
How the kind art,† that, of unvalued price,
The famed and only picture, easy, gives,
Refined her touch, and, through the shadow'd piece,
All the live spirit of the painter pour'd.

* The Academies of Sciences, of the Belles Lettres, and of Painting.

† Engraving.

Coyest of arts, how Sculpture northward deign'd
A look, and bade her Girardon arise.
How lavish grandeur blazed; the barren waste,
Astonish'd, saw the sudden palace swell,
And fountains spout amid its arid shades.
For leagues, bright vistas opening to the view,
How forests in majestic gardens smiled.
How menial arts, by their gay sisters taught,
Wove the deep flower, the blooming foliage train'd
In joyous figures o'er the silky lawn,
The palace cheer'd, illumed the storied wall,
And with the pencil vied the glowing loom.*
'These laurels, Lewis, by the droppings raised
Of thy profusion, its dishonour shade,
And, green thro' future times, shall bind thy brow;
While the vain honours of perfidious war
Wither abhorr'd, or in oblivion lost.
With what prevailing vigour had they shot,
And stole a deeper root, by the full tide
Of war-sunk millions fed? Superior still,
How had they branch'd luxuriant to the skies,
In Britain planted, by the potent juice
Of Freedom swell'd? Forced is the bloom of arts,
A false uncertain spring, when Bounty gives,
Weak without me, a transitory gleam.
Fair shine the slippery days, enticing skies
Of favour smile, and courtly breezes blow;

* The tapestry of the Gobelins.

Till arts, betray'd, trust to the flattering air
Their tender blossom: then malignant rise
The blights of Envy, of those insect clouds,
That, blasting merit, often cover courts:
Nay, should, perchance, some kind Mæcenas aid
The doubtful beamings of his prince's soul,
His wavering ardour fix, and unconfined
Diffuse his warm beneficence around;
Yet death, at last, and wintry tyrants come,
Each sprig of genius killing at the root.
But when with me imperial Bounty joins,
Wide o'er the public blows eternal spring;
While mingled autumn every harvest pours
Of every land; whate'er Invention, Art,
Creating Toil, and Nature can produce.'
   Here ceased the Goddess; and her ardent wings
Dipt in the colours of the heavenly bow,
Stood waving radiance round, for sudden flight
Prepared, when thus, impatient, burst my prayer:
   'O forming light of life! O better sun!
Sun of mankind! by whom the cloudy north,
Sublimed, not envies Languedocian skies,
That, unstain'd ether all, diffusive smile:
When shall we call these ancient laurels ours?
And when thy work complete?' Straight with her hand,
Celestial red, she touch'd my darken'd eyes.
As at the touch of day the shades dissolve,
So quick, methought, the misty circle clear'd,
That dims the dawn of being here below:

The future shone disclosed, and, in long view,
Bright rising eras instant rush'd to light.
'They come! great Goddess! I the times behold!
The times our fathers, in the bloody field,
Have earn'd so dear, and, not with less renown,
In the warm struggles of the senate fight.
The times I see! whose glory to supply,
For toiling ages, Commerce round the world
Has wing'd unnumber'd sails, and from each land
Materials heap'd, that, well employ'd, with Rome
Might vie our grandeur, and with Greece our art.
'Lo! Princes I behold! contriving still,
And still conducting firm some brave design;
Kings! that the narrow joyless circle scorn,
Burst the blockade of false designing men,
Of treacherous smiles, of adulation fell,
And of the blinding clouds around them thrown:
Their court rejoicing millions; Worth, alone,
And Virtue dear to them; their best delight,
In just proportion, to give general joy;
Their jealous care thy kingdom to maintain;
The public glory theirs; unsparing love
Their endless treasure; and their deeds their praise.
With thee they work. Nought can resist your force:
Life feels it quickening in her dark retreats:
Strong spread the blooms of Genius, Science, Art;
His bashful bounds disclosing Merit breaks;
And, big with fruits of glory, Virtue blows
Expansive o'er the land. Another race
Of generous youth, of patriot sires, I see!

Not those vain insects fluttering in the blaze
Of court, and ball, and play; those venal souls,
Corruption's veteran unrelenting bands,
That, to their vices slaves, can ne'er be free.
'I see the fountains purged! whence life derives
A clear or turbid flow; see the young mind
Not fed impure by chance, by flattery fool'd,
Or by scholastic jargon bloated proud,
But fill'd and nourish'd by the light of truth.
Then, beam'd through fancy the refining ray,
And pouring on the heart, the passions feel
At once informing light and moving flame;
Till moral, public, graceful action crowns
The whole. Behold! the fair contention glows,
In all that mind or body can adorn,
And form to life. Instead of barren heads,
Barbarian pedants, wrangling sons of pride,
And truth-perplexing metaphysic wits,
Men, patriots, chiefs, and citizens are form'd.
'Lo! Justice, like the liberal light of Heaven,
Unpurchased shines on all; and from her beam,
Appalling guilt, retire the savage crew,
That prowl amid the darkness they themselves
Have thrown around the laws. Oppression grieves;
See! how her legal furies bite the lip,
While Yorkes and Talbots their deep snares detect,
And seize swift justice thro' the clouds they raise.
'See! social Labour lifts his guarded head,
And men not yield to government in vain.
From the sure land is rooted ruffian force,

And the lewd nurse of villains, idle waste;
Lo! raised their haunts, down dash'd their maddening bowl,
A nation's poison! beauteous order reigns!
Manly submission, unimposing toil,
Trade without guile, civility that marks
From the foul herd of brutal slaves thy sons,
And fearless peace. Or should affronting war
To slow but dreadful vengeance rouse the just,
Unfailing fields of freemen I behold!
That know, with their own proper arm, to guard
Their own bless'd isle against a leaguing world.
Despairing Gaul her boiling youth restrains,
Dissolved her dream of universal sway:
The winds and seas are Britain's wide domain;
And not a sail, but by permission, spreads.
'Lo! swarming southward on rejoicing suns,
Gay colonies extend; the calm retreat
Of undeserved distress, the better home
Of those whom bigots chase from foreign lands.
Nor built on rapine, servitude, and woe,
And in their turn some petty tyrant's prey;
But, bound by social Freedom, firm they rise;
Such as, of late, an Oglethorpe has form'd,
And, crowding round, the charm'd Savannah sees.
'Horrid with want and misery, no more
Our streets the tender passenger afflict.
Nor shivering age, nor sickness without friend,
Or home, or bed to bear his burning load;
Nor agonizing infant, that ne'er earn'd

Its guiltless pangs; I see! the stores, profuse,
Which British bounty has to these assign'd,
No more the sacrilegious riot swell
Of cannibal devourers! right applied,
No starving wretch the land of freedom stains:
If poor, employment finds; if old, demands,
If sick, if maim'd, his miserable due;
And will, if young, repay the fondest care.
Sweet sets the sun of stormy life; and sweet
The morning shines, in Mercy's dews array'd.
Lo! how they rise! these families of Heaven!
That! chief,* (but why—ye bigots!—why late?)
Where blooms and warbles glad a rising age;
What smiles of praise! and, while their song ascends,
The listening seraph lays his lute aside.
'Hark! the gay muses raise a nobler strain,
With active nature, warm impassion'd truth,
Engaging fable, lucid order, notes
Of various string, and heart-felt image fill'd.
Behold! I see the dread delightful school
Of temper'd passions, and of polish'd life,
Restored: behold! the well dissembled scene
Calls from embellish'd eyes the lovely tear,
Or lights up mirth in modest cheeks again.
Lo! vanish'd monster land. Lo! driven away
Those that Apollo's sacred walks profane:

* The Foundling Hospital.

Their wild creation scatter'd, where a world
Unknown to nature, Chaos more confused,
O'er the brute scene its Ouran-Outangs pours;*
Detested forms! that, on the mind impress'd,
Corrupt, confound, and barbarize an age.
'Behold! all thine again the Sister-Arts,
Thy graces they, knit in harmonious dance.
Nursed by the treasure from a nation drain'd
Their works to purchase, they to nobler rouse
Their untamed genius, their unfetter'd thought;
Of pompous tyrants, and of dreaming monks,
The gaudy tools, and prisoners, no more.
'Lo! numerous domes a Burlington confess:
For kings and senates fit, the palace see!
The temple breathing a religious awe;
E'en framed with elegance the plain retreat,
The private dwelling. Certain in his aim,
Taste, never idly working, saves expense.
'See! silvan scenes, where Art alone pretends
To dress her mistress, and disclose her charms:
Such as a Pope in miniature has shown;†
A Bathurst o'er the widening forest ‡ spreads;
And such as form a Richmond, Chiswick, Stowe.
'August, around, what public works I see!
Lo! stately streets, lo! squares that court the breeze,

* A creature which, of all brutes, most resembles man. *See Dr. Tyson's Treatise on this animal.*

† At his Twickenham Villa.

‡ Okely woods, near Cirencester.

In spite of those to whom pertains the care,
Ingulfing more than founded Roman ways,
Lo! ray'd from cities o'er the brighten'd land,
Connecting sea to sea, the solid road.
Lo! the proud arch (no vile exactor's stand)
With easy sweep bestrides the chasing flood.
See! long canals, and deepen'd rivers join
Each part with each, and with the circling main
The whole enliven'd isle. Lo! ports expand,
Free as the winds and waves, their sheltering arms.
Lo! streaming comfort o'er the troubled deep,
On every pointed coast the lighthouse towers;
And, by the broad imperious mole repell'd,
Hark! how the baffled storm indignant roars.'
As thick to view these varied wonders rose,
Shook all my soul with transport, unassured,
The Vision broke; and, on my waking eye,
Rush'd the still ruins of dejected Rome.

END OF VOL. I.